Contemporary American Trauma Narratives

Contemporary American Trauma Narratives

Alan Gibbs

EDINBURGH
University Press

© Alan Gibbs, 2014

Edinburgh University Press Ltd
The Tun – Holyrood Road
12(2f) Jackson's Entry
Edinburgh EH8 8PJ
www.euppublishing.com

Typeset in 11.5/13 Ehrhardt by
Servis Filmsetting Ltd, Stockport, Cheshire,
and printed and bound in the United States of America

A CIP record for this book is available from the British Library

ISBN 978 0 7486 4114 7 (hardback)
ISBN 978 0 7486 9408 2 (webready PDF)
ISBN 978 0 7486 9407 5 (paperback)
ISBN 978 0 7486 9409 9 (epub)

Contents

Acknowledgements

I owe numerous friends and colleagues thanks for indulging me in lengthy conversations about the contents of this book. Amongst colleagues in the School of English, University College Cork, I am especially grateful to Graham Allen, Lee Jenkins, and Barry Monahan for comments, suggestions and encouragement along the way. Rachel MagShamhráin, Silvia Ross and David Ryan also provided helpful comments that fed into Chapters 2, 3 and 4, respectively. Katie Ahern, Conor Dawson, and Dan O'Brien provided invaluable feedback on chapter drafts. Tamás Benyei provided especially insightful comments on some material that eventually found its way into the Introduction and Chapter 2. The School of English administrative staff – Anne Fitzgerald, Jennifer Crowley, Elaine Hurley, and Carol Power – deserve special praise for being always efficient and supportive, as do the patient editorial and publicity staff at Edinburgh University Press.

The College of Arts, Celtic Studies, and Social Sciences, University College Cork provided me with a period of research leave, a contribution towards publications costs, and travel bursaries towards a number of conferences, for all of which I am very grateful. I would also like to thank the organisers of conferences in Chichester, Belfast, Cork, Reykjavik, and Lincoln for the opportunity to deliver papers and receive feedback on early drafts of sections of this book. These conferences also enabled me to meet and exchange ideas with numerous fellow delegates, and I would like to thank, in particular, Clare Hayes-Brady, Adam Kelly, and Philip McGowan for useful general discussions regarding contemporary literature, and Anne Whitehead, Kalí Tal and Susannah Radstone for more theoretical discussions and further recommended readings.

Thanks finally to Mona and Dan Clarke, who were always there when we needed them, and pre-eminently to Bronagh Clarke who not only donated what little spare time she had to give surpassingly helpful feedback on the entire book, but without whose love, support, advice and encouragement this work would not have been possible.

For Bronagh, who made it easier, and to Nathaniel, who made it, joyously, more difficult.

The Trauma Paradigm and Its Discontents

In her influential book, *Trauma and Recovery* (1992), Judith Herman extensively discusses the phenomenon of 'post-traumatic stress disorder'. In the Afterword added to the 1997 second edition, Herman refers to 'PTSD'. The difference is minor, perhaps, but telling, suggesting that in the short intervening period the concept had come to such broad public awareness in America – helped not least by the success of books such as Herman's – that the abbreviation now sufficed as an identifier. Post-traumatic stress disorder was first defined – or, as its critics insist, invented – through its inclusion in the 1980 third edition of the American Psychiatric Association's (APA) *Diagnostic and Statistical Manual of Mental Disorders* (*DSM-III*), while its reach was significantly widened in the 1994 fourth edition. During the last two decades of the twentieth century, and on into the beginning of the twenty-first, PTSD and trauma have become ubiquitous terms of diagnosis in America and across the West reaching far into the culture, and effecting 'the rise of what is becoming almost a new theoretical orthodoxy' (Radstone, 'Trauma Theory' 10).

The following study examines the trauma paradigm both as a critical or 'theoretical orthodoxy', and through its manifestation in a variety of American prose narratives. The general position taken is that while trauma initially provides an illuminating perspective upon American cultural production, its creeping ubiquity as a critical paradigm eventually becomes limiting. As the trauma paradigm was more widely disseminated through American culture during the late twentieth century, so a tendency developed to read everything through its increasingly monolithic and programmatic critical prism. This in turn began to influence the form of cultural products, such that an identifiable 'trauma genre' emerged, a self-reinforcing circuit of fictional and non-fictional prose narratives that existed in tandem with a supporting critical structure. The events of 11 September 2001 only served to strengthen this relationship, with the emergence of a glut of cultural production seemingly based on aesthetic models approved by existing trauma theory, and often subsequently praised by critics subscribing to those same theories.

Later chapters in this study examine some of the earlier twentieth-century literary manifestations of trauma (Chapter 1); more recent challenges to dominant paradigms of trauma representation, with the analysis of Mark Z. Danielewski's *House of Leaves* (2000) in Chapter 2; postmodernist writers' attempts to comprehend the events of 9/11 (Chapter 3); trauma in memoirs of service personnel in both Gulf Wars (Chapter 4); and the manifestation of trauma in three recent American counterfactual novels in the final chapter. An important founding principle of these chapters is to ascertain whether texts, in their depiction of trauma and its effects, evade the more formulaic prescriptions of dominant trauma theory or, conversely, tend to conform to them and even borrow from them. Firstly this introduction traces the construction and growing hegemony of post-traumatic stress disorder in America, and the effect of this emerging dominance on the critical theory of the period. The work of Cathy Caruth, enormously influential in cultural and literary studies from the mid-1990s onwards, is examined in detail here, while key concepts in her work on trauma are critiqued. This introduction also focuses on the problematic clashing origins of cultural trauma theory, drawing as it does on diverse areas including Holocaust studies, post-structuralism, and the roots of PTSD as a concept in the experience of Vietnam veterans. The aesthetic prescriptions of cultural trauma theory are also examined, along with a more detailed analysis of the mutually reinforcing critical-practitioner trauma genre mentioned above, before a final section considers alternatives to the narrow, Caruthian-PTSD critical perspective on trauma.

POST-TRAUMATIC STRESS DISORDER: ITS INVENTION AND DISSEMINATION

Rehearsing a full genealogy of trauma and PTSD is beyond the scope of this study and, in any case, covered more than adequately in a number of existing works.[1] In order to demonstrate some of the contradictions and difficulties in applying concepts from dominant trauma theory, however, it would be useful to consider the ways in which PTSD has been constructed, and certain resultant incoherencies in its epistemology. A cornerstone to this critique is that PTSD is not discovered but invented, and that the collection of symptoms into a unified syndrome is artificial and self-perpetuating, with clinical diagnoses reinforcing the syndrome's defining power. Whereas much of the literature of PTSD presents traumatic memory as something discovered, Allan Young argues instead that 'the traumatic memory is a man-made object. It originates in the scientific and clinical discourses of the nineteenth century; before that time there is unhappiness, despair, and disturbing recollections, but no traumatic memory, in the sense that we know it today' (141). A number of commentators have noted particular motivations behind the invention of PTSD that lay outside strictly clinical findings, in particular the effect of the advocacy of Vietnam veterans' pressure groups. As Richard McNally observes, 'the very fact that the movement to include the diagnosis in *DSM-III* arose from Vietnam veterans' advocacy groups working with anti-war psychiatrists prompted concerns that PTSD was more of a political or social construct, rather than a medical disease discovered in nature' (1). Ben Shephard's *A War of Nerves* delineates the lobbying involved in having PTSD accepted into *DSM-III* and likewise locates the origins of PTSD as a concept in post-Vietnam politics. Vietnam, he claims, 'helped to create a new "consciousness of trauma" in Western society' (355). Shephard is highly critical of the widespread adoption of PTSD, pointing out the dangers of using this set of concepts arising from particular geographical and temporal circumstances as a universal and standardised diagnostic tool. According to Shephard, the veterans groups' skilful lobbying obscured any sense that they were merely a special interest group through the construction of a 'wider category of trauma and shrewdly presenting their case in a way designed to appeal to the new psychiatry' (366). They thus proposed an inclusive category of trauma of which combat stress was just one subset. This sharpened into PTSD, and thus '[a] bridge was forged between "war neurosis" and the victims of civilian trauma that had never really existed before' (367). This was 'a new, unitary kind of "trauma"' (367), which gained widespread credibility through its inclusion in *DSM-III*, and a rapid authority in the field of cultural trauma studies.

PTSD, as its critics readily avow, quickly developed a momentum of its own, as what was essentially a socio-political as much as a medical category acquired official status. It is useful to consider Ian Hacking's concept of looping here, as it describes how people begin to change their behaviour and conform to ways in which they have been defined and treated by dominant social forces (34). As a result, they begin to form new, socially constructed group identities. Indeed, McNally likens PTSD to one of Hacking's 'interactive kinds', whereby sufferers begin to be grouped together and are 'affected by the very process of classification itself' (McNally 11). In other words, an iatrogenic circuit reinforces the strength of PTSD as increasing numbers of people fall within its reach, a process compounded with PTSD's much wider diagnostic criteria in *DSM-IV* (1994). McNally cites as an example the PTSD diagnostic criterion of the flashback. In the earlier twentieth-century literature of trauma there is no mention of flashbacks, and according to McNally it is only after the emergence of the flashback as part of film culture that it becomes connected with trauma. The flashback is first constructed and then widely disseminated as a trauma symptom, after which its presence becomes finally self-fulfilling, as 'people experience their trauma as photographic reenactments' (11). This flashback, in turn, becomes a cornerstone of claims, discussed below, that traumatic memory is precisely literal. PTSD according to this analysis is thus 'not "discovered" in nature, but co-created via the interaction of psychobiology and the cultural context of classification' (11).

Nevertheless, numerous articles and studies in the cultural studies field have taken the construction or invention of PTSD on its own terms, as something instead discovered. Moreover, the concept of PTSD and wider ideas of trauma have been readily transported back in time – as if the concept had existed as a condition for decades and even centuries before 1980 – and also spatially, as UNICEF and other western organisations carried out studies of PTSD in Third World countries (Shephard 387). This notwithstanding that '[t]he disorder is not timeless, nor does it possess an intrinsic unity' (Young 5). Given its recent occurrence, the specific and particular context of PTSD's creation has been remarkably overlooked by too many commentators eager to observe its manifestation across a range of social, historical and cultural phenomena. It is, perhaps, a growing awareness of the actually diffuse and fractured character of trauma and its symptoms that has produced recent critiques of the metanarrative that PTSD seemed to provide. As Young suggests, PTSD is in fact not unified but 'glued together by the practices, technologies, and narratives with which it is diagnosed, studied, treated, and represented and by the various interests, institutions, and moral arguments that mobilized these efforts and resources' (5). The mention of moral arguments here is particularly interesting; the tendency in dominant trauma theory to conflate the moral with the analytical, the ethical with the aesthetic, is examined further later in this chapter. Above all, though, Young correctly challenges the falsely simple genealogy (and therefore dubious validity) of PTSD, and thus its unjustifiable universal application. Specific problems with these attributes of trauma and PTSD are addressed in more detail below. First, though, it would pay to take a closer look at the work of Cathy Caruth, which has been so thoroughly influential in the adoption of trauma in cultural and literary studies.

CATHY CARUTH: THE RHETORIC OF TRAUMA STUDIES

The content of Caruth's work – key concepts and manifestations of trauma that she claims as typical – is assessed further below, whereas the main focus of this section is a short formal analysis of the rhetorical strategies found throughout her work, and the degree to which slippages obfuscate gaps in her arguments. Caruth's two major publications in the mid-1990s – an edited collection, *Trauma: Explorations in Memory* (1995), and a monograph, *Unclaimed Experience: Trauma, Narrative, and History* (1996) – set out the key ideas for what has been adopted into a dominant set of theories, cultural trauma theory as such, in the humanities. As the following aims to demonstrate, however, a number of key arguments are based around logical gaps and lacunae. Bearing in mind that broadly the same concepts concerning trauma are outlined, and using the same rhetorical strategies, in Caruth's influential introductory essays in the *Trauma* collection, the following focuses on that text rather than the lengthier exposition contained in *Unclaimed Experience*.

In terms of rhetoric, one of the most striking strategies in Caruth's writing is a continual shift from hypothesising to definitive statement, but with a missing logical argument bridging the two. For example, the first introduction begins with a notably cautious set of claims, as Caruth admits that 'the precise definition' of PTSD is 'contested', but suggests that there is general agreement regarding

> a response, *sometimes* delayed, to an overwhelming event or events, which takes the form of repeated, intrusive hallucinations, dreams, thoughts or behaviors stemming from the event, along with numbing that *may have* begun during or after the experience, and *possibly* also increased arousal to (and avoidance of) stimuli recalling the event. (4, emphasis added)

The italics here demonstrate how Caruth's claims at this juncture are relatively modest, a point sometimes missed by more enthusiastic followers of her work. Almost immediately, however, is a much more far-reaching set of claims, as trauma is proclaimed to be by definition belated:

> the pathology cannot be defined either by the event itself – which may or may not be catastrophic, and may not trau-

matize everyone equally – nor can it be defined in terms of a *distortion* of the event . . . The pathology consists, rather, solely in the *structure of its experience* or reception: the event is not assimilated or experienced fully at the time, but only belatedly. (4, original emphases)

This bears serious consideration, given that this is perhaps the most frequently quoted passage in Caruth's entire oeuvre, and almost always approvingly. And yet the absent argument – there is only assertion – by which we arrived at this point is never noted, let alone questioned.

Similar lack of substantiation follows in the argument concerning the alleged exact match between traumatic nightmares and the events which inspired them, and this time Caruth is a good deal less cautious, insisting upon a 'literal return of the event' (5), and the 'nonsymbolic nature of traumatic dreams and flashbacks, which resist cure to the extent that they remain, *precisely*, literal' (5, emphasis added). This particular claim, as we shall see later in this chapter, has come in for severe criticism, albeit generally not from those working in the cultural studies realm in which Caruth has been so influential. The italics are added in the second quotation above to emphasise again the rhetorical slippage: there is no proof in the preceding argument that justifies the use of 'precisely', but it is a term continually employed in Caruth's discourse, as a rhetorical reinforcement of arguments that are in fact highly contestable. Moreover, points apparently made through such rhetoric are used as foundations for subsequent claims. Thus the literality which was shown in the previous passage to be 'precisely' true of trauma is the basis of Caruth's next claim, that belatedness is another necessary component of traumatic experience: '[i]t is this literality and its insistent return which thus constitutes trauma and points towards its enigmatic core: the delay or incompletion in knowing, or even seeing, an overwhelming occurrence that then remains, in its insistent return, absolutely true to the event' (5). More extravagant claims are then extrapolated: '[i]t is indeed *this truth of traumatic experience* that forms the center of its pathology or symptoms; it is not a pathology, that is, of falsehood or displacement of meaning, but of history itself. If PTSD must be understood as a pathological symptom, then it is not so much a symptom of the unconscious, as it is a symptom of history' (5, emphasis added). These are grand claims indeed and again demonstrably underpinned by assertion rather than argument, as suggested by the italicised phrase, which apparently relies merely upon the alleged proof provided in the previously quoted passage.

The ascribed inevitability of a latency period in traumatic memory – that is, an indefinite duration of amnesia regarding the traumatic event – arises again in Caruth's subsequent discussion of Freud, who '*seems to describe* the trauma as the successive movement from an event to its repression to its return' (7, emphasis added). Again the disingenuous tentativeness of 'seems to describe' transforms, on the next page, to traumatic experience characterised by 'the *fact of latency* . . . an inherent latency within the experience itself' (8, emphasis added). Ruth Leys has pointed out the tendentiousness of this 'appropriat[ion of] Freud's concept of *Nachträglichkeit*' (271), which is again achieved through rhetorical slippage whereby debate about the validity of latency as a concept underpinning trauma is dispelled, and this assumption is used as a departure point for a discussion regarding latency's constitution. Astonishingly, the succeeding passage claims that even the complex character of latency is instantly emptied of doubt: 'The historical power of the trauma is not just that the experience is repeated after its forgetting, but that it is only in and through its inherent forgetting that it is first experienced at all' (8). What we encounter in Caruth's writing is a series of slippages where initial conjecture is transformed into certainty, which then becomes the basis for subsequent, largely unsubstantiated arguments. The tenuousness of this rhetoric is perhaps most starkly revealed a little later, when Caruth attempts to reconcile her reading of Freud with her affiliation to de Manian post-structuralism. Again, the logical leaps coupled with an absence of evidence are striking: '[i]f repression, in trauma, is replaced by latency, this is significant in so far as its blankness – the space of unconsciousness – is paradoxically what *precisely* preserves the event in its literality. For history to be a history of trauma means that it is referential *precisely* to the extent that it is not fully perceived as it occurs' (8, emphasis added). The repetition of 'precisely' here in fact demonstrates nothing more clearly than the desperately abstract and diffuse nature of the arguments being proffered here. It reveals, moreover, the ultimately insurmountable difficulties involved in reconciling Freudian thought and post-structuralism (not to mention the discourse of PTSD). Given the widespread influence and acceptance in the humanities of Caruth's work, however, especially with regard to belatedness and the unrepresentability of trauma, it would appear that the rhetorical strategies outlined above have been sufficient to persuade many unwary critics and readers.

It is not difficult to discover this critical practice of unquestioningly using Caruth's arguments. Whenever trauma is discussed in Richard Gray's *After the Fall*, for example, he blithely endorses Caruth's position that trauma has rendered events unavailable to memory. Caruth is continually cited as 'an authority in the field' (53) as if that settles debate. This appeal to Caruth's authority produces formulaic readings and an acceptance of certain deeper consequences of her arguments, such as the necessary 'structural connection' between the Holocaust and 9/11 in terms of the representation of trauma (54). Similarly, Gray reproduces conventional arguments regarding the purported – but arguably illusory – so-called paradox of trauma, whereby the sufferer 'has to achieve some kind of resolution, however fragile or fleeting, between the imperative of silence (since trauma is that for which there is no language) and the imperative of speech (since trauma is that which demands language as an alternative to emotional paralysis)' (54). Second-hand employment of Caruth's ideas in this way has, through repetition, only served to strengthen the sense that this particular way of conceiving the representation of trauma is the only way. The following section examines some of the key foundations of Caruthian thought and PTSD (since there is a significant overlap), in an initial attempt to assess their validity.

INTERROGATING THE CORNERSTONES OF TRAUMA AND PTSD

Belatedness/*Nachträglichkeit*

The idea that trauma is always characterised by a temporary or permanent latency period of amnesia, during which the source of the originating trauma is unavailable to the sufferer's memory, derives from the work of Freud, who introduced the concept of *Nachträglichkeit*, or belatedness, in *Project for a Scientific Psychology* (1895). According to Caruth's influential reading of Freud, after this period of forgetting, memories belatedly return. Regardless of whether or not we remain convinced by Freud's account of *Nachträglichkeit*, bound as it actually is to particular temporal and geographical circumstances despite its claims for universality, Caruth's reading has been criticised as further distorting Freud's concept. Ruth Leys suggests that Caruth's 'model of trauma as defined by latency is much closer to the model of an infectious disease, in which an "incubation period" or period of delay intervenes between the initial infection and the subsequent appearance of symptoms, than to Freud's concept of *Nachträglichkeit*' (271).

With the concept of repression, Freud clearly allows that trauma is often banished from consciousness deliberately and knowingly, rather than unconsciously erased through amnesia, as the currently more popular dissociative model insists. In *Unclaimed Experience*, for example, Caruth – perhaps the chief exponent of the dissociative model – quotes *Beyond the Pleasure Principle*, where Freud discusses how trauma sufferers may be 'more concerned with *not* thinking of [traumatic memories]' (in Caruth 61). This formulation, where *not* thinking of something clearly acknowledges that there is an awareness of something *not* to think about, thus suggesting conscious repression, is nevertheless discussed by Caruth in terms of a memory that is involuntarily unavailable: 'trauma is suffered in the psyche precisely, it would seem, because it is *not* directly available to experience' (61, original emphasis). Despite lapses such as this (again indicated by the return of a phrase such as 'precisely, it would seem') the concept of belatedness retains a relentless hold upon trauma theory in the humanities.

Outside the humanities, straightforward notions of belatedness have been more readily criticised and debunked as fallacy. McNally, for example, notes that earlier clinical writing on trauma did not insist upon a period of amnesia following the traumatic incident. Indeed, even the original definitions of PTSD 'emphasized that traumatic experiences were all too memorable, an assertion fully consistent with the scientific literature' (8). In the revised version of *DSM-III* and then *DSM-IV*, however, 'psychogenic amnesia' (9) was incorporated as a possible symptom, and the idea of the repressed memory gained much widespread support. As McNally observes, this position suggests that there is something unique to traumatic memory about not remembering every event. More commonly, however, failures of memory occur simply because information was never encoded to begin with, a phenomenon which connects rather than distinguishes between ordinary and traumatic memory. As McNally elaborates, an insistence on belatedness also depends in part upon a simplistic model of memory:

> Because the mind is not a video recorder, not every aspect of a traumatic experience will get encoded into memory: this is especially true when an event is rapidly unfolding as in an automobile accident or a sudden assault. Accordingly, failure to encode every aspect of a traumatic experience – including an 'important' one – must not be confused with an inability to recall an aspect that has been encoded. (9)

Thus the traumatic event may be unavailable not through a failure of memory, but because it was never encoded in the first place. This challenges the popular idea that traumatic memory is different in this respect, whereas in fact events in life are frequently insufficiently encoded into memory to allow accurate recall. As Katherine Hodgkin and Susannah Radstone suggest, the apparent disruptions of traumatic memory may be common to all types of memory: 'the characteristic features of "traumatic memory" – its elisions, interruptions and reinventions – need bear no specific relation to an event, but rather can be seen to characterise the workings of memory in general' (97).

Notwithstanding critiques such as McNally's, a number of trauma theorists have attempted to provide support for the notion of dissociation and belatedness through appeal to neuroscience. Bessel van der Kolk is perhaps the most prominent of these, insisting that evidence of key elements such as dissociation and belatedness is provided in studies of brain patterns (as is – as discussed in the following section – literal recall of trauma in nightmares and flashbacks). In Caruth's collection, for example, van der Kolk mentions (but does not cite) research which allegedly demonstrates 'that dissociation of traumatic experience occurs as the trauma is occurring . . . Many trauma survivors report that they automatically are removed from the scene; they look at it from a distance or disappear altogether, leaving other parts of their personality to suffer and store the overwhelming experience' (168). The appeal to attributes such as the metaphysical rather than clinical 'other parts of their personality' is not the least cause of disquiet regarding such claims. Ann Kaplan takes particular issue with van der Kolk's arguments by drawing on recent and more extensive neuroscience which suggests that in many cases there is no evidence of amnesia or belatedness. Instead, 'the victim is conscious of the trauma. In this case, in a sense, two circuits happen at the same time: a circuit . . . where the cortex is bypassed; and a circuit that includes the cortex, so that trauma does find its way into memory' (38). Evidence is far from compelling either way: as McNally and others have suggested, the neuroscience makes little distinction between traumatic and regular memory, with events sometimes recalled and sometimes forgotten in both instances. More directly relevant here, as Kaplan points out, research demonstrates that it is quite possible for 'trauma to be in conscious memory' (38). The key point is that the dominant model in the humanities, which follows Caruth's insistence upon belatedness, is far too rigid, partial, and exclusionary, since 'things are more complex. How a victim will respond depends on the particular situation, on an individual's specific psychic history and formation, and on the context for the event' (38). This is clearly borne out by the literature, whether scientific studies demonstrating the importance of predisposition, testimony of remembered but consciously repressed trauma, or fictional treatments which violate the formulaic model set out by

Caruth. In particular, the event's context, not least a society's propensity for understanding trauma according to a widely circulated symptomatology, is an element thoroughly overlooked in mainstream trauma studies.

As Kaplan and others have suggested, trauma functions in far more complex ways than Caruth's model or definitions of PTSD allow. The belatedness model which argues for the blocking of access to traumatic memories by amnesia, either temporarily or permanently, is actually rare in sufferers' experience: 'frequently the subject does have memories, or partial memories, of what happened. But at the same time, what one remembers may be influenced by fantasies and desires, or by a wish that things had been different. Subsequent events may subtly have an impact on memory' (Kaplan 42). This latter point, that trauma is reworked in memory and affected by the sufferer's fantasies, is supported by Radstone's observations that traumatic memory is far more active than the dissociation model allows: 'a memory becomes traumatic when it becomes associated, later, with inadmissible meanings, wishes, fantasies, which might include an identification with the aggressor . . . it is not an event, which is by its nature "toxic" to the mind, but what the mind later does to memory' ('Trauma Theory' 17). Not only is traumatic memory present and active, but it may also include fantasy identification with the perpetrator. Furthermore, perpetrators themselves can experience trauma, an issue that is discussed at greater length below. We also revisit belatedness later in this chapter, but suffice to say for now that traumatic memory is clearly a good deal more complex and inconsistent than the belatedness model allows.

Literality: Flashbacks and Nightmares

Debates about the distinctions between traumatic and regular memory also inform our next area of controversy, this time concerning theorists who allege that another unique element of traumatic memory is the exactly literal quality of recollection in the flashbacks and nightmares of trauma sufferers. Caruth's work is again central to this concept, although her claims once more depend on rhetorical slipperiness. In *Unclaimed Experience*, Caruth describes how the significance of trauma is that its characteristic of inaccessibility is, 'paradoxically, precisely what preserves the event in its literality' (17–18). This unfounded notion of literality is, to borrow Caruth's language, precisely what slips through here, with no actual evidence that traumatic memory is necessarily literal. Caruth later repeats the assertion, describing trauma as 'the unmediated occurrence of violent events' and 'the literal return of the event' (59), and attempts to explain the allegedly literal quality of the traumatic memory as a consequence of the overwhelmingly sudden impact of the event upon the sufferer: 'the painful repetition of the flashback can only be understood as the absolute inability of the mind to avoid an unpleasurable event that has not been given psychic meaning in any way. In trauma, that is, the outside has gone inside without any mediation' (59). A number of critics find such assertions simplistic, but Caruth's claim has had widespread consequences in the realms of cultural, aesthetic and literary criticism. Not least, as discussed later in this chapter, the allegedly literal character of the traumatic memory means that trauma in art and literature is considered by Caruthian theory to be unrepresentable, or only representable through the employment of radically fragmented and experimental forms.

But is there compelling evidence for the literal quality of traumatic memory? Wulf Kansteiner suggests that in her belief in literality, Caruth 'finds herself in contradiction with most of the empirical and theoretical work on trauma' (203). Leys similarly takes issue with van der Kolk's claim that the sufferer is unable to process the trauma, which instead imprints itself literally on the brain but 'defies all possibility of representation' (16). Leys notes that 'There is no consensus in the field of memory research regarding such a claim' (7), and declares van der Kolk's 'literalist view of trauma' to be 'not only theoretically incoherent but also poorly supported by the scientific evidence' (16). Those working in the clinical sciences are similarly unconvinced. McNally, for example, rejects the insistence of van der Kolk that the trauma dream exactly replays the event. As he points out, van der Kolk et al. 'simply asked their PTSD patients . . . whether their nightmares matched the combat events the patients had experienced in Vietnam' (7), with predictable results. The idea that a nightmare can 'literally replay the sensory aspects of the traumatic experience' (McNally 7) is thus a fallacy, not least because 'the standard against which the dream is compared – the trauma as recalled by the dreamer when awake – is itself a fallible reconstruction of the event' (McNally 7). This underlines the overstatement and oversimplification in the theories of van der Kolk, which regard the sufferer's experience of trauma as largely passive, and ignore the partiality and incorporation of fantasy actually entailed in memory work. As Melvin Lansky notes, nightmares, like other dreams, contain coded and complex reworkings of past events, often merged, often conflating traumatic episodes, often employing dream work to incorporate narcissistic fantasies, and all requiring the same interpretive work as regular dreams (10). Claims such as van der Kolk's, however, despite the lack of convincing scientific or clinical evidence, have proved highly influential amongst Caruth and her followers, to the extent that to suggest traumatic memory is not precisely literal is an unorthodox position in cultural trauma theory.

Punctual versus Insidious Trauma

One further controversy in trauma studies concerns whether traumatic events are necessarily sudden – that is, 'punctual', to borrow the commonly used term – or whether they can also be slow, gradual and insidious. The insistence that trauma is the result of a sudden and overwhelming event is fundamental to Caruth's theories, and has been highly influential in the work of myriad critics and theorists. *Unclaimed Experience*, for example, develops a punctual model of trauma that 'is experienced too soon, too unexpectedly, to be fully known and is therefore not available to consciousness until it imposes itself again, repeatedly, in the nightmares and repetitive actions of the survivor' (4). The sudden, overwhelming character of the event is here posited as the reason for trauma's belatedness and its manifestation in flashbacks and so on. Paradoxically, while the cause of trauma thus becomes (possibly temporarily) unavailable to consciousness because of 'its very unassimilated nature', for Caruth, a single 'simple violent or original event in an individual's past' (4) remains the inevitable presence behind traumatised behaviour. This rigidity is perhaps surprising, given certain roots of Caruth's trauma theory in Holocaust Studies, and the generally insidious nature of trauma suffered by victims of the Shoah.

Laura Brown's essay 'Outside the Range', which somewhat incongruously appears in Caruth's *Trauma* collection, by contrast sets out an important challenge to the notion that trauma is always the result of a single event. Brown's professional capacity as a psychotherapist brought her into contact with numerous female trauma sufferers whose experience was not, as *DSM-III* insists, 'outside the range of human experience', but provides instead, as she puts it, a 'picture of "normal" traumatic events' (101). In other words, Brown discovered that many American women's experiences were daily blighted by abusive situations that, while part of their everyday life, were nevertheless traumatic. The event-based model in *DSM-III* was therefore found wanting: '[t]he range of human experience becomes the range of what is normal and usual in the lives of men of the dominant class; white, young, able-bodied, educated, middle-class, Christian men. Trauma is thus that which disrupts these particular human lives, but no other' (101). From this, Brown (in conjunction with Maria Root) developed the notion of 'insidious trauma' (107), which diverges from the punctual model in accepting 'everyday' chronic conditions as potential causes of trauma. Brown's perspective is shared by Herman, whose clinical experience with trauma sufferers led her to conclude that, 'There is a spectrum of traumatic disorders, ranging from the effects of a single overwhelming event to the more complicated effects of prolonged and repeated abuse' (3). This feminist branch of trauma theory has done much to challenge the punctual model, to the extent that *DSM-IV* took greater account of post-traumatic conditions brought on by insidious or chronic exposure to stress.

While Brown's argument is convincing, there is a slight western bias; in the list cited above ('white, young, able-bodied, educated, middle-class, Christian men'), she does not mention 'western' or 'American' except by implication, and there are similarly exclusionary references to 'our culture' (103) and 'this society' (107). On one hand, this is laudable, in that Brown seems to be attempting a localised theory of trauma, thus resisting the temptation to universalise, a common thread in much trauma theory. On the other, it is therefore curious that Brown overlooks the colonial experience as a key marker of insidious trauma, especially since her article has been highly influential upon theorists attempting to develop non-punctual models of trauma as a means to discuss postcolonialism. In a double issue of *Studies in the Novel* on representations of postcolonial trauma published in 2008, for example, Brown's work on insidious trauma is repeatedly cited. The introductory article by co-editors Stef Craps and Gert Buelens makes this link between postcolonial and insidious trauma explicit: 'Routinely ignored or dismissed in trauma research, the chronic psychic suffering produced by the structural violence of racial, gender, sexual, class, and other inequities has yet to be fully accounted for' (3–4). Numerous contributors to the issue subsequently draw on a broader definition of trauma highly influenced by Brown's insights. I return to her work and its implications below and in subsequent chapters.

It is worth noting briefly how debates around belatedness, literality, and punctual versus insidious trauma have influenced literary representations and trauma criticism in an American context. Belatedness and amnesia are typically expressed through a variety of literary and narrative strategies that are understood to formally represent the symptom. These may include, as subsequent chapters examine in more detail, fragmented narratives characterised by analepses; digressions, diversions and prevarications in narrative trajectory; and dispersal or fragmenting of narrating personae. Experimental forms have been even more insistently prescribed in the representation of the allegedly literal character of traumatic memory. Caruth asserts that trauma 'is marked, not by a simple knowledge, but by the ways it simultaneously defies and demands our witness', a characteristic which demands that trauma must 'be spoken in a language that is always somehow literary: a language that defies, even as it claims, our understanding' (*Unclaimed Experience* 5). This huge claim, that the representation of trauma depends necessarily upon apparently experimental artistic and literary forms, has had lasting effects on both trauma literature and criticism in contemporary America, imposing formulae that have in turn produced a narrow approved trauma aesthetic. An appreciation that trauma can take an insidious as well as a punctual form underlies several recent representations of trauma. As well as the postcolonial context discussed below, Chapter 4 examines this phenomenon in conjunction with the portrayal of perpetrator trauma in recent narratives by members of the American armed forces involved in both Gulf Wars.

To summarise the widespread influence of both Caruth's writings and the popular dissemination of the concept of PTSD, it is worth briefly reiterating the way in which some of the criticism draws in a broadly unquestioning fashion upon these discourses. In Laurie Vickroy's influential study *Trauma and Survival in Contemporary Fiction*, for example, there is no investigation into the conceptual origins of PTSD; it is instead introduced merely with the comment that PTSD 'can be a widespread cultural phenomena [sic]' (13). Comparing this to the careful genealogies of trauma and PTSD found in, for example, works by Young, Leys, or Roger Luckhurst, where the concepts' epistemologies are minutely examined, it becomes evident that too much second-generation theory and criticism is unaware of the concept's contested origins. The potentially ideological motivations behind *DSM* definitions and theoretical works by writers such as Herman, Caruth and van der Kolk are allowed to pass unchallenged. It is arguably this inadequate understanding of the conceptual origins of PTSD that has helped to construct a network of formulaic and universalising criteria for the representation of trauma in the literary realm.[2]

TRAUMA THEORY, ETHICS, AND THE PERPETRATOR

PTSD and Caruthian trauma theory are not only built on questionable foundations, but also include elements that make the two theories difficult to reconcile with each other. In particular, the contrasting roots of these two discourses produce a series of awkward questions about the ethical dimension to trauma. The development of PTSD is heavily imbricated with the fallout from America's excursion into Vietnam, and thus focuses to a large degree upon perpetrator trauma. More often than not, PTSD amongst American Vietnam veterans is linked to guilt at their culpable role in the horrors they witnessed. Cultural trauma studies, on the other hand, are traceable not only to Freud but also to Holocaust Studies. For obvious reasons, Holocaust scholars are much more reluctant to countenance the traumatic experience of the perpetrator. 'There is an absolute obscenity in the very project of understanding,' Claude Lanzmann, director of the acclaimed Holocaust testimony film, *Shoah*, explains in Caruth's collection with regard to the perspective of the perpetrator, 'I cling to this refusal of understanding as the only possible ethical and at the same time the only possible operative attitude' (204). While this is a perfectly understandable position for Holocaust survivors and scholars to take, it does produce a problem when contemporary trauma theorists and critics attempt to assimilate or conflate the concept of PTSD with a trauma theory heavily influenced by Holocaust Studies. There are a number of consequences of this attempt to reconcile the two, perhaps the most notable being the discomfort regarding the experience of the perpetrator, important to the concept of PTSD but shunned by cultural trauma theory.

A wider consequence of trauma theory's roots in Holocaust Studies is the incorporation of a moral dimension absent from PTSD. For example, one key ethical element of trauma theory is the insistence that only silence is acceptable in the face of unspeakable horror, again echoing the perspective of Holocaust Studies. This position risks translating an ontological inability to speak into an ethically-driven absolute refusal to communicate, as Jenny Edkins suggests: '[w]hat survivors have witnessed has long been recognised as "unimaginable" and "unspeakable", although these epithets have often served as an excuse for neither imagining it nor speaking about it' (*Trauma* 2). This moral prescriptiveness has become such an underlying imperative of the theory, often to the exclusion or marginalisation of detached analysis, that literary trauma criticism faces certain limitations.

The effects of this ethical dimension are felt most strongly in trauma studies when moral judgements begin to overlap with value judgements and/or phenomenological observations. In comparing critical (rather than popular) reactions to *Schindler's List* and *Shoah*, Andreas Huyssen notes that the former's appeal to a mass audience is seen by numerous critics to produce a misleading representation, 'thus fostering forgetting: Hollywood as fictional substitute for "real history"', whereas 'Lanzmann's refusal to represent . . . is said to embody memory in the proper way precisely because it avoids the delusions of a presence of that which is to be remembered' (69). Mention of 'the proper way' here is telling, demonstrating precisely this shading of ethical and value judgement. Implicit or explicit value judgements such as these, deriving from moral considerations and under which 'mass cultural representations are not considered proper or correct' (69), are all too common in trauma criticism. Moral judgements also shade into phenomenological ones in both trauma theory and Holocaust Studies, as is detectable in Dori Laub's essay on testimony in Caruth's collection. Here, Holocaust survivors' accounts written at or shortly after the events they describe nevertheless 'become receivable only *today* . . . it is only now, *belatedly*, that the event begins to be historically grasped and seen' (69, original emphasis). Initially this belatedness is therefore perceived as an intrinsic trait, which 'underscores the fact that these testimonies were not transmittable, and integratable, at the time' (69). This observation, however, immediately transforms into a moral prescription: '[i]t is all the more imperative to recognize and to enhance today the value and the momentous contributions of the testimonies and the witnesses who preserved evidence often by risking their lives' (69). It is, of course, impossible to argue with the sentiment here, but the rhetorical shift eliding a slippage from critical observation in the first quotation to ethical demand in the second needs to be pointed out, since it is of a kind with questionable strategies seen elsewhere in literary trauma criticism.

Anne Rothe has commented on this narrowly prescriptive critical mode which demands that Holocaust representations (and by extension trauma narratives) 'must cause suffering approximating that of the victims', that is, emotional affect rather than political action, a requirement Rothe dismisses as 'impossible and hence nonsensical' (161). This may be linked of course, to the insistence of Caruth and others that trauma must be transmitted rather than represented by the text (this imperative is discussed further below and in Chapter 2). The link between the Holocaust and the wider trauma model is noted by Rothe herself: '[a]s American Holocaust discourse became paradigmatic for trauma culture at large, the idea that audiences must suffer with, and even as, the victims emerges as the dominant mode of reception advocated . . . for other representations of extremity' (161). This demand is, Rothe notes, 'absurd and unethical' and 'grounded in the fallacious analogy between the experience of the Holocaust and the consumption of its representation' (161). Again, this is clearly true of the wider field of trauma literature and its prescribed reception. Rothe argues that the trauma paradigm desocialises and thus depoliticises suffering, but it is also worth pointing out that, as the example of 9/11 demonstrates, vicarious suffering – corralled and transformed into a sense of collective victimhood – may also be employed to provide spurious justification for undesirable political action, such as the invasions of Afghanistan and Iraq, and the domestic crackdown on civil liberties. This use of collective trauma is explored more fully in Chapter 3.

As suggested above, the moral phenomenon that the conflation of PTSD and Caruthian trauma theory most struggles to account for is perpetrator trauma. While this difficulty stems in large part from PTSD's origins in the experience of Vietnam veterans, Radstone points out a difficulty of reconciling the moral dimension of trauma theory even with Freud's work. This is in relation to trauma theory's absolutism that the traumatic event necessarily takes the form of an assault from without, thus conferring victim status upon the sufferer: 'whereas psychoanalysis takes the "darker side of the mind" for granted, emphasizing the ubiquity of inadmissible sexual fantasies, for instance, trauma theory suggests, rather that the "darkness" comes only from *outside*' ('Trauma Theory' 19, original emphasis). In other words, despite the debt Caruth's model of trauma owes to the undecidabilities of de Man's deconstructive practice, 'it nevertheless offers a theory of the subject which retreats from psychoanalysis's rejection of a black-and-white vision of psychical life to produce a theory which establishes clear, not to say Manichean binaries of "inside" and "outside", "trauma" and "normality", and "victims" and "perpetrators"' ('Trauma Theory' 19). This underlines the moral obstacles which trauma theory has self-constructed in terms of adequately considering the potentially traumatic experience of the perpetrator. Chapters 3 and 4 further develop this critique, examining the extent to which trauma theory's blind spot regarding the perpetrator has enabled the transformation of perpetrators into victims. The texts discussed depict members of the American armed forces who are in an invidious and liminal position, as potential or actual perpetrators of violence but also subject to the aggressive demands of a military hierarchy.

Finally, with regard to the problematic moral strictures of trauma theory, we should consider in a little more detail the argument that the trauma paradigm necessarily depoliticises social inequalities. This is not an original observation; as Antonio Traverso and Mick Broderick comment, 'with its pervasive medical connotations, most probably due to its entrenched origin in the physical and psychological health sciences, the expression trauma continuously tends to psychologize, and therefore, potentially, depoliticize the discussion and analysis of socio-historical phenomena and their representation' (9). This echoes earlier observations from Laura Brown's essay, where she notes that envisaging trauma as extraordinary – that is, 'outside the range' – safely brackets it, giving the illusion that it is not part of normal life, and allowing us to become instead of everyday sufferers, 'spectators, titillated by the thrill of risk, safe behind our imaginary psychic barriers' (108). Rothe borrows from this notion, noting the existence of a large network of 'trauma kitsch' in America that finds a basis in the sensationalist exploitation of traumatic subjects in talk shows. Rothe argues that trauma kitsch omits 'the socio-economic contexts of oppression, victimization, and violence by representing these quintessentially political subjects as individual tragedies,' and as a result encourages a 'teary-eyed sentimentality' which 'covertly reinforces the power structures that have created the represented injustices' (45). Significantly, this depoliticised sentimentality regarding individual traumas is supported by and ideologically attuned to key tenets of dominant models of trauma theory, hence the growing number of critiques from postcolonial theorists, who object to a set of theories that distracts from political inequalities.

It may be argued that this depoliticising dimension of trauma discourse took an even darker turn in the political reaction to the events of 9/11. In this case the Bush administration employed a paradigm of collective trauma precisely to decontextualise and therefore simplify and depoliticise alleged reasons for the attack. As David Holloway observes, '[d]escribing 9/11 as a "trauma" in this way implied a breakdown in embedded models of communal identity, particularly in symbols and signifiers of national "American" belonging' (61). As the mass media took to describing 9/11 in terms of 'a loss of American innocence or impregnability, as a turning point in American history and as a fundamental reconfiguring of what it meant to be a citizen of the United States' (61), attention was turned away from any historical or political role America may have had in helping to precipitate the attacks. This depoliticised construction of a sense of victimhood and epochal change, acquired through the collective trauma paradigm, and aligned with the 'uncritical patriotism that flooded TV screens, radio airwaves, magazines and newsprint after 9/11' (62), was potentially useful for the neoconservatives as a way to further their agendas while simultaneously obscuring how their policies contributed towards constructing the conditions for 9/11 in the first place.

The next section examines the aesthetic criteria which have been laid down by dominant trauma theory, but first it is worth noting that there is a necessary link between these criteria and the moral imperatives of trauma theory discussed above. Some of this should be clear already, since the ethical cautions of Caruthian theory discouraging the representation of trauma in any straightforward way necessarily entail the employment of experimental literary forms. This link is noted, for example, by Luckhurst, who describes a generally held view that since trauma freezes time, it therefore rules out the possibility of narration, and can only be 'an aporia in narrative, and any narrative temporalization is an unethical act. Severe trauma can only be conveyed by the catastrophic rupture of narrative possibility' (81). Similarly, Leys points out the ethical drives behind ostensibly aesthetic criteria in her discussion of Dori Laub, who suggests that experiencing from the inside an event such as the Holocaust precludes witnessing it. As a result, Leys suggests, 'the subject's not-knowing of the trauma – his inability to speak or represent his experience – is what *guarantees* the return of the truth in the patient's traumatic repetitions. From this perspective, the concept of trauma as literal provides an essentially *ethical* solution to the crisis of representation posed by trauma' (252, original emphasis). Trauma is thus reified, according to post-Holocaust aesthetic–ethical criteria, as something that cannot be represented but which nevertheless relentlessly returns unbidden. As Michael Rothberg suggests, such an approach endangers sacralising the Holocaust (and, by implication, trauma more generally) since it 'removes the Holocaust from standard historical, cultural or autobiographical narratives and situates it as a sublime, unapproachable object beyond discourse and knowledge' (*Traumatic Realism* 4). We might take this further and argue that the apparently ontological, epistemological or aesthetic prohibitions regarding the representation of trauma, as discussed in the next section, in fact mask moral issues, and that what really drives theorists to suggest that trauma is unrepresentable, or representable only in certain ways, is ultimately an ethical imperative.

CRITERIA FOR THE REPRESENTATION OF TRAUMA

The narrow way in which trauma has been defined, according to a sometimes contradictory synthesis of Freudian thought, PTSD, elements of Holocaust studies, and the post-structuralist-inflected work of theorists such as Caruth, has proved problematic. The key difficulty concerning us here is that a prescriptive understanding of trauma based on this range of popularised work has come to limit representations of trauma's effects, and to produce an identifiable critically-approved aesthetic. This is an aesthetic related to ways in which trauma has been most commonly encountered in a clinical context. Herman, for example, notes how in therapy an avoidance of the traumatic memories in the patient 'leads to stagnation in the recovery process, while approaching them too precipitately leads to a fruitless and damaging reliving of the trauma' (176). Both of these dynamics may be readily found in the fictional literature of trauma, as sufferer-narrators either deny, mislead, or elide details of traumatic events (generally only temporarily), or gradually edge towards confronting their pasts. What I am referring to as the 'trauma genre' draws in relatively unquestioning ways upon a simplified and restricted range of those aspects of trauma theory most widely disseminated into European and, especially, American culture. These include the punctual model of trauma critiqued above, which in literature typically produces characters who suffer symptoms such as involuntary flashbacks, nightmares, and cycles of repetitive, often self-destructive behaviour, without having access to memories of the originating cause. The aesthetic and thematic norms of the trauma genre thus clearly attest to the inevitability of belatedness. Concepts such as *Nachträglichkeit* and concomitant symptoms such as nightmares, or the assertion that trauma is aesthetically unrepresentable, are thus sufficiently dominant in contemporary trauma theory that simplified versions of them have found their way into the wider culture, and from there into the aesthetic of the trauma genre.

While these symptoms undoubtedly characterise many sufferers' encounters with trauma, however, to suggest that this is the only model devalues the experience of and the recovery from trauma. As Ann Kaplan and Ban Wang suggest, an aesthetic model based on this limited conception of trauma – for example, on the insistence that it is unrepresentable – also risks cordoning off and reifying historical atrocities: '[i]t is a mistake to think that investment in the abysmal, unrepresentable quality of trauma is the only way to be fair to the traumatized and injured' (12). As they point out, this narrow trauma aesthetic also betrays a western bias in favour of avant-garde forms, which loses sight of 'the practical question of why we need to remember historical trauma in a broader context' (12). This emerges especially clearly in neo-realist postcolonial representations of trauma. Craps and Buelens, for example, argue that an exclusive valuing of experimental forms marginalises many non-western trauma representations: '[w]ithin trauma studies, it has become all but axiomatic that traumatic experiences can only be adequately represented through the use of experimental, (post) modernist textual strategies' (5). In many of the essays in the special issue of *Studies in the Novel* that they co-edited, by contrast,

> an attachment to realism and indigenous literary practices is interpreted as a deliberate eschewal of the Western discourse of unspeakability, recourse to which is seen as politically debilitating. These contrasting appraisals of the appropriateness and effectiveness of (post)modernist forms for the representation of traumatic experiences provide a welcome

reminder of the importance of attending to the political and cultural contexts in which literary testimonies are produced and received. (5)

Thus in the African texts discussed by Robert Eaglestone, 'there is a real sense that there can be comprehension, that a story must be told and can and should be grasped by others in the West' (82). Moreover, there is an urgent political imperative to narrate traumas in order to educate western readers. Such a perspective tallies with Greg Forter's critique of Caruth, which argues that the silence that the aesthetic of dominant trauma theory more or less enforces on the sufferer perpetuates a defeatist admission of the inevitability and universality of trauma (280, 282). From the tacit, or even sometimes explicit, endorsing of a universal template for the presentation of traumatised pathologies, has emerged a dominant aesthetic that is similarly attenuated, western-biased, and which risks making trauma sublime, part of 'the mystified circle of the occult, something untouchable and unreachable' (Kaplan and Wang 8).

Ethical issues once more cloud the aesthetic according to this model, since the moral injunction against straightforward or realistic representation of trauma is a vital component of the general aesthetic criteria. According to this perspective, trauma texts should aim to transmit or convey trauma rather than represent it, and if they are to represent it, then it should be done according to the most indirect and experimental aesthetic forms possible. Generally confirming Caruth's assertion that trauma is necessarily beyond representation, the trauma genre aesthetic is thus, as Luckhurst suggests, 'uncompromisingly avant-garde', as writers are encouraged to seek structures that are 'experimental, fragmented, refusing the consolations of beautiful form, and suspicious of familiar representational and narrative conventions' (81). Critics' often favourable appraisals of such work have enabled the emergence of an identifiable canon of approved trauma literature, conforming to various conventions. Luckhurst correctly notes that strongly prescriptive aesthetic programmes such as these have effectively shaped a genre: 'texts are often brought together by critics as exemplary works because they are held to share a particular trauma aesthetic . . . Because a traumatic event confounds narrative knowledge, the inherently narrative form of the novel must acknowledge this in different kinds of temporal disruption' (88). Luckhurst clearly has in mind here a literary practice which employs certain disruptive formal techniques of postmodernism – most familiarly, perhaps, fragmented, non-linear chronologies, repetition, shifts in narrating voice, and a resultantly decentred subjectivity – in order to represent or attempt to transmit trauma. Some of the founding postmodernist novels, including Gabriel García Márquez's *One Hundred Years of Solitude* and Günter Grass's *The Tin Drum*, indeed employ what were then startlingly disruptive techniques partly in order to represent the effects of historical traumas upon their protagonists. In America, similar techniques were used in texts such as Kurt Vonnegut's *Slaughterhouse-Five*, E. L. Doctorow's *The Book of Daniel*, and Toni Morrison's *Beloved*, all of which are discussed in Chapter 1. These and other initiator texts unwittingly helped to construct certain conventions for the literary treatment of trauma. As Luckhurst suggests, a problematic reification of representational modes occurred when the originality of these progenitor texts was lauded by critics:

[t]here is something of a contradiction . . . in affirming the centrality of innovation whilst identifying a specific (and sometimes prescriptive) trauma aesthetic. Paradoxically, the aesthetic means to convey the singularity of a traumatic aporia has now become highly conventionalized, the narratives and tropes of traumatic fiction easily identified. (89)

While foundational trauma texts such as these employed a pioneering aesthetic to politically radical effect, once these techniques were recognised as conventions by critics and adopted as techniques by writers their effect was blunted.

A broad injunction exists in cultural trauma theory, discouraging writers from attempting to represent trauma. Instead, the approved ethical–aesthetic approach is to aim to transmit the trauma to the reader. Theory regarding this point manifests in several ways, but is often built on questionable epistemological foundations. Kalí Tal, for example, asserts that '[a]ccurate representation of trauma can never be achieved without recreating the event since, by its very definition, trauma lies beyond the bounds of "normal" conception. Textual representations . . . are mediated by language and do not have the impact of the traumatic experience' (15). She goes on to argue that texts indeed should seek to transmit affect onto the reader rather than attempt to represent or recreate the trauma. Given the influence of post-structuralist thought in both Caruth's and Tal's work, this argument is a little surprising. The post-structuralist observation that reality, general quotidian existence, cannot be captured in language or literature has been widely accepted, and so to plead the representation of trauma as a special case is clearly dubious.

The notion of transmissibility, and the demand that trauma writers should seek to transmit rather than represent, has been criticised on other grounds, not least that transmissibility is no more possible than representation. Kansteiner, for example, witheringly dismisses transmissibility, or second-hand trauma, observing that there is actually a 'vast, unchartered psychological territory that lies between the experience of extreme trauma on the one hand and the much more frequent encounter with representations of violence on the other' (195). Rothe similarly criticises Caruth and Dominick LaCapra (specifically the latter's notion of 'empathic unsettlement') for colluding with the 'empirically unsustainable idea' that successful trauma artefacts might communicate trauma 'so that the reader of this oxymoronically unmediated trauma narrative can experience it in its literal totality' (162). Indeed, if trauma cannot be adequately represented in language – which is, in any case, a still disputable point – then the notion of transmission is equally debatable. The transmission of affect onto a reader that a trauma text may perform will vary so much depending on context and the disposition of the reader that to suggest it somehow mimics the original experience of trauma is deeply problematic. Perhaps Caruth's theories regarding transmission are initially attractive precisely because as readers of trauma texts we desire affect and emotional response. The transmission argument effaces the representational dimension of trauma narratives, focusing instead on supposedly innovative forms, while suggesting that such texts grant us unmediated and direct access to trauma. It is clearly absurd to elide this categorical difference between the experience of a trauma sufferer, a witness, and the second-hand reader, but this is a major motivating force behind cultural trauma theory.

AESTHETIC CRITERIA OF TRAUMA THEORY: TWO CASE STUDIES

This section briefly considers two studies of trauma texts, Laurie Vickroy's *Trauma and Survival in Contemporary Fiction* and Anne Whitehead's *Trauma Fiction*, and the relationship between these works and the prescriptive aesthetic models laid down for the representation of trauma. Vickroy's book begins relatively cautiously, as she observes various formal affinities between first modernism, and then postmodernism, and the representation of trauma, wherein certain 'stylistic innovations . . . have proved effective in approximating for readers the psychic defenses that pose obstacles to narrating and recovering from trauma' (xi). Problems begin to emerge when these fragmentary techniques assume such importance for Vickroy that they become essential. Texts must follow these formulae, otherwise she omits discussion of 'worthy and important works (such as Maya Angelou's *I Know Why the Caged Bird Sings*) that do not yet emphasize formal innovations, testimonial influences, or the symptoms and defenses common to conflicted traumatic memory' (xi). The move towards a more prescriptive mode of trauma criticism continues when Vickroy argues that traumatic content must be fulfilled through experimental form: '[d]iscoveries about the nature of traumatic experience as overwhelming, alien, amnesiac, and often incomprehensible have *necessitated* new historiographic, testimonial, and representational approaches to help interpret and reconfigure the enigmatic traces of evidence and memory' (1, emphasis added). Such is Vickroy's valuing of these allegedly experimental approaches that she is quick to extend aesthetic judgements to the point that popular culture treatments of trauma are dismissed. Instead, there is a correct (implicitly high cultural) way to represent trauma: '[t]rauma narratives go beyond presenting trauma as subject matter or character study. They internalize the rhythms, processes, and uncertainties of traumatic experience within their underlying sensibilities and structures' (3). This line of argument is pursued later in the chapter, where Vickroy's reference to an '[a]uthentic trauma fiction' (21) begins more overtly to embed problematic value and ethical judgements.

Vickroy also subscribes to the notion that it is essential for trauma to be transmitted rather than represented: 'trauma narrativists enlist their readers to become witnesses to these kinds of stories through the unconventional narrative translations of traumatic experience and memory that give them a different kind of access to the past than conventional frameworks' (20). In this vein, she discusses the use of multiple voices and narrators in Toni Morrison's *Beloved* and Larry Heinemann's *Paco's Story*, and claims that '[w]hen readers absorb these stories through the division of voice . . . they experience something analogous to splitting' (27–8), that is, a dual experience of normal memory and non-integrated traumatic memory. As with the argument above, the notion that a reader can vicariously share the experience of the original sufferer (even if it is 'analogous') cannot but appear as an overstatement designed firstly to defend the idea of trauma fiction per se (something which preoccupies Vickroy throughout), and secondly to elide the actual difficulties inherent in the notion of transmission.

Whitehead's monograph occupies similar ground to Vickroy's, but her criticism is generally a good deal less prescriptive and more nuanced. Thus while Whitehead adopts some of the overriding ethical concerns of Caruth and synthesises them into something approaching a model for trauma fiction, it is a markedly broader and less prescriptive framework than Vickroy's. On the one hand, Whitehead affirms Caruth's reading of trauma by extrapolating it into an aesthetic whereby, 'if trauma is at all susceptible to narrative formulation', then this is only possible through 'a literary form which departs from conventional linear sequence' (6). On the other, statements such as the following indicate a much greater sense of caution: '[n]ovelists have frequently found that the impact of trauma can only be adequately represented by mimicking its forms and symptoms, so that temporality and chronology collapse, and narratives are characterised by repetition and indirection'

(3). It is this reluctance to construct a model of validated trauma writing embedded in the phrase 'have frequently found' that helps to make Whitehead's textual analysis more convincing. Whitehead is similarly more measured than Vickroy with regard to the affinities between postmodernism and the representation of trauma, arguing that postmodernism's

> innovative forms and techniques critique the notion of history as grand narrative . . . Trauma fiction emerges out of post-modernist fiction and shares its tendency to bring conventional narrative techniques to their limit. In testing formal boundaries, trauma fiction seeks to foreground the nature and limitations of narrative and to convey the damaging and distorting impact of the traumatic event. (82)

A key point, though, is that unlike Vickroy, Whitehead discusses tendencies rather than seeking to construct a definitive model of trauma fiction which would normalise these strategies, thus leaving the specificity of the texts intact.

Before considering the trauma genre and trauma genre criticism in the next section, it is worth noting that despite the dominance of a Caruthian model for the representation of trauma, other aesthetic possibilities exist. Indeed, to adopt a narrow and formulaic critical approach derived from Caruth's strictures is to overlook the variety of trauma writing in contemporary literature, American and world-wide. The following section, amongst other things, discusses what I term 'traumatic metafiction', that is, writing which is more likely to undermine or parody existing conventions of trauma writing and to challenge accepted theories regarding the representation of trauma and its effects. This may be carried out, as we shall see, through the development of narratives which violate the kind of accepted trajectory mentioned above, or through formal devices that more fully and precisely dramatise issues related to narrating trauma. At the opposite end of the spectrum of trauma representation, although similarly resisting the increasingly programmatic tendencies of the trauma genre, we find a return to a form of realism. As we might expect, a significant part of the effect of this mimetic tendency is to contest the dominant definition of trauma as something which is, in its exceptional nature, sublime and beyond representation. This challenge to assertions that trauma is therefore only representable through experimental discourse may be found, for example, in the deadpan realist prose of recent works by writers such as Carol Shields and Lorrie Moore or, as discussed in Chapter 5, the emergence of novels drawing on ideas from literary naturalism.

As the discussion of Vickroy above suggested, realism has sometimes been perceived as a debased form aligned with a low culture aesthetic, but increasingly trauma theorists and critics are recognising its potential. Craps and Buelens, and Eaglestone, as cited previously, point out the importance of realist narrative for many postcolonial trauma writers, while Luckhurst notes a healthy subgenre of realist trauma narratives in the West:

> [b]eyond post-structuralist trauma theory and its trauma canon, a wide diversity of high, middle and low cultural forms have provided a repertoire of compelling ways to articulate that apparently paradoxical thing, the trauma narrative. These work from a different aspect of the same problem: if trauma is a crisis in representation, then this generates narrative *possibility* just as much as *impossibility*. (83, original emphasis)

Kaplan and Wang agree (contra Vickroy), that 'mainstream narrative or imagistic interpretations of trauma . . . merit more than a simplistic negative judgment' (9), and argue that 'It is overhasty to dismiss representation and narrative on grounds of inadequacy and failure' (12). Thus 'it is necessary that a choice be made between inadequate telling and relegating of trauma to a mystified silence' (12). Trauma is, evidently, difficult to narrate, but it is also difficult to transmit through the literary text, and so conflated ethical–aesthetic value judgements should not be unthinkingly deployed as a means to dismiss realist trauma narratives out of hand. There are, it seems, alternatives to the ostensibly experimental fragmented narratives of the postmodernist trauma writers. Besides the problematic contemporary American mode of writing and criticism comprising the trauma genre, the following considers some of these alternatives, in particular this embracing of a form of realism.

THE TRAUMA GENRE

In an article for *Studies in the Novel* Shane Graham questions certain formulaic perspectives on trauma which insist that only 'anti-narrative representational methods can be used to convey the paradox-laden disruptions to temporality and language of a traumatic event', and ruefully notes an MLA call for papers. These papers were required to appreciate that 'attempts to represent a traumatic event must employ "anti-narrative modernist forms" including the "disruption of linear chronology, fragmentation, narrative self-consciousness . . . [and] non-closure"' (129). This provides a telling example of the hegemony in trauma theory of a particular and restrictive conception of how trauma should operate in the literary text. The following discusses how this perspective has helped to shape the trauma genre, which affects both criticism and cultural representations of trauma.

The development of the trauma genre is in some ways connected with responses to the events of 11 September 2001. Before that point, forms of trauma writing had begun to emerge that challenged the growing dominance of the trauma genre. One of these, what I term traumatic metafiction, is characterised by a very self-aware and parodic treatment of trauma, and is discussed in detail in Chapter 2 in relation to Mark Z. Danielewski's *House of Leaves*. Although a somewhat reductive interpretation, it is apparent that in the shock following 9/11 writers and commentators fell back onto conventional and reassuring ways of thinking about trauma, most notably PTSD and the Freudian-Caruthian models discussed above. These models, with their prescriptions about narrative form, produced a trauma genre aesthetic that became interwoven with 9/11. Ann Keniston and Jeanne Quinn argue that 'the first novels about 9/11 featured formal innovations – self-reflexive meta-narratives, disrupted temporality, multiple viewpoints' (4). This is in essence correct, but Keniston and Quinn fail to mention that these so-called innovations were in fact adopted from a well-established body of existing trauma literature. The emergence of traumatic metafiction, a more sceptical model, was thus prevented or diverted by the reassertion of this form of trauma theory and a formulaic mode of representation, the 'ready-to-wear trauma' (Farrell 31) of the trauma genre.

The literature of the trauma genre exists in a vicious circle with the reinforcing criticism, which looks approvingly on every new literary text that emerges to reconfirm the theories. This self-perpetuating process in contemporary American writing and criticism is worth examining here in order to enable us to appreciate the power of the trauma genre in shaping the way American culture now thinks about trauma. One telling example in this respect is the controversy surrounding Binjamin Wilkomirski's faked Holocaust memoir, *Fragments*. Originally published as an autobiography, *Fragments* was later revealed to be fictional, a trauma genre text that replicated numerous genre clichés or representational conventions with sufficient accuracy to be initially accepted as genuine testimony: '[l]iterary critics considered *Fragments* a genuine Holocaust memoir precisely because it was a collage of tropes, compiled from many of the same primary sources from which they had generated their expert discourse, and thus proved a better fit with dominant theories of trauma and Holocaust aesthetics than actual memoirs' (Rothe 147). In the text, Wilkomirski lays claim to a latency period during which he was unable to recall or write about his experiences. The text also includes familiar techniques such as fragmented chronology and splitting of the narrative voice at moments of thematic crisis. *Fragments* is thus only the most notorious example of writers adopting what had, by the end of the twentieth century, become generic conventions in order to produce their own convincing accounts of trauma. While *Fragments* was vilified as a forgery, plenty of fictional trauma texts have embodied similar strategies, drawing from existing theory, and have thereafter been celebrated by critics for providing evidence to validate those same theories.

Other authors writing in the 1990s and afterwards may be identified as perpetuating what soon became increasingly conventional methods of representing trauma, to the extent that such writing constructs an identifiable (and critically supported) genre. Chapter 1 discusses some of the twentieth-century texts which unwittingly helped to construct some of the norms of trauma representation, but when effects drawing upon this established aesthetic are evident in later texts – Anne Michaels's *Fugitive Pieces*, Siri Hustvedt's *What I Loved*, Don DeLillo's *The Body Artist* and Jonathan Safran

Foer's *Everything is Illuminated* to name but four examples – the once disruptive or disorientating effect upon the reader is inevitably lessened through familiarity. All four of these novels employ tropes including abrupt ellipses, non-linear chronology, and shifts in narrating voice, which by the mid-1990s had become familiar to readers. This means that when a reader acquainted with the tropes of the trauma genre encounters the breach in the narrative between parts one and two of *What I Loved*, the revelation regarding the death of the protagonist's son is actually predictable. These texts, and other ostensibly unconventional works, have nevertheless drawn significant praise from critics. Daniel Mendelsohn, for example, applauded the appearance in *Everything is Illuminated* of 'some of the most complex technical tricks you're likely to encounter in recent fiction', which, he argues, comprise 'a remarkably effective way of dwelling on an issue of considerable urgency in Holocaust literature: the seemingly hopeless split between history and narrative, between what happened and what can be told'. In an even more rapturous review, Francine Prose, in *The New York Times*, declared that '[n]ot since . . . *A Clockwork Orange* has the English language been simultaneously mauled and energized with such brilliance and such brio,' and went on to praise Foer's formal strategies: 'the structure reveals itself slowly, in stages, and each one of these small revelations is a source of surprise and pleasure.' As we shall see in Chapter 1, however, the non-linear, fragmentary and repetitive structure of *Everything is Illuminated*, built around incremental revelations, actually becomes a staple of the trauma genre, having been formulated in the preceding decades.

This is not to dismiss these texts out of hand. Indeed, a number of these works, for all their use of genre aesthetics, also present an equivocal challenge to certain dominant elements of trauma theory. *The Body Artist*, for example, through its parodic imitation of popular trauma discourse (in the simulation of a pretentious magazine interview with its protagonist, Lauren), and its ambiguous refusal of the neat closure provided by a conventional narrative model of trauma and recovery (given that Lauren arguably remains traumatised at the novella's end), demonstrates an awareness of debates in the field, but also a willingness to engage with and critique rather than adopt them. The problem emerges when authors adopt formal and thematic genre conventions without DeLillo's scepticism, as well as their texts existing in a close and self-reinforcing relationship with trauma genre criticism. Authors and critics may be held equally to blame in this respect, the former for too unquestioningly adopting narrative forms and themes derived from dominant, simplified and popularised aspects of trauma theory, the latter for finding confirmatory evidence of their theories in the works of these and other trauma authors. In particular, critics are not infrequently guilty of mounting tendentious readings of novels for precisely this aim. In seeking to bestow moral and aesthetic value on a particular type of writing, critics have thus typically exaggerated the alleged subversive qualities of what has in fact become a strikingly codified way of representing trauma. The parodic and ambiguous elements in *The Body Artist* identified above, for example, have been largely overlooked by critics who insist on imposing a conventional recovery ending. Anne Longmuir, for instance, although she acknowledges ambiguous elements in the novella, insists that Lauren is finally able to 'work through her own grief and trauma' (534).

Clearly, a wider range of options than the narrow aesthetic that characterises the trauma genre is available for writers, and these options have not been entirely ignored. Another mode adopted by some contemporary writers may be classed as a return to realism, drawing in part upon certain non-fiction techniques that have recently been (re)popularised through factual trauma memoirs. This new realism arguably now represents a more effective technique for jolting the reader than over-familiar postmodernist effects. Its tendency to adopt a deadpan or jaded narrating tone, for example, convincingly mimics the disconnected voice of the traumatised protagonist. Accomplished works that deal with trauma without recourse to the sometimes meretricious effects of trauma genre literature belie the latter's narrow and prescriptive aesthetic. Carol Shields's *Unless*, for example, communicates a thoroughly convincing and affecting depiction of family trauma, but the predominant register in the novel is realist, being chronologically linear, and defiantly non-experimental. Despite her refusal to employ the prescribed formal elements of the trauma genre, Shields is nevertheless clearly versed in the theoretical issues at stake. PTSD and its treatments are specifically – and knowledgably – mentioned in the novel, while towards its end her narrator, Reta, states 'I'm not sure I believe in the thunderclap of trauma' (269), and expresses her doubts about 'the filigree of fine-spun theory' (269) not only regarding the necessarily overwhelming intrusion of trauma, but also the existence of the latency period upon which PTSD and Caruthian theory depends. Unlike novels characterised above as trauma genre, *Unless* engages with existing theory but refuses to conform to any doctrinal formal requirements regarding the representation of trauma. Shields's writing provides an essential example of a violation of the reinforcing circle of experimental literary techniques and, more importantly, suggests that the narrow genre aesthetic represents merely one way in which trauma might be addressed. Critics who hold too rigidly to this programmatic model of writing may thus be missing crucial exceptions to their rule and, indeed, lagging well behind actual literary practice.

A similarly sceptical, downbeat, disconnected but realist narrating voice can be found in the work of Lorrie Moore, most notably in her *A Gate at the Stairs* (2009). Like Shields, Moore provides a highly persuasive account of family trauma and, as she explained in an interview with *The Believer*, the potentially traumatising effect of broader political decisions, 'the way that the workings of governments and elected officials intrude upon the lives and minds of people who feel generally safe from the immediate effects of such workings'. This overwhelming impact of global politics on the individual and its thematic treatment through a form of neo-naturalism – which also clearly informs Moore's writing – is discussed further in Chapter 5. Like Shields, Moore achieves her effects without employing the range of postmodernist techniques generally demanded by the trauma genre. She demonstrates an awareness of debates, but critiques prescriptive assumptions regarding representation, not only through an apparently anachronistic realist mode, but also, for example, when characters openly state that when it comes to traumatic events, rather than therapeutic remembering, it may be 'good to forget' (243). As Elizabeth Anker suggests, *A Gate at the Stairs* thus 'stages a type of rejoinder to other literary treatments of 9/11, probing whether their heady preoccupation with the spectacle . . . has impeded forms of mournful reckoning, with the outcome of silencing valuable critique as well as contrition' (481). Moore thereby subtly disparages more generic 9/11 texts and produces a narrative which successfully reflects on the wider fallout of subsequent American foreign policy, especially compared to other texts that 'spectacularized the lingering trauma of 9/11 through sublime enthrallment'. Instead, 'Moore resists either romanticizing 9/11's tragedies or distancing them through such a redemptive prism' (Anker 480).

As suggested above, one of the most serious consequences of the full absorption into mainstream western culture of many of the principal concepts of dominant trauma theory – in the form of a loose collection of ideas associated with PTSD – is that these theories have begun demonstrably to influence the ways in which writers of fiction engage with the subject. It is hardly contentious to argue that writers are both learning about trauma from popularised theory and following the aesthetic strictures of trauma theory in order for their works to pass for realistic and convincing representations of the pathology. As Naomi Morgenstern suggests, '"[t]rauma" has become central not only to debates about psychoanalysis, but more generally to a postmodern understanding of subjectivity, and that means that many authors are more or less self-consciously writing trauma narratives' (70). Without wishing to overstate this claim, some of the previously cited works, alongside examples such as Nicole Krauss's *Great House* and Yann Martel's *Beatrice and Virgil*, seem at the very least calculated to cater for a readership now well versed in the formal aesthetic of trauma literature.

This almost incestuous process may be seen to work in both directions, and one of the most dismal aspects of the interdependency between contemporary fiction and criticism in the trauma genre is that the employment of elements from theory by fiction writers has been taken by critics as evidence of the validity of their positions. Indeed, a number of reviewers and critics in the field have constructed what amounts to a critical practice based on a search for elements in literary texts which endorse accepted tenets of trauma theory. This 'checklist criticism' mimics aspects of clinical practice where PTSD developed according to a 'checklist of symptoms' which made it 'easy for both doctor and patient to read, [since] there were also standardised packages of diagnostic questionnaires and psychometric devices' (Shephard 385). And just as with clinical practice, so in the cultural domain this has arguably led to a vicious circle, whereby dominant theoretical staples inspire works of fiction which are in turn taken to prove trauma theory's validity. Examples of this critical practice are plentiful. For instance, Whitehead finds that in *Fugitive Pieces*, 'In the childhood experiences of Jakob, Michaels encapsulates Caruth's notion of "missed" or "Unclaimed experience",' thus confirming a value in the fictional work's employment of the theoretical principle (53).[3]

While the influence of the trauma genre is easily locatable in the practices of writers and critics in the field, it also pervades popular cultural reading practices. Luckhurst, for instance, notes of Oprah's Book Club that texts

> have to conform to [a] narrative model of tribulation and ultimate moral uplift. The reading mode encouraged is one of complete identification, affective connection rather than aesthetic analysis . . . Identification through affect produces a circuit where Oprah's choice guarantees a book's authenticity and the book reinforces Oprah's privileging of trauma subjectivity. (134)

Albeit at an arguably lesser level of formal sophistication, the broad demand for trauma writing here is once more the transmission of affect rather than the communication or representation of trauma. Again, the potentially depoliticising effect of this demand is not difficult to perceive. Rothe notes how the dominant trauma aesthetic is increasingly formulaically applied in popular trauma narratives, here in child abuse memoirs of dubious authenticity, wherein the abuse is characteristically 'represented as occurring in the narrated present and depicted in horrific detail by an uncomprehending naïve child's voice' (120). Formulaic narrative trajectories of trauma such as these have become, she argues, ubiquitous in America: '[a]lthough these fabricated accounts of victimhood were generated in diverse contexts, their resemblances indicate that the trauma-and-redemption story paradigm emplotted in melodramatic good-versus-evil conflicts and embodied in the flat characters of innocent victim and evil villain has thoroughly saturated the public sphere' (157). As the above should demonstrate, this may indeed be the case not only in the realm of the popular 'misery memoir' but also in the supposedly avant-garde and self-consciously literary representations of trauma which studiously construct impenetrable barriers between victims and perpetrators.

ALTERNATIVE TRAUMA PARADIGMS

As Kansteiner observes, 'a number of theorists have called for an intellectual approach to trauma that brings the abstract, counter-representational traditions' of Caruth and her fellow travellers 'in contact with alternative perspectives on trauma which have developed in other professional contexts and which are generally committed to the paradigm of realism' (206). Already, we have considered a number of writers and theorists whose work might fall into this category, including Shields and Moore, and critics such as Radstone, Leys, Rothberg, and Luckhurst. Rothberg's is among a growing number of voices seeking recognition for more realist representations of trauma, and part of my analysis of counterfactual fictions in Chapter 5 is similarly orientated towards investigating this aspect of a form of neo-realism or neo-naturalism.

Alternative approaches to the study of trauma have also been extensively advocated – if not always successfully practiced – in notable editions of academic journals, most significantly in the special editions devoted to the subject of *Studies in the Novel* (2008) and *Continuum* (2010). Both these issues, as mentioned above, aimed to broaden trauma theory's parameters, in particular to look beyond western examples or the application of western theoretical models to writing from elsewhere on the globe. While they share a partial failure in developing and applying entirely new critical idioms – indeed, some of the articles contained therein lapse into surprisingly conventional practice – their potential contribution to new forms of trauma criticism and theory should not be overlooked. As Rothberg suggests in his 'Response' to the *Studies in the Novel* articles, however, there remains a concentration on individual character, rather than an adoption of some of the collective or culture-wide perspectives that the contributors initially appear to advocate. Instead, there is much of the same focus on forms that are falsely identified as 'experimental' in numerous Euro-American texts, whereas the different forms of trauma identified here, especially the insidious and the collective, should surely be appreciated as manifesting in different ways, using distinct and often more realist narrative forms. There is also scant attempt to adapt contemporary narratological analyses to trauma texts.[4]

A central argument of this study is that a number of divergent narrative forms for the representation of trauma can be found in contemporary American texts, and these texts are deserving of a less formulaic set of critical approaches than has hitherto been employed. Chapter 1 offers a brief sketch of a selection of twentieth-century precursor or foundational trauma texts, including J. D. Salinger's 'For Esmé – with Love and Squalor', Joseph Heller's *Catch-22*, Kurt Vonnegut's *Slaughterhouse-Five*, Toni Morrison's *Beloved*, E. L. Doctorow's *The Book of Daniel* and some of Tim O'Brien's Vietnam narratives. The chapter analyses some of the key paradigms that these trauma texts helped to construct, including extreme chronological and narrating fragmentation, formal employment of repetition, the radical decentring of narrating subjectivity, and the belated revelations of traumatic incidents. A contrast is drawn in this chapter between the originally shocking effects of these deliberately disjointed narratives, and trauma texts from later in the century that employ similar, but by now derivative, representational practices. Chapter 2 focuses in detail upon the idea of traumatic metafiction, mainly through Mark Z. Danielewski's *House of Leaves* (2000). Danielewski's novel is interpreted here as a culmination of numerous postmodernist trauma concerns, both formal and thematic. As a traumatic metafiction, the text is partly orientated as a parody of trauma genre texts, but the experimental form of narrating voice, in particular the complex interpolated narration Danielewski employs, is equally worthy of notice as a strikingly original vehicle for narrating trauma.

Chapter 3 focuses on postmodernist responses to 9/11, primarily Art Spiegelman's short graphic memoir, *In the Shadow of No Towers*, and Jonathan Safran Foer's novel, *Extremely Loud and Incredibly Close*. The chapter argues that responses to 9/11, cultural or political, may be placed somewhere on a spectrum between historicism and decontextualisation; that is, respectively, those texts which integrated the events of 9/11 into an ongoing geopolitical historical narrative, and those which saw them, by contrast, as an outrageous and unprecedented limit event. In this respect, Keniston and Quinn argue that 'while the initial experience of 9/11 seemed unprecedented and cataclysmic, the experience of incommensurability generated a culture-wide need for explanatory narratives, not simply as a means of countering the trauma, but as a means for refusing incommensurability, prompting attempts to place 9/11 into a historical framework' (3). Keniston and Quinn suggest that this 'history of literary representations of 9/11' takes the form of a 'transition from narratives of rupture to narratives of continuity' (3), but this conception depicts change that is both universal and smooth, and is thus slightly misleading on both counts. As Chapter 3 maintains, right-wing commentators aided the Bush administration in perpetuating the 'rupture' view and, as Spiegelman's text angrily delineates, using the resultant feelings of victimhood as a spur to military action. Chapter 4 examines the consequences of this military action in more detail, focusing on a selection of American narratives from the Gulf Wars of 1991 and 2003 onwards. The texts consulted here include those written by male and female service personnel and officers, and embedded reporters. Issues of race, gender, and class are particularly important in this chapter, in terms of demonstrating starkly different reactions to similarly stressful incidents. The chapter focuses in particular on the service personnel's peculiar status as potential perpetrators of traumatic acts, yet generally stripped of more than rudimentary agency. This status, alongside their general experience of insidious rather than punctual trauma, sometimes produces unusual manifestations and representations of trauma.

The final chapter examines the depiction of trauma in three counterfactual novels which respond in some way to post-9/11 America: Paul Auster's *Man in the Dark*, Michael Chabon's *The Yiddish Policemen's Union*, and Philip Roth's *The Plot Against America*. The chapter treats these works as, to varying degrees, experimental novels which, moreover, mark some sort of return to a form of naturalism. All three novels feature protagonists who struggle to maintain agency, beset as they are by forces greater than themselves, in a way familiar from earlier forms of naturalism and also to be found in other novels of the period (for example in Cormac McCarthy's *The Road*, Lorrie Moore's *A Gate at the Stairs* and Andre Dubus III's *The Garden of Last Days*). In *After the Fall* Richard Gray argues that a key failing of a number of American post-9/11 novels is that while they recognise the need for new forms and modes of articulation, they actually retreat to old, comforting ideas, especially that of the family (30). I take Gray's call for new forms literally here – but depart significantly in terms of the kind of text consequently found – and understand the realism/ neo-naturalism of the writers considered in this chapter to be a form of reaction against the prevailing anti-realist trauma aesthetic. In these cases, the combination of neo-naturalism with counterfactual history represents precisely a new way of thinking about the traumas of early twenty-first century American life.

NOTES

1. Ruth Leys's *Trauma: A Genealogy* and Roger Luckhurst's *The Trauma Question* are particularly recommended in this respect.
2. Indeed, even some of the originating theory is elusive when it notes the way in which the development of PTSD as a set of diagnostic criteria came about following Vietnam. Herman, for example, notes how a 'five-volume study [*Legacies of Vietnam* by Egendorf et al.] on the legacies of Vietnam *delineated* the syndrome of post-traumatic stress disorder and demonstrated beyond any reasonable doubt its direct relationship to combat exposure' (27, emphasis added). Thereafter, in 1980, 'the characteristic syndrome of psychological trauma became a "real" diagnosis' for the first time, as the APA 'included in its official manual of mental disorders a new category, called "post-traumatic stress disorder" ... Thus the syndrome of psychological trauma, periodically forgotten and periodically rediscovered through the past century, *finally attained formal recognition* within the diagnostic canon' (28, emphasis added). Italics in the above quotations highlight what is being elided

here with regard to the construction rather than the alleged discovery or recognition of PTSD.

3. Other examples of checklist criticism abound in the explosion of writing about trauma texts in the last fifteen or so years. Some of these, concerning readings of Foer's *Extremely Loud and Incredibly Close* by Francisco Collado-Rodriguez, Sien Uytterschout and Kristiaan Versluys, are discussed in more detail in Chapter 3.

4. Mieke Bal's work is one of surprisingly few attempts to analyse trauma aesthetics using contemporary narratological tools. Her work, however, for all its innovations regarding narratology, draws too acceptingly on the dominant trauma theories criticised in this chapter. For example, in distinguishing between the contrasting effects upon narrative of repression and dissociation, she cites as authoritative the work of Bessel van der Kolk and Onno van der Hart. Bal claims that in terms of the representation of memory, '[i]n narratological terms, repression results in ellipsis – the omission of important elements in the narrative – whereas dissociation doubles the strand of the narrative series of events by splitting off a sideline' (ix). This is a useful observation, but is limited through its origin in psychoanalytic trauma theory. In fact, textual representation of the effects of dissociation, as the following chapters suggest, is much more varied than Bal's formulation indicates.

CHAPTER I

Twentieth-Century Trauma Narratives: Some Paradigmatic Texts

Delineating an exhaustive genealogy of literary representations of trauma in the twentieth century is beyond the scope of this chapter or the aims of this book. Even if, as with this study, one restricts the scope to manifestations in American literature, it is immediately obvious that trauma has become so ubiquitous that – at the very least – a full-length study would be required just to describe its emergence. Even in an American context one is immediately faced with the question of how far back in time we should search for origins of the trauma paradigm. No matter that PTSD, as the Introduction described, only comes into being through its definition in 1980, since this has encouraged some contemporary critics and theorists to find earlier prototypes. According to this perspective, some of the canonical American texts of the nineteenth century may be fancifully refigured as depictions of the traumatised legacy of the Puritans (as in *The Scarlet Letter*), or of later religious crises (much of Melville's oeuvre). Similarly, the slave narratives of Frederick Douglass, Harriett Jacobs et al. may now be understood in part as catalogues of traumatised responses. And, going further back, perhaps we might reinterpret Mary Rowlandson's narrative of removals as a paradigmatic response to traumatic events.

As suggested, such questions are beyond the scope of this chapter but also, in their imposition of a contemporary framework upon historical works from quite different contexts, such reinterpretations are dangerously tendentious. Instead, this chapter engages with the more modest, but essential, task of tracing some of the key formal and thematic characteristics of trauma representation that emerge in the latter half of the twentieth century. As we shall see in later chapters, many of these characteristics become entrenched as archetypes by the end of the twentieth century, and on into the twenty-first. The following chapter divides broadly into two parts. The first part focuses on trauma representations deriving from America's involvement in armed conflicts across the globe, and considers key works by J. D. Salinger, Joseph Heller, Kurt Vonnegut and Tim O'Brien. Secondly, the chapter examines two of the most influential works concerning other manifestations of trauma, Toni Morrison's *Beloved* and E. L. Doctorow's *The Book of Daniel*.

A few overarching patterns discernible from these texts and the critical responses they elicited are especially relevant to this study as a whole. In particular, we shall see that there is a different relationship between content and form in this first generation of trauma texts, from the latter half of the twentieth century, compared with many from the early twenty-first century. In this first generation, traumatic content is paramount and is communicated with a detectable urgency. Often sufferers themselves, these authors depict trauma as intrusive and compelling. While numerous experimental forms are employed in order to represent the effects of trauma upon the individual, these experiments in form are produced by or respond to the traumatic content that is to be communicated. Form in these works is clearly subordinate to content. The frequently devastating effect produced by these works makes this apparent, but the hierarchy is also confirmed in, for example, interviews with authors, or by their evident need to revisit and rework traumatic themes. Repetition within individual works or across a range of texts reveals a compulsion to find appropriate artistic means to register trauma's impact. One might think in this respect of the circling narrative of Heller's *Catch-22*, the autobiographical and semi-fictionalised themes and variations within Tim O'Brien's published oeuvre, Henry Roth's *Mercy of a Rude Stream* series (1994–8) and its preceding thirty years' worth of constantly reworked manuscript drafts, or Toni Morrison's revisiting the story of Margaret Garner in her fictionalised account,

Beloved, and her later collaborative opera. In short, innovative and experimental forms employed by these and other trauma writers of the twentieth century are a means to an end, developed precisely in order to represent the compulsive material.

By contrast, this study suggests that in many texts of the late twentieth and into the twenty-first century, a fascination with the experimental forms employed in the representation of trauma becomes the primary motivation for literary production. There emerges at this time a preoccupation with formal devices that become established methods of depicting trauma, including fragmentation, dislocation, and repetition. This has been encouraged by the type of trauma criticism which stresses a 'need for a narrative form which does not succumb to closure and coherence, but retains within itself the traces of traumatic disruption and discontinuity' (Whitehead 142). One should ask, perhaps, precisely for whom this 'need' arises. Clearly, in principle we are talking here about the victim or sufferer, but in practice, especially in fictional works, it is arguably the case that ostensibly experimental forms are employed primarily to demonstrate the fiction writer's superior powers of representation, and the trauma critic's highly developed empathy. Traumatic content, in these instances of trauma genre writing, becomes subservient to form, as writers become preoccupied more with the sublime jouissance of representing trauma, than with trauma's actual impact. Once the formal means become ends in themselves, trauma is relegated from a subject of committed study (as in the works discussed in this chapter) to a vehicle for these practices and, thus, aestheticised and ossified.

Western society's broad fascination with trauma is also, undoubtedly, a major factor in the way in which the formal tropes of trauma writing become overly familiar. This is reflected in trauma's proliferation across art forms and popular culture, as well as in the explosion of critical and theoretical studies, of which this present study is, however disapproving, a part. In turn, this proliferation has helped to produce a situation where what were once the experimental and disorientating narrative forms of trauma – and, at a wider level, postmodernism – have become both blunted and unmoored from their original purpose. Trauma literature produced under such circumstances becomes what I am terming the 'trauma genre', or what others have labelled 'trauma kitsch'. Given the historical circumstances of the beginning of the twenty-first century in the US – most significantly, the perceived collective trauma of 9/11, and the alleged rupture this causes in American society – the transformation of trauma literature into a formulaic kitschy genre is surprising. In reaction to 9/11 one might, instead, have expected an urgent and serious renewed engagement with trauma and its representation. As Chapter 3 in particular discusses, however, unquestioning assumptions about the 'collective trauma' of 9/11 – whose western bias decontextualises and limits the events and their consequences – in fact encourages a retreat to a facile bricolage of accepted representational practices disingenuously masquerading as experimental and avant-garde.

While this chapter discusses a number of influential thematic and formal elements found in twentieth-century trauma texts, it also examines certain less recognised characteristics of these foundational works. Perhaps as a result, these elements have been less frequently or less obviously assimilated by later trauma texts. These often interdependent characteristics include, firstly, a not infrequent focus upon the trauma or guilt of the perpetrator, especially with regard to the war combat narratives discussed here. Secondly, we shall observe the way in which these texts often depict post-traumatic reactions as a constant, insistent, and conscious presence, rather than, as dominant trauma theory would insist, being characterised by *Nachträglichkeit*, the latency period during which the traumatic event is unavailable to consciousness. Finally, a number of the texts in this chapter represent the kind of insidious trauma discussed in the introduction in relation to Laura Brown's theories that depart from the dominant model's insistence on sudden, event-based trauma. Indeed, it is striking that the incremental type is the predominant form of trauma discussed in these works, suggesting that it is in fact the event-based model of Caruth and her supporters that is atypical. As we shall see, the common experience of war combat trauma, on the side of both victim and (apparent) perpetrator, would appear to be more often insidious than sudden.

The works of the first four authors discussed in this chapter – J. D. Salinger, Joseph Heller, Kurt Vonnegut and Tim O'Brien –

are tied together by this focus on combat trauma. This means that the discussion centres on certain shared characteristics, including elements such as perpetrator trauma and the generally insidious character of combat trauma, thus anticipating a number of the characteristics of war narratives explored in Chapter 4. Related to this thematic focus is an examination of the way in which many of these paradigmatic twentieth-century trauma texts imbricate the broad sweep of history with the personal, in part reflecting the history of bloody conflicts that marks much of the twentieth and twenty-first centuries. Texts such as *Catch-22*, and even more so *The Book of Daniel*, *Beloved*, and the work of Tim O'Brien draw on actual historical events, often as a means of exploring the overwhelming and traumatic effect of wider historical events upon the individual or the family. Likewise, the description of the 'Children's Crusade' in *Slaughterhouse-Five*, a thirteenth-century attempt to kidnap 30,000 German and French children into slavery on the pretext that they were going to fight in Palestine (11–12), in many ways anticipates similar examinations of the traumatic effect of history upon the family in the works of Philip Roth and Paul Auster, discussed in Chapter 5. As we shall see, many of the founding or paradigmatic twentieth-century trauma texts therefore locate on the porous borders between fiction and nonfiction, or autobiography. This location, found by a number of authors to be crucial to the communication of trauma, is replicated in a number of twenty-first century texts.

J. D. SALINGER, 'FOR ESMÉ – WITH LOVE AND SQUALOR' (1953)

J. D. Salinger's 'For Esmé – with Love and Squalor' is a striking attempt to employ experimental techniques which later become familiar in the depiction of trauma, such as fragmented, non-chronological narration, and shifts in narrating subjectivity. Perhaps the most influential element, however, in this and Salinger's other stories concerning the war trauma of various members of the Glass family, is the degree to which the narrative draws on his own experiences. In common with O'Brien's work discussed later in this chapter, Salinger draws an indistinct line between his own experiences and those of the war-traumatised characters in this story. Paul Alexander notes that even outside his own literary output, Salinger made fluid distinctions between his life and his work. Alexander describes Salinger, in 1987, looking back on his younger self and describing that self in the third person (286–7), having already been known for talking about Holden Caulfield as a real person. '[A]t least following World War II,' Alexander concludes, 'Salinger was not always able to make strict distinctions between fiction and memory' (287). The link here is interesting: Alexander causally relates Salinger's evidently traumatising experiences of ferocious fighting in Bavaria in the Second World War to a growing lack of distinction between reality and fiction, the real and the imagined. In 'Esmé', the blurred distinction between autobiography and fiction – evident at least at the beginning of the story – represents one of a number of effects deployed by Salinger which, deliberately or not, enable the communication of Sergeant X's trauma.

The implication that the story as a whole is a simulation of that which Sergeant X writes for Esmé provides an early, if tentative, example of what might be termed inscription, wherein the narrating act is interpolated, in whole or part, into the text itself. Combining this effect with the story's autobiographical shading – as protagonist, narrator and author inextricably overlap – suggests that a considerable degree of narrative complexity is a necessary means towards the representation of trauma. That this is now a conventional perspective regarding the representation of trauma is in large part due to experiments carried out by writers such as Salinger. As with other examples of inscription, the effects include a sense of decentred subjectivity, most strikingly in the change in narrative voice to heterodiegetic for Sergeant X's war narrative; X claims sardonically to have 'disguised myself so cunningly that even the cleverest reader will fail to recognise me' (77). More significantly, the inscribed narration also (re)introduces an unusual temporal dimension to the narration, and through this an appreciation of the insidious effect of trauma upon X, as well as the time required for his recovery. Combined with repetition – another facet of trauma narrative that becomes much more familiar later in the twentieth century – the narrative strategies also convey a cautious set of gestures towards the protagonist's recovery from war trauma. Most significantly, the phrase 'faculties intact' reoccurs: Esmé uses it at the end of her meeting with Sergeant X, he quotes it at the beginning of his narrative, fearing that 'he was a young man who had not come through the war with all his faculties intact' (77), and again at the story's conclusion, where the inscribed narration gives a tentative indication of recovery, as further suggested by the fracturing of the penultimate word: '[y]ou take a really sleepy man, Esmé, and he *al*ways stands a chance of becoming a man with all his fac – with all his f-a-c-u-l-t-i-e-s intact' (85). The unspeakable effect of trauma is shown gradually to become comprehensible and bearable.

Salinger's 'Esmé' thereby provides us with an early example of trauma and recovery conveyed through a series of linked disruptive narrative strategies, not the least of which is the measure of inscribed narration. Of course, even some of these strategies for communicating trauma could be traced back to earlier narratives – in the case of Salinger, for example, to Hemingway, who spoke encouragingly to Salinger about his war writing. The point is, this story provides us with a prototype for writing about war trauma, and a range of effects for conveying trauma which only later in the century become overly familiar. This employment of a range of disruptive narrative effects now commonly associated with postmodernism as a means for conveying traumatic material is even more apparent in the following text.

JOSEPH HELLER, *Catch-22* (1962)

While innovations in the representation of trauma in Salinger's 'Esmé' are relatively tentative, *Catch-22* is by contrast a fully paradigmatic trauma text, certainly one of the most influential in terms of formal means used to depict war and trauma. Indeed, the entire structure of *Catch-22* can be interpreted as narrative procrastination, slowly circling around the central trauma of Yossarian's witnessing of Snowden's agonising death. Through this spiralling narrative the reader experiences an extraordinary degree of repetition, with gradual additions to the Snowden story, whose totality is nevertheless deferred until the penultimate chapter of this lengthy novel. Circling as a form of evasive narration becomes a classic trope of trauma narrative, as we shall see. The repetitive, circular trajectory of Heller's novel helps to explain the seemingly irrational behaviour of its central protagonist, Yossarian, whose reaction to the madness and bureaucracy of the war surrounding him is to indulge his overriding drive for self-preservation. Having witnessed Snowden's violent and bloody death first-hand, Yossarian reacts in apparently solipsistic fashion, believing that the war primarily constitutes a personal threat to his self, as the following (typical) exchange illustrates:

> "They're trying to kill me," Yossarian told [Clevinger] calmly.
> "No one's trying to kill you," Clevinger cried.
> "Then why are they shooting at me?" Yossarian asked.
> "They're shooting at *everyone*," Clevinger answered. "They're trying to kill everyone."
> "And what difference does that make?" (24)

If Yossarian feels individually persecuted, he also believes that he is partly responsible for Snowden's death, due to his failure to treat Snowden's fatal but initially hidden injury. It is tempting to interpret Yossarian's delayed comprehension of the degree of Snowden's injuries – he initially 'treat[s] Snowden for the wrong wound' (353) – as a symbolic rendering of his *Nachträglichkeit*, or delayed experience of trauma. Indeed, Alberto Cacicedo is one of a number of critics to insist precisely that, arguing that the novel is a representation of Yossarian's recovery of memory: 'throughout the novel Yossarian is as much in the dark as is the reader about the actuality of Snowden's death. The novel circles around and around the death precisely because Yossarian can neither remember it nor forget it' (359). While the novel's structure in some ways simulates the recovery of a memory, however, this is directed at protecting the reader from too sudden exposure to the truth of the trauma, rather than specifically mimicking Yossarian's psyche. Indeed, Cacicedo is only forced into awkward and paradoxical formulations such as this: '[t]he fictional character and the real novelist must revisit the traumatic event over and over again precisely because it has determined their lives in profound ways; yet, because of its horrific power, the event has also erased itself from their consciousness' (361) because of a dogmatic adherence to the concept of *Nachträglichkeit*. In fact, there is nothing in Yossarian's behaviour after this incident to suggest that its memory is blocked from conscious recall. Quite the opposite: the memory of Snowden's death is insistently present in Yossarian's consciousness throughout, and much of the novel concerns his traumatised acting out – the aforementioned solipsistic paranoia – and his unsuccessful attempts to suppress the incident from overwhelming conscious memory. Yossarian may act out, but he remains lucid about and conscious of why he is doing so, in a way that mimics, and arguably inspires, the absurd paradoxical logic that thematically and structurally underpins the novel. Interestingly, even in such a paradigmatic, foundational trauma text as Heller's, a model of trauma contingent on *Nachträglichkeit* demonstrably fails to apply.

As we shall see, in much of Tim O'Brien's war writing there are allusions to traumatic incidents at the start of the work, which are revisited and gradually filled in throughout the succeeding narrative. We might trace such strategies back to *Catch-22*, where the earliest allusion to the principal traumatic incident, the death of Snowden, is in the fourth chapter, when Yossarian silences his squad's briefing with the question, 'Where are the Snowdens of yesteryear' (43). As the novel progresses, the reader is granted access to Yossarian's recurring flashbacks to Snowden's death, in gradually greater detail. Heller uses the narrative structure of the traumatic memory repeating with incremental additions to construct a linguistic shorthand, which forms a screen, partially obscuring the full memory. In Chapter 17, the memory of Snowden's death again briefly intrudes, as Yossarian is momentarily reminded of 'the way Snowden had frozen to death' while mortally wounded in the aeroplane:

"I'm cold," Snowden had whimpered. "I'm cold."
"There, there," Yossarian had tried to comfort him. "There, there." (180)

It is telling that this short exchange is what intrudes most often from Yossarian's memory of the traumatic incident. Yossarian's shame regarding his impotence constructs a shorthand for the entire episode. As we revisit the incident throughout the novel and more is gradually revealed, Snowden's 'I'm cold' remains a constant synecdochic reminder of Yossarian's failure to save his compatriot.

This construction of a codified shorthand synecdoche for the full memory also becomes paradigmatic in the representation of trauma. Traumatic narratives are, as already suggested, typically built around what Genette terms repeating narrative, where a single past episode is narrated more than once and, generally in the case of trauma narratives, numerous times. This repetition frequently combines with a shorthand signification which stands synecdochally for the entire memory, which is usually too terrible to bear. If it is Snowden's 'I'm cold' and Yossarian's 'There, there' in *Catch-22*, we might also think of the repeated refrain of 'So it goes' in Vonnegut's *Slaughterhouse-Five*, or 'impossible, of course' in O'Brien's *In the Lake of the Woods*, both of which sardonically denote a variety of atrocities. Outside war trauma narratives, Henry Roth's semi-autobiographical *Mercy of a Rude Stream* series uses numerous shorthand codifications for traumatic sexual experiences in the past of the protagonist, Ira, fixating, for example, on the 'pork-pie hat' of a child molester he encounters at the age of ten (*A Star Shines* passim), or the 'green, blistery walls' (*Diving Rock* 213) of the room where Ira and his sister later commit incest. A full, finally graphic, description of Snowden's death is only granted in the penultimate chapter of Heller's novel. It is characterised again by numerous repetitions of the 'I'm cold'/'There, there' codification (461–4), which by now refers back to – and begins to explain more fully – earlier evocations. The key point regarding the repetitions is that the entire structure of *Catch-22* – its circling narrative which gradually adds more detail, and complementary elements such as the shorthand codification of the memory of the death of Snowden or Yossarian's solipsistic paranoia – is predicated on Heller's portrayal of war trauma.

Besides the final full disclosure in the scene depicting Snowden's death, the novel's traumatic themes emerge a little earlier, in

Chapter 39, 'The Eternal City', wherein Yossarian spends a night wandering a Rome resembling the worst imaginings of Dante. One of the longest in the novel, this chapter provides the bleakest manifestation of the traumatic horrors which have hitherto been broached only tangentially or by allusion. Accompanying Yossarian's wandering through night-time Rome, the reader witnesses a gradually deepening circle of violence, abuse and oppression. This includes a multiple rape of a drunken woman (437), a dog and then a child being mercilessly beaten (438), a civilian being brutally abducted by police (439), and finally the rape and murder of an Italian maid by Aarfy, a member of Yossarian's squadron (441). It is as if the limited comforts of the novel's foregoing carnivalesque humour are suddenly dissolved, as the reader is more fully exposed to the horrors of Yossarian's experience of wartime Europe. Rome, in this chapter, becomes a physical correlative to traumatic memories of the death of Snowden; just as we have previously circled this event throughout the novel before the truth is finally revealed, so here we witness Yossarian's descent into the circles of Hell. While the notion of spiralling descent in this chapter again reinforces the novel's general structural basis in repetition, the incidents Yossarian encounters are also inherently repetitious. The drunken woman is repeatedly raped; a soldier in convulsions is placed on a car bonnet then back on the ground, and then back on the bonnet; the dog and then the boy are repeatedly beaten. The novel's deeper spiralling structures are similarly reflected at the level of language: finding himself stepping on a plethora of human teeth, Yossarian '*circled* on tiptoe the grotesque debris' (439, emphasis added); he sees inhabitants vanish 'into the deepening *layers* of darkness' (440, emphasis added), and then notes that a streetlight is not working, 'the glass *globe* broken' (440, emphasis added). The bleak and repetitive imagery in this chapter reinforces the novel's themes and structures, while preparing the reader for the long-delayed narration of Yossarian's most traumatic experience, the death of Snowden. As we shall explore further in the next chapter, a spiralling descent towards traumatic disclosure sometimes, as here, represented physically, becomes a recurring structure in the literature of trauma.

KURT VONNEGUT, *Slaughterhouse-Five* (1969)

Published at the height of the Vietnam War, but set, like *Catch-22*, during World War II, Vonnegut's *Slaughterhouse-Five* has long been interpreted as a formally rich evocation of trauma. Susanne Vees-Gulani's article, suggestively entitled 'Diagnosing Billy Pilgrim: A Psychiatric Approach to Kurt Vonnegut's *Slaughterhouse-Five*', relies on a familiarly rigid model of trauma, which is used to diagnose the novel and its central protagonist. This sometimes produces formulaic and overly neat conclusions, such as that Vonnegut's writing of *Slaughterhouse-Five* was 'a therapeutic process that allows him to uncover and deal with his trauma. By using creative means to overcome his distress, Vonnegut makes it possible for us to trace his path to recovery' (176). As we shall see, this rather simplifies the book's complex construction.

The novel concerns Billy Pilgrim, a reluctant US soldier held during the Second World War as a German POW. Like Vonnegut, Billy witnesses the devastating fire-bombing of Dresden, which leaves him in a permanently dissociative traumatised state. He is prone to fantasies (although the novel remains playfully ambiguous regarding whether these might actually be true) that he travels, albeit involuntarily, in time, and is regularly abducted by aliens from the planet Tralfamadore. That Billy suffers from trauma, and that it is considerably more serious than suggested by the narrator's bathetic description of it as 'a mild nervous collapse' (18), is unquestionable. His pathology is relatively conventional for the condition, including narcolepsy, melancholia, and hallucinations (after his capture, Billy sees 'Saint Elmo's fire, a sort of electronic radiance around the heads of his companions and captors' [46]). Billy also experiences associative flashbacks, as when, at his wedding, the facial expressions of the barbershop quartet remind him of the appalled reactions of the four German guards who, 'in their astonishment and grief' on witnessing the devastation wrought on Dresden, had themselves 'resembled a barbershop quartet' (130). This memory, moreover, takes the similarly conventional form of a haunting; as Billy's new wife, Valencia, remarks, 'You looked as though you'd seen a *ghost*' (126, original emphasis).

What is perhaps most interesting about Billy's relatively conventional trauma symptoms and their manifestation in *Slaughterhouse-Five* is that Vonnegut has confirmed that he was influenced in writing the book by theoretical reading he had carried out in the then-emerging field of trauma. While the novel's autobiographical narrator describes how difficult it was for a long time to write about the subject, in subsequent interviews Vonnegut has also broached the problem of dealing with the subject:

> it took me a long time and it was painful. The most difficult thing about it was that I had forgotten about it. And I learned about catastrophes . . . that there is some device in our brain which switches off and prevents us from remembering catastrophes above a certain scale. I don't know whether it is just a limitation of our nervous system, or whether it's actually a gadget which protects us in some way. But I, in fact, remembered nothing about the bombing of Dresden although I had been there, and did everything short of hiring a hypnotist to recover the information. ('Conversation with Musil' 128)

Given that this interview emerged in 1980, the same year as the publication of *DSM-III*, which first fully defined PTSD, Vonnegut's confirmation of certain tenets – most notably the period of *Nachträglichkeit* – is striking, if fortuitous. Although Vonnegut describes how his own experience of trauma feeds into the work, this is also an early instance of a writer drawing on theory in order to deliver ostensibly convincing portrayals of trauma. Given that Vees-Gulani cites the novel as attesting to the validity of dominant ideas concerning trauma and recovery, Vonnegut's drawing upon trauma theory perhaps marks an initial, tentative turn of a circle which only later, with the full emergence of the trauma genre, becomes vicious.

There is considerably more to *Slaughterhouse-Five*, though, than the confirmation of an emerging consensus regarding trauma. Indeed, as Kevin Brown suggests, the novel's apparent narrative trajectory of trauma and therapy-inspired recovery is deceptive and decidedly more heterodox than others have argued, since Tralfamadorian philosophy is a denial of the reality of death, and therefore a damaging turn to egoism rather than a positive escape or recovery (106). While *Slaughterhouse-Five* superficially offers the reader a conventional trauma-and-recovery narrative, any form of recovery is actually equivocal. Billy's escape into fantasies of travel through time and between planets is ultimately of very limited benefit; more broadly, 'Tralfamadorian determinism and passivity' (Vanderwerken 47), that is, a form of escapism, are revealed as empty and defeatist. The novel's continual refrain of 'so it goes', for example, is borrowed from the Tralfamadorians, and is employed every time Billy encounters some appalling act of violence, atrocity, or tragedy. The phrase reflects the Tralfamadorians' non-chronological and therefore non-teleological understanding of the universe. Since time, for them, is non-linear, death does not constitute any kind of loss. Clearly, though, this is Billy's escapist strategy for circumventing feelings of anguish associated with the traumatising death or injury of others that he encounters.

The novel's fragmented subjectivity – both in terms of the narrator(s) and the chief protagonist – further complicates its critique of escapism as a response to trauma. *Slaughterhouse-Five* is characterised by numerous breaks in the fictional narrative for authorial or autobiographical interjection. Unlike in twenty-first-century texts where the device has become overly familiar, these episodes disrupt the reading experience. This protean sense of subjectivity is produced by the playful autobiographical form adopted in the first and final chapters, and occasional apparently autobiographical interjections in the intervening chapters. On one level, the fractured subjectivity constructed in part through the blurring of fiction and autobiography mirrors the uncertain sense of self experienced by trauma sufferers such as Billy. At a deeper level, this blurring is a typical disorientating strategy of the postmodernist text, what Brian McHale identifies as 'ontological flicker' (207). The complex ontology of Vonnegut's text thus serves as one of the ostentatiously metafictional devices which underscore the difficulty of representing traumatic effects using realist discourse. Reflecting its traumatic theme, the novel's overall form embraces fragmentation from a fractured sense of subjectivity right through to ontological aporia.

The autobiographical address in *Slaughterhouse-Five* thus enables metafictional consideration of the problems of writing about traumatic memory. 'When I got home from the Second World War twenty-three years ago, I thought it would be easy for me to write about the destruction of Dresden, since all I would have to do would be to report what I had seen,' comments the narrator in the opening chapter, foreshadowing remarks quoted from the Musil interview above. But traumatic memory is found to be inaccessible: 'not many words about Dresden came from my mind then . . . And not many words come now, either' (2). The autobiographical narrator thereby explains why experimental forms are sought for representing trauma, and while this anticipates the strictures of later theory regarding non-realist trauma discourse, Vonnegut is rare in using direct metafictional voice to discuss the reasons for these devices in the text itself. Unlike a number of trauma writers following the explosion of theory, Vonnegut, as metafictional comments throughout *Slaughterhouse-Five* confirm, carefully considers form, but it remains subordinate to theme. 'There are almost no characters in this story,' he interjects, 'and almost no dramatic confrontations, because most of the people in it are so sick and so much the playthings of enormous forces' (119). This is one of a number of telling comments, of particular interest since it not only addresses the relationship between the novel's non-dramatic form and its traumatised content, but also anticipates the potential for the 'enormous forces' of history to overwhelm and traumatise the individual. This phenomenon is discussed in more detail in relation to Philip Roth's *The Plot Against America* and what I term neo-naturalism in Chapter 5.

Billy's excursions through time and to Tralfamadore represent an attempted retreat or escape from the trauma produced by these 'enormous forces'. Teleological chronology, which, through cause and effect, produces trauma, is challenged not only through the narrative's structure (as in *Catch-22*) but also in the anachronistic experience of the protagonist, who 'has come unstuck in time' (17). The novel's anachronistic structures are thus more radical than the kind of temporal fragmentation typically found in other trauma books. Billy's time travel is an apt symbol for his mental state, not only acting as 'a metaphor for Billy's repeatedly re-experiencing the traumatic events he went through in the war' (Vees-Gulani 177), but actually literalising his condition. As the narrator explains,

'Billy is spastic in time, has no control over where he is going next, and the trips aren't necessarily fun. He is in a constant state of stage fright, he says, because he never knows what part of his life he is going to have to act in next' (17). This quotation points specifically to this literalisation, since it anticipates symptoms of trauma identified in *DSM-III*. That Billy's trips are not usually 'fun' gestures towards the common symptom of the unwelcome intrusion of the past and its unsettling effect on the present, while his 'stage fright' demonstrates that he lives in a present permanently unsettled by the past, in other words in a state of constant hyperarousal.

Perhaps the most revealing example of the relationship between Billy's anachronistic experience of time and his traumatised state occurs when he comes 'unstuck' and begins to experience a war film backwards. This reversal not only continues the dramatisation of Billy's trauma in literal terms, but also anticipates later representations of trauma, some of which are also connected to the Second World War (for example, Foer's *Extremely Loud and Incredibly Close*, Martin Amis's *Time's Arrow*, and Sandra Gilbert's essay 'Writing Wrong'). Billy watches as

American planes, full of holes and wounded men and corpses took off backwards from an airfield in England. Over France, a few German fighter planes flew at them backwards, sucked bullets and shell fragments from some of the planes and crewmen . . . The formation flew backwards over a German city that was in flames. The bombers opened their bomb bay doors, exerted a miraculous magnetism which shrunk the fires, gathered them into cylindrical steel containers, and lifted the containers into the bellies of the planes. (53)

And so the experience continues: the bombs are dismantled into their constituent minerals that are buried in the ground, until Billy extrapolates further, as '[e]verybody turned into a baby, and all humanity, without exception, conspired biologically to produce two perfect people named Adam and Eve' (54). As with the later works (and Foer's in particular echoes this) the fantasised reversal represents a way of stripping trauma of its teleological power, a not uncommon reaction to trauma, as Judith Herman observes:

'[s]ometimes people reenact the traumatic moment with a fantasy of changing the outcome of the dangerous encounter' (39). The futility of this, however, is underlined by the imagined reversal going to conspicuously absurd lengths. Indeed, a careful reading demonstrates that Billy's attempt to use this reversal to escape from traumatic events is tacitly acknowledged to fail: although a lengthy passage relates Billy's reversed experience of the film, preceding this he is described as seeing it backwards, 'then forwards again' (53). Even from the outset, the fantasy of escape is denied.

This dual proffering and refusal of escape is a crucial organising principle of *Slaughterhouse-Five*. Billy's adventures, the excursions to Tralfamadore and his embracing of the Tralfamadorians' non-teleological perception of time initially seem, like the war film's reversal, to offer escape. 'The most important thing', Billy significantly states, that he learned on Tralfamadore, 'was that when a person dies he only *appears* to die. He is still very much alive in the past, so it is very silly for people to cry at his funeral. All moments, past, present, and future, always have existed, always will exist' (19). Billy's discoveries on Tralfamadore seem to have convinced some critics that he successfully uses these fantasies to recover from trauma. Vees-Gulani, for example, argues that, 'Tralfamadorian philosophy, which opposes trying to make sense out of occurrences, helps Billy deal with the horrible events and their consequences by reinterpreting their meaning' (179–80). The problem is that this conceives of Billy coping with traumatic events precisely by denying them or emptying them of meaning, yet he remains grotesquely affected by his horrific memories. Billy is thus only able 'to avoid some of the distress he feels when facing death' (Vees-Gulani 180) because he almost entirely withdraws from quotidian existence, and denies himself choice, agency, and responsibility. As we shall see in Chapter 5 in relation to Auster's *Man in the Dark*, this denial of one's own agency, a constricted response arising from the fear of traumatic occurrences repeating, is a familiar but doomed strategy for coping with trauma. Refusing agency is therefore just another form of escape that the narrative of *Slaughterhouse-Five* demonstrates to be an ultimately futile response to trauma.

Despite Billy's adoption of the Tralfamadorians' ostensibly

comforting non-teleological model of chronology, other strategies in the novel continually undermine any attempted fantasised retreat from trauma. Vonnegut's autobiographical interjections are crucial in this respect, such as this characteristically sudden reversion to homodiegetic narration when Billy is amongst the American POWs: 'I was there. So was my old war buddy, Bernard V. O'Hare' (49). The sudden transformation of the narrator into 'the author of this book' (91), even if only momentary, disabuses us from any comforting sense that we are reading an escapist fable. This reading is clearly at odds with that offered by Vees-Gulani:

> Billy's story allows an indirect and detached exploration of the effects of the Dresden bombing because the character is mostly fictional. The narrator's story parallels Vonnegut's on one level, but on another level, it is an integral part of a work of fiction. Removing himself from the factual to the fictional plane by creating the narrator allows Vonnegut a degree of distance from himself and his experience. (182)

Far from 'removing himself' from this work of fiction in the form of a narrator, however, the narrator of this fictional work actually 'becomes', as Jerome Klinkowitz observes, 'the real Kurt Vonnegut. A lifetime of instruction that the narrator of a novel is not the author thus flies out the window' (84). Rather than 'removed', which raises the question of why an author would be present in a fictional work in the first place, Vonnegut continually inserts himself, and thus shocks the reader out of any comforting sense that *Slaughterhouse-Five* is mere fiction. In this sense, Vonnegut's novel offers a classic example of historiographic metafiction, or a prototypical one of traumatic metafiction. When the POWs encounter Dresden for the first time, 'Somebody behind [Billy] in the boxcar said, "Oz." That was I. That was me. The only other city I'd seen was Indianapolis, Indiana' (108). Crucially, this insertion of the author figure ontologically disarms the reader, banishing in an instant the escapism of fiction. This is a key point in relation to the novel's overarching strategies, since this refusal of escapism runs precisely counter to what Billy is attempting. As Cacicedo suggests, this continual insertion of the autobiographical narrator into the novel itself 'demonstrate[s] precisely the distance between Billy's serenity and his own restless, inevitable grappling with the evil of the world' (358). While we may have become firstly, accustomed to and secondly, jaded by autobiographical–fictional hybridity, at the time Vonnegut writes *Slaughterhouse-Five*, the novel's effects remain disorientating. The book's approach to trauma – offering science-fiction escapism and then subversively undermining such a comforting option through the insertion of an authorial voice – is highly original. Ultimately, Vonnegut's 'short and jumbled and jangled' book, whose form reflects that 'there is nothing intelligent to say about a massacre' (14), ably critiques political ideologies that would support warfare, while simultaneously dramatising the acute damage wrought by traumatic experience. The passage above continues, '[e]verybody is supposed to be dead, to never say anything or want anything ever again. Everything is supposed to be very quiet after a massacre' (14). The ideas that trauma produces nothing so effectively as silence and that there is, in any case, nothing to say about war, prove extremely influential for subsequent war trauma writers, as we shall see with the next example.

TIM O'BRIEN'S VIETNAM WAR TRAUMAS

Like Vonnegut, Tim O'Brien vociferously rejects meaning when it comes to war stories. 'A true war story is never moral. It does not instruct, nor encourage virtue, nor suggest models of proper human behavior,' he explains in an oft-quoted section from the chapter entitled 'How to Tell a True War Story' in *The Things They Carried*. He concludes, '[i]f at the end of a war story you feel uplifted, or if you feel that some small bit of rectitude has been salvaged from the larger waste, then you have been made the victim of a very old and terrible lie' (68–9). If war is meaningless, this nihilism extends to a rejection of narratives that deliver conventional recovery from trauma. O'Brien, like Vonnegut, refuses the apparent comfort of escapism; his writing, as Robin Silbergleid suggests, 'does not function as therapy' (152). *Going After Cacciato* (1978), for example, is predicated on the failure of Paul Berlin's imaginary narrative of desertion to Paris to provide enduring relief from the various traumas he has suffered as a combat troop in Vietnam; even at the end of the novel, 'Paul has fully revisited his own traumatisation and the deaths of others, yet he remains unresolved to them' (Heberle 142). This section positions O'Brien as a bridge between some of the twentieth-century war writers discussed previously and those of the twenty-first century. Where Heller and Vonnegut evolved certain experimental strategies for communicating war trauma, O'Brien develops these in extended and sometimes radical ways. O'Brien's typical themes – the persistence of trauma, guilt and perpetrator trauma, and the insidiousness of war trauma – are represented through a range of strikingly experimental forms. These include blurred author-narrator-protagonist subjectivities, extreme ontological and generic flicker between autobiographical memoir and fiction, and a form of inscribed and/or interpolated narration which brings O'Brien's writing into the realm of traumatic metafiction.

Although there are brief instances of perpetrator trauma in Heller and, more so, Vonnegut, the general perspective that pertains in America regarding World War II as the 'Good War' means that this issue rarely surfaces. By contrast, writing on America's involvement in neo-colonial wars such as those in Vietnam and, as we shall see in Chapter 4, Iraq, has produced a much more sustained engagement with the notion of perpetrator trauma. This complex condition arises numerous times in O'Brien's oeuvre. Most interestingly, issues of perpetration and guilt are sometimes muddied, repositioning invading US forces as the victim, albeit with a measure of self-conscious irony. For example, in *Cacciato*, in response to seeing a 'skinny blank-eyed' Vietnamese girl being treated by the company doctor for wounds inflicted by the Americans, Paul Berlin reflects on what she thinks of when she looks at him: 'could she somehow separate him from the war?' (248). Paul has suffered traumatic incidents as both victim and perpetrator, and it is as if he now seeks an empathic link with the girl. But it is she, the colonised and exoticised other, rather than Berlin, the invader, who is expected to extend empathy. If this seems to attempt an inversion of victim and perpetrator, as Berlin seeks sympathy from those who are oppressed by the US forces, O'Brien frames it in such a way that the reader is aware of the irony of repositioning an American soldier as victim. This is not necessarily or universally true, as we shall see in Chapter 4, of similar attempted inversions in Iraq narratives, but O'Brien's soldier-protagonists occupy a moral position in a 'murky middle' (*Cacciato* 250) which tends to guard against simplistic depictions of them as victims.

This morally 'murky middle' is a phenomenon we return to repeatedly in O'Brien's writing, and it is marked by an obscuring of distinctions between victim and perpetrator. In *In the Lake of the Woods*, for example, another victim-perpetrator, the soldier John Wade, experiences Vietnam as a morally complex location 'where every object and every thought and every hour seemed to glow with all the unspeakable secrets of human history' (73). In Vietnam, Wade's initially innocent magic tricks become incrementally darker: '[h]e pulled a lighted cigar from his ear. He transformed a pear into an orange. He displayed an ordinary military radio and whispered a few words and made their village disappear. There was a trick to it, which involved artillery and white phosphorous, but the overall effect was spectacular' (65). Wade, now transformed thanks to his penchant for tricks into 'Sorcerer', begins to revel in a place where 'elaborate props were always on hand – exploding boxes and secret chemicals and numerous devices of levitation – you could *fly* here, you could make *other* people fly' (72–3, original emphasis). The grotesquely blurred distinctions between Wade's harmless illusions performed to entertain the men and the murderous technologies of war refigured as 'magic' reveal America's role in Vietnam as problematising distinctions between victim and perpetrator for the individual soldiers.

O'Brien's determined employment of non-linear, often repetitive or elliptical chronologies in his work radically transforms strands found in earlier war writing. Repetition, both within and between texts, the 'rhizomatic proliferation of contiguous relationships in the stories of *The Things They Carried* (and, indeed, across the entire body of O'Brien's work)' (Lustig 85), clearly demonstrates the lasting traumatic effect of O'Brien's time in Vietnam. Regardless of manifold formal and thematic variations in O'Brien's work, the one constant which is obsessively worked over throughout is the individual and collective scar of Vietnam.

This is emphasised through deliberate eschewing of progression, as O'Brien resists what would be, for the reader, satisfying forms of recovery from trauma in a similar fashion to his refusal of meaningful war stories. The structures of repetition underline how O'Brien's protagonists are, like himself, mired in a trauma which 'is constantly recirculated in different forms with different outcomes, without linear progression or closure' (Heberle 33). *Cacciato* develops the pattern of repetition with addition that we encountered in *Catch-22*. The book begins thus:

> It was a bad time. Billy Boy Watkins was dead, and so was Frenchie Tucker. Billy Boy had died of fright, scared to death on the field of battle, and Frenchie Tucker had been shot through the nose. Bernie Lynn and Lieutenant Sidney Martin had died in tunnels. Pederson was dead and Rudy Chassler was dead. Buff was dead. Ready Mix was dead. (9)

These euphemistic vignettes introduce us to most of the incidents that have produced Paul Berlin's traumatised state, but they are extremely brief, and omit any painful detail of this 'bad time'. The yawning gaps in these opening narratives are only gradually revisited during the course of the novel; following Emily Dickinson's dictum, Berlin revisits the causes of his post-traumatic stress 'at a slant'. Besides Berlin's ultimately thwarted fantasy narrative of escape, the novel is otherwise structured around completing analepses which flesh out the traumatic events when Paul feels ready to do so. This is not to suggest that Paul has forgotten the events, but it is the major task of the narrator to summon up the strength of will to narrate the traumatic episodes fully. For example, although this opening passage alludes to how 'Billy Boy had died of fright,' it is only in Chapter 31 that the reader fully encounters the awful detail regarding his death. Here it is revealed how much was covered up by the initial brief description, as Billy Boy in fact has his foot blown off by a mine, after which he dies of a heart attack combined with shock on witnessing his initial injuries (208–9).

Form is again firmly subordinate to content, used to represent trauma as experienced in conscious memory, but deliberately suppressed. Events scantly recounted in elliptical narration are revisited throughout the subsequent narrative, as completing analepses fill in most of the initial gaps. Similar to *Catch-22*, O'Brien's work frequently employs a spiralling narrative structure, with selective and fragmented additions to initially synecdochal memories which gradually reveal traumatising events to the reader. *In the Lake of the Woods* is similarly structured around this principle: both Wade's past in Vietnam and the ambiguous fate of his wife, Kathy, are revisited throughout the novel, with gradually more (but never complete) information added. Heberle notes that in *Tomcat in Love* O'Brien again employs this structure, repeating events and adding more each time, so that events which 'appear briefly as allusions or truncated scenes' in the first chapter are 'repetitively elaborated throughout the rest of the novel' (269).

If O'Brien's use of repetition as a means to represent traumatic effects only slightly extends patterns constructed by earlier war writers, his experiments in this field regarding subjectivity and generic hybridity go considerably further. Indeed, taken collectively, O'Brien's writing may be regarded as the apotheosis of the play of narrating/authorial subjectivities as a means of representing trauma. This combines with strategies of repetition, as similar or identical incidents recur across *If I Die in a Combat Zone*, *The Things They Carried*, and *Going After Cacciato*, reinforcing the sense that O'Brien is haunted by traumatic memories. Furthermore, these works are positioned differently in terms of levels of fictionality, suggesting a scepticism towards the notion of truth in the narration of trauma. Experiencing an insidiously traumatising war environment – this could be Vietnam or, as we shall see later, Iraq – notions of truth are markedly difficult to grasp or to maintain. O'Brien conveys this uncertainty both through his strikingly protean subject positions, and the use of inscribed narration.

Unstable subjectivity is found in *Combat Zone*, where the visceral terror of walking through minefields is conveyed through the employment of a second-person voice. If you step on a mine, the narrator asks, '[w]ill you scream or fall silent? Will you be afraid to look at your body, afraid of the sight of your own red flesh and white bone?' (123). The second-person voice here suggests a kind of alienation from self and, moreover, a bodily self-disgust that again problematises easy divisions of victim and perpetrator. *The*

Things They Carried takes these experiments in subjectivity a stage further, since although it is overtly labelled textually and paratextually as a work of fiction, it clearly has a heavy autobiographical basis and is narrated by one 'Tim O'Brien'. As Tina Chen suggests, '[w]hile the narrator is named "Tim," and it is tempting to read him as synonymous with the real Tim O'Brien, there are distinctions between the narrator and the author that prevent any easy assignment of authorial intention or identity' (79 n.3). Similarly, *In the Lake of the Woods* is framed by a narrator who employs a series of philosophically complex discursive footnotes, and who, although he is unnamed, shares experiences with the Tim O'Brien of 'The Vietnam in Me'. Thus O'Brien extends his enquiry into the nature of a 'True War Story', which can apparently only be narrated through a range of works grouped around the unstable border between fiction and autobiography.

As if deliberately extending strategies employed by Vonnegut in *Slaughterhouse-Five*, O'Brien deploys complex metafictional experiments in mutable identity in order to challenge ontological distinctions between 'fiction' and 'autobiography'. Here we should link O'Brien's experiments in liminal subjectivity with his employment of a form of inscribed narration, which together position O'Brien as an early exponent of what I am terming 'traumatic metafiction'. A similar point is made by Robin Silbergleid, who understands O'Brien's writing in the context of 'an emergent postmodern genre situated at the boundary between autobiography and metafiction' (131). Silbergleid even coins the slightly different term 'autobiographical metafiction' (130) in order to discuss the effects of hybridity in O'Brien's work.[1] O'Brien's continual binary of ratifying concepts of truth (through using narrators who share his name) and then undermining them (through presenting alternative and contradictory descriptions of specific incidents) is key to this autobiographical or traumatic metafiction. And a cornerstone of O'Brien's traumatic metafiction is his use of inscribed narration, wherein the narrating act is brought back into the text itself and performed. Silbergleid argues that the call to autobiographical reference draws on what in Foucault and Barthes represents a kind of author function. This performative act is used as a means of grounding traumatic material:

we use the author to stabilize the text, to limit what it might mean. In this way, the rebirth of the author – evidenced by the use of author protagonists in contemporary fiction – becomes a strategic means by which writers who represent trauma earn credibility and the trust of their readers, offering an illusion of stability in texts that otherwise thrive on ambiguity and multiplicity. (Silbergleid 140–1)

This is a useful way of conceiving how postmodernist trauma writers give firmer foundations to their texts. To a limited extent the author function is performed, through inscription into the traumatic metafictional text, as a means of granting authenticity to a depiction of trauma. As 'illusion' suggests, however, these foundations are always destabilised by the playful metafictional techniques O'Brien simultaneously employs, which tend to undermine the text's epistemological and ontological grounds.

What Silbergleid conceives of as a relatively stable 'autobiographical metafiction', I characterise as a more experimental 'traumatic metafiction'. This differing terminology is based on distinctions in ontology: what Silbergleid would understand as a reinsertion of an author function in O'Brien's work, I read as shading into inscribed narration. Rather than the insertion of a stabilising author figure, O'Brien's work is marked by the destabilising of the narrator. Examples of this abound in O'Brien's work, and as with other practitioners it has multiple and complex effects. These include – as Silbergleid suggests above – granting a dimension of authenticity, but more importantly in terms of the type of insidious trauma O'Brien is attempting to represent, inscribed narration crucially reintroduces a temporal dimension to the narrating process. One of the most striking examples of this type of narration occurs in the 'Step Lightly' chapter of *Combat Zone*, which fittingly 'includes O'Brien's only writing contemporaneous with his residence in the war' (Heberle 41). As well as the shifts to second-person voice, as cited above, O'Brien employs a temporally positioned narrating discourse in order to convey the gradually traumatising effect of creeping through minefields:

In the three days I spent writing this, mines and men came together three more times. Seven more legs, one more arm. The immediacy of the last explosion – three legs, ten minutes ago – made me ready to burn the midsection of this report. (126)

As Lustig observes, 'O'Brien's usual stance of posterior narration shifts to one of implied simultaneous narration' (88). The reader experiences the immediately perilous and traumatising situation in which the narrator here both exists and inscribes. O'Brien, here as conflated author and narrator-protagonist, according to strategies identified by Silbergleid, is represented as a more or less simultaneous narrator (certainly according to Genette's terminology). Conventional realist narration is shattered in order to represent the immediate but insidious accumulation of traumatic affect. As explored further in Chapter 2, this form of writing – an inscribed narrating that incorporates a temporal dimension to the telling – is an important element in the representation of insidious trauma. Form is once more at the service of theme. Inscribed narration, with its temporal character, functions as a specific method of representing the kind of insidious trauma which has conventionally been overlooked or marginalised by the event-based model of trauma.

Finally regarding O'Brien, it should be noted that his traumatic metafiction demonstrates an awareness of the conventions of trauma depiction and even an occasional willingness to parody them. As Heberle notes, despite the way in which the form of O'Brien's writing, as we have seen in this chapter, 'mimics the phenomena of constriction, intrusion, hyperarousal' (xxi) – that is, conventionally acknowledged symptoms of trauma – we also encounter, in *Tomcat*, a sheer excess of adherence to traumatised acting out. This helps to subvert 'the conventional solemnity of the subject', just as its protagonist's 'sob stories parody trauma therapy itself' (Heberle 283). O'Brien's perspective on trauma theory is thus complex, veering from endorsement to parody: while John Wade in *Lake* is 'nearly a textbook case of PTSD' for whom 'constriction has become a way of living' (Heberle 15), the 'sometimes manic narrative voices' of the protagonists of *The Nuclear Age* and *Tomcat* 'nearly parody hyperarousal' (Heberle 14).

As we shall see with Mark Danielewski in the next chapter, parody of trauma discourse such as this can constitute a key element of traumatic metafiction. O'Brien's relationship with theory is further complicated by his direct engagement with it, and with trauma theorists' regular endorsement of his work. Heberle points out that Judith Herman cites *The Things They Carried* as Vietnam testimony, despite its avowed (if contentious) fictional status (32). The favour is returned in *Lake*, adding yet another layer of complexity, when the narrator quotes Herman's *Trauma and Recovery*. While this quoting of theoretical material might appear derivative, O'Brien's metafictional approach and the overt self-consciousness with which he treats such material mean that his engagement with theory is often sceptical and parodic. John Wade in *Lake*, for example, represents such an ostentatious composite of textbook trauma clichés that it would be foolish to take his character, or the citing of Herman et al. in the highly metafictional 'Evidence' chapters, at face value. The point to bear in mind for our discussion of later trauma writers is that O'Brien clearly draws on trauma theory both to validate his writing and to challenge the discourse through parody. His work skilfully undermines overarching narratives of trauma, and the postmodernist techniques he uses are very much a part of his incredulity towards this particular metanarrative. It is therefore ironic that theorists such as Herman and Jonathan Shay have been inclined to take O'Brien's metafictional parody at face value, and as validating their theories, since O'Brien's trauma texts in fact deliberately undermine foundations of knowledge, alongside numerous cherished myths about subjectivity.

TONI MORRISON, *Beloved* (1987)

While tracing a genealogy of war trauma narratives illuminates certain crucial developments in the trauma paradigm, there are other key texts, especially in terms of constructing formal strategies revisited by writers in the twenty-first century. Two further influential novels in this respect are considered in the following: Toni Morrison's *Beloved* and E. L. Doctorow's *The Book of Daniel*. Morrison's novel has already been widely identified in recent critical writing as a paradigmatic trauma text, which 'helped establish some of the basic narrative and tropological conventions of trauma fiction. It was soon regarded as a formative text in literary trauma studies' (Luckhurst 90). Notably, even at this relatively foundational stage, one can perceive an interplay between theories of trauma and literary practice that has recently become much more – and much more damagingly – entrenched. Morrison herself admits to drawing on Freudian theory in her writing, while *Beloved* was seized upon enthusiastically by commentators as a working out of many of the most prominent elements in trauma theory. Laurie Vickroy, for example, argues that the novel 'incorporates the gaps, uncertainties, dissociations, and affects that characterize traumatic experience in attempting to re-create the visceral details of living in extraordinary circumstances', and, again validating certain narrow models of trauma representation, she lauds the way in which 'Morrison avoids standard chronology and linear storytelling, seeking out the paths of elicited survivor memories that are characterized by the struggle to both remember and forget' (178–9). Comments such as these bring to mind Luckhurst's observation that '[t]he remarkable symmetry of *Beloved* with a psychoanalytic post-structuralism gone Gothic means that the text has become an easy form of exemplification for a certain kind of cultural theory' (97).

Clearly *Beloved* is a particularly rich trauma text, in terms of both content and formal experimentation, hence its influence on trauma criticism and later literary texts, but its aesthetic extends beyond the rather limited set of accepted trauma representational practices. Morrison's novel has more to offer than these narrow paradigms, for example in its dramatisation of trauma's major problematic as presence and insistence rather than absence. This section uncovers some of the more overlooked elements of Morrison's representation of trauma, alongside ways in which the novel's paradigmatic status becomes problematic, when its experimental forms are appropriated for less suitable content. Firstly, it should be acknowledged that *Beloved* also draws upon and develops some of the key characteristics of trauma writing discussed in the preceding sections. In particular, *Beloved* is striking and much remarked upon in terms of its disrupted narrative, whereby the novel's chronology is structured according to characters' associative memories of trauma rather than adhering to a realist, linear chronology. Morrison also significantly pluralises the novel's narrating voice. To an extent, this, like the fractured chronology, simulates the psychic experience of the protagonists, as in the celebrated sequence where the disembodied voices of Sethe, Denver and especially Beloved merge and overlap, sometimes so indistinctly that is it unclear who speaks (200–17). The novel is also replete with another paradigmatic marker of the trauma text, in its heavy formal basis in varieties of repetition. Repetition in *Beloved* is broadly similar to what we encountered in *Catch-22* and *In the Lake of the Woods*, concerning traumatised characters who may approach traumatic memories only indirectly. This is most evident in the 'circling' episode, where Sethe finally confesses her role in Beloved's death to Paul D (148–65). Here, the figurative spiralling towards traumatic memory is physically realised, as Sethe '[c]ircl[es] him the way she was circling the subject' (161).

While these attributes have been extremely influential, there are several more unconventional elements in *Beloved*'s representation of trauma which have too often been ignored. One of these, Morrison's emphasis on the insistent presence of traumatic memory, is particularly significant in running counter to prevailing theoretical perspectives. This characteristic is conveyed through a diverse array of narrative strategies. The dangerous fluidity of memory and its constant impinging upon the present, for example, is emphasised through shading from iterative to singulative narration, as when Paul D first returns to Sethe.[2] The narrator here first describes how Sethe '*might be* hurrying across a field, running practically, to get the chamomile sap from her legs. Nothing else *would be* in her mind' (6, emphasis added), before shifting to the single occurrence of the reunion with Paul D. This is interesting, not only because the second sentence is actually misleading, attempting but failing to conceal how Sethe's mind is in fact plagued with traumatic flashbacks, but also because of the implication that the everyday life of the iterative is prone to sudden intrusion by elements from Sethe's past.

The looming presence of memory in *Beloved* is also related to the associative structure of the book mentioned above regarding chronology, in the evident sense that one undesired memory inevitably brings forth others. This characteristic of traumatic memory is alluded to near the start of the novel, when Sethe is described as having 'worked hard to remember as close to nothing as was safe. Unfortunately her brain was devious' (6). The insistence of conscious traumatic memory is later represented in more detail. Given the strikingly unconventional depiction, this is worth quoting at length:

> She shook her head from side to side, resigned to her rebellious brain. Why was there nothing it refused? No misery, no regret, no hateful picture too rotten to accept? Like a greedy child it snatched up everything. Just once, could it say, No thank you? I just ate and can't hold another bite? I am full God damn it of two boys with mossy teeth, one sucking on my breast the other holding me down, their book-reading teacher watching and writing it up. I am still full of that, God damn it, I can't go back and add more. Add my husband to it, watching, above me in the loft – hiding close by – the one place he thought no one would look for him, looking down on what I couldn't look at at all. And not stopping them – looking and letting it happen. But my greedy brain says, Oh thanks, I'd love more – so I add more. And no sooner than I do, there is no stopping. (70)

In emphasising insistent presence, this passage plays on metaphors of plenitude employed elsewhere in the book – for example with regard to Beloved's ravenous appetite – while the numerous repetitions of 'and' and 'also' underline the accumulative process of Sethe's memory. But there is an irony in Sethe's repeated insistence that she is 'full', for this is a negative plenitude, a traumatic one of abjection and possession. As Jean Wyatt suggests, 'There are no gaps in Sethe's world, no absences to be filled in with signifiers; everything is there, an oppressive plenitude' (477). Plenitude, even as here a negative or oppressive one, suggests that passages such as this evoke presence. It is the insistence and full consciousness of Sethe's traumatic memory which forces her to be perpetually engaged with the 'serious work of beating back the past' (73). The insistence of memory is underlined, moreover, by the novel's persistent theme of haunting; given the way in which it evokes these notions of insistent memory, it is appropriate that the novel refers to the baby ghost as a 'presence' (104). The ghost's insistent presence mirrors that of traumatic memory in *Beloved*, along with the negative plenitude of memory which engulfs Sethe.

While this presence may appear to be understood according to conventional trauma theory through the notion of intrusion, this is complicated in *Beloved* by the degree to which Sethe is clearly conscious of this memory process. As Jill Matus concedes, the trouble for Sethe is that she cannot control the memories that return: '[i]t is not repression of memory that presents the problem here, but Sethe's consciousness of the amorality of her memories' (106). This suggestion that memory represents a series of conscious choices for Sethe is significant, since it means that we must establish a distinction between memory and narration: 'Sethe may choose not to tell or to "tell things halfway" only, but that does not mean she does not remember them' (Matus 108). The key point, which again underlines that no matter how paradigmatic it has become, *Beloved* is a non-formulaic representation of trauma, is that while Sethe possesses (and is possessed by) 'overwhelming and abundant recall of the past' (Matus 109), she does not always choose to narrate it. More generally, the textual representation of trauma which involves gaps that are filled in by completing analepses can be misidentified by critics as simulating the recovery of unconscious memory. What it may actually represent is, as in *Catch-22*, the narrator's gradual revelation of the truth or, as in *Beloved*, the peeling back of a conscious repression of memory. Significantly, these strategies represent not an inability to recall, but a refusal to tell, to narrate, in anything other than hesitating, oblique, indirect fashion. All the indications, metaphorical and otherwise, of presence in *Beloved*, including the ubiquitous ghost and the trope of negative plenitude, point in this direction.

Beloved also provides us with another highly pertinent example of traumatic affect that is gradual rather than, as dominant trauma theory leads us to expect, sudden in its impact. We shall not dwell on this overly here, as insidious trauma is discussed at greater length elsewhere in this study (see, especially, Chapter 4). It is worth mentioning, however, as it is arguably connected to the unusual 'negative plenitude' depiction of trauma discussed above. In other words, the ex-slaves' perpetual consciousness of trauma may be linked to the fact that for them it has consisted of an accumulation of incidents of abuse rather than a single, sudden event 'outside the range of normal experience'. As Laura Brown's argument (see Introduction) leads us to recognise, 'normal experience' for the African-Americans in *Beloved* consists precisely of exposure to regular, horrific and traumatising brutality. In *Beloved* this is seen both in the frequent examples of physical abuse, and through schoolteacher's insidious erosion of the slaves' already limited freedoms and sense of self-worth. Physical and psychological brutalisation is such a part of the slaves' everyday life that in Morrison's unusual treatment of trauma in *Beloved*, the memories can never be anything other than insistently present.

If one problem of *Beloved*'s paradigmatic status is that is has marginalised the unconventional elements in Morrison's portrayal of trauma, another is the appropriation of some of its techniques and strategies. Clearly, the narrative strategies Morrison develops to tell Sethe's story are closely connected to themes of race and slavery; equally, they are specific to the speaking position of African-Americans. Ironically, precisely because of this novel's deserved impact, its narrative techniques have been unmoored and reused without an understanding of their organic interdependence with the novel's thematic context. Morrison's development of the trope of the ghost, of trauma as haunting, for example, has been excessively and sometimes inappropriately borrowed by later trauma writers seeking similar effects. As a result, devices including fragmented chronology and subjectivity have become almost ubiquitous in later trauma texts. While Morrison was not, as this chapter has already suggested, necessarily the first to draw upon such ideas, the commercial and critical success of *Beloved* was instrumental in their becoming paradigmatic. Moreover, as the foregoing discussion of the overlooked specificities of traumatic memory in *Beloved* should suggest, their employment here is oriented towards the particular and the local, temporally, culturally, and ethnically. There is little reason why forms Morrison finds necessary for representing the traumas of nineteenth-century ex-slaves, African-American men and, especially, women, will function when taken out of that context. Rafael Pérez-Torres's reading is comparatively rare in noting the experimental narrative strategies employed in *Beloved*, but understanding them not as relevant to trauma per se, but to the specific structures of oppression in nineteenth-century America: '[t]here is a crossing of genres and styles and narrative perspectives in *Beloved* that suggests it filters the absent or marginalised oral discourse of a pre-capitalist black community through the self-conscious discourse of the contemporary novel' (129). Critiques such as this are relatively uncommon, however, in challenging the universalising of Morrison's techniques.

There are clear dangers in elevating something quite as unusual as *Beloved* – in terms of its narrative structures and challenging content – as a paradigm. Inevitably, one will discover that to appropriate elements of such a work is simultaneously overly timid and prone to unforeseen risks. In short, once these techniques – which are, as discussed, specific to the tale Morrison feels compelled to narrate – become more generally employed, their original effect is skewed. Moreover, these relocated strategies, through being repeatedly reused, soon lose their shocking or disorientating power, as the more obviously imitative texts of the twenty-first-century trauma genre have begun to demonstrate.

E. L. DOCTOROW, *The Book of Daniel* (1971)

Like *Beloved*, E. L. Doctorow's *The Book of Daniel* may reasonably be considered a paradigmatic trauma text. This novel synthesises a number of crucial thematic and formal attributes of the trauma text, including the question of perpetrator trauma and guilt; repetition and fragmented chronology; fragmented subjectivity, and its relationship with inscribed narration; further challenges to the insistence on sudden or punctual trauma; and a blurring of the lines between autobiography, history and fiction.

This final point is particularly significant in Doctorow's novel in terms of forms being developed as a means to narrate traumatic content. The admixture of autobiography, history and fiction facilitates Doctorow's meditation on the traumatising effect of vast historical forces upon individuals and families. The novel is narrated – using both homodiegetic and heterodiegetic voice – by Daniel Isaacson, who looks back to the McCarthy period of the 1950s, and the persecution and eventual execution of his working-class Jewish parents as alleged Russian spies. Daniel and his sister Susan, children at the time of their parents' deaths, are, like their parents, predominantly portrayed as victims of reactionary historical forces then sweeping America. To this extent, *The Book of Daniel* provides a theme to which we shall return in Chapter 5, especially in regard to discussion of Philip Roth's formally and thematically similar autobiography-fiction hybrid, *The Plot Against America*. Indeed, just as Roth does in his later work, Doctorow depicts much of this effect on the individual of irresistible political forces through the work's form, as it carefully meshes history and fiction. This focus and form are both suggested by Doctorow's insistence that despite numerous similarities, the novel is about the 'idea of the Rosenbergs', rather than being merely a fictionalised account (Carmichael 131). Indeed, the text's hybridity is a good deal more complex than a mere blending of history and fiction, constituting, rather, a 'monstrous novel – a fragmented, hybridized narrative that combines multiple genres (autobiography, personal memoir, historical description, sociology, political theory, and pornography to name but a few)' (Rasmussen 216). This hybrid form is perfectly suited to portraying the unusual, equivocal type of trauma that here concerns Doctorow. Daniel is a victim, certainly, but also, as we shall see, able rapidly to become a persecutor, especially in terms of his sadistic misogyny.

In terms of gaining a deeper understanding of the relationship between this novel's complex form and its representation of trauma, a selected critical history is useful. The radical form and content of *The Book of Daniel* are clearly linked, as has been noticed at least as far back as Geoffrey Galt Harpham's 1985 reading, but it is only more recently that trauma has been advanced as the key nexus between the two. Michelle Tokarczyk's essay makes some connections in this respect but also, being published in 1987, predates the explosion of theory regarding cultural manifestations of trauma. As such, the article inclines towards laboriously psychoanalysing the characters, all of whom rather straightforwardly display 'the psychological traits of survivors' (3). More recent readings, notably those of Naomi Morgenstern, Aaron Derosa, and Eric Dean Rasmussen, have employed more sophisticated theoretical bases, in focusing explicitly on Doctorow's formal rendering of trauma.

One key element in this representation of trauma, and the one which probably strikes readers most immediately, is the constant alternating between first- and third-person (or, respectively, autodiegetic and heterodiegetic) narrating voice. This pattern is established from the start of the novel, which begins in heterodiegetic, shifts ambiguously towards the end of the first paragraph, and in the second paragraph relocates abruptly to present tense and autodiegetic narration. Doctorow thus immediately constructs a radically unstable and disorientating structure. Some critics have attempted to discern a pattern to these shifts; according to Susan Brienza, 'Daniel swerves abruptly from first person to third at moments of emotional crisis. At such times he needs distance and detachment' (177). Derosa likewise suggests that Daniel's narrative 'enacts a traumatic recovery process where Daniel places himself as both patient and analyst' (471). Given the disorientating frequency of these shifts, however, neither their pattern nor their effect might be as clear-cut as these critics propose. In this respect, Rasmussen's understanding of the shifting voices may be more convincing, since it also implicates the reader in this matrix through taking into account Daniel's rarer use of second-person address. Discussing the incident where Daniel threatens to burn his wife, Phyllis, with their car's cigarette lighter, Rasmussen notes that she 'is not the only pedagogic subject in this scene; readers, too, are being instructed' (210). Taking the reader into account in terms of Doctorow's shifting narrating voice seems appropriate. Daniel is a confrontational character in any case, and the use of second-person voice explicitly challenges the reader as voyeur. In the scene in which he threatens his wife with the cigarette lighter, he then confronts the reader: '[s]hall I continue? Do you want to know the effect of three concentric circles of heating element glowing orange in a black night of rain upon the tender white girlflesh of my wife's ass? Who are you anyway? Who told you you could read this? Is nothing sacred?' (62) This scene, along with the use of second-person voice before Daniel's imagined recreation of his parents' execution, clearly implicates the reader as morbidly fascinated with violence and trauma. Given the later twentieth-century and early twenty-first-century popularity of talk-show trauma kitsch, this seems prescient.

The shifts in narrating persona are also heavily imbricated with this novel's innovative engagement with the key mode of traumatic metafiction, the inscribing of the narrating act. The second paragraph of the novel thus refers not only to the moment but also to the very tools of inscription: '[t]his is a Thinline felt-tip marker, black. This is Composition Notebook 79C made in the USA by Long Island Paper Products, Inc. This is Daniel trying one of the dark coves of the Browsing Room' (3). The continual reminders that what we are reading purports to be the protagonist's Ph.D. thesis presents an act of inscribed narrating that serves to underline the traumatised character of Daniel. Significantly, Daniel's experience of trauma is doubled in the use of inscribed narration; he seems to re-experience trauma symptoms – as evidenced in the abrupt switches between autodiegetic and heterodiegetic voice – as he writes of the causal events. Doctorow's is itself an originating text of traumatic metafiction in the sense that it is amongst the first in which the reader actually witnesses the transcription of narrating into writing, something conventionally elided. Crucially, this more complex subtype of what Genette would term 'interpolated narrating' introduces a temporal element to the narrating of Daniel's traumatic past. This is significant when one remembers that when Daniel begins narrating his story (inscribing his thesis) his sister Susan is alive, which is not the case as he finishes his narrating act. This passage of time underlines that the traumatising process Daniel suffers is both gradual and ongoing. This is reflected elsewhere in the novel: the Isaacsons' arrest, interrogation, trial, appeals and execution are drawn out, rather than sudden. Indeed, much of their traumatising effect lies not in the overwhelming character of a sudden event, but precisely in the agonising slowness of the FBI's persecution of the family. Daniel also explicitly states that the children were never actually told, but only became slowly aware of their parents' deaths. Inscription thus operates in *The*

Book of Daniel partly as a means to convey the gradual and insidiously cruel nature of the children's traumatisation by the state. As in O'Brien, this also offers a challenge to the prescriptive branch of theory that insists on instantaneity of causation. As we shall see, especially in the next chapter, this is a model of critique taken further by certain subsequent writers.

Linked to the novel's focus on insidious trauma, innovative formal means are also employed to enable the depiction of perpetrator trauma. Despite his profound experience of victimisation Daniel is a notably unsympathetic protagonist, prone to self-absorption, resentful anger and, the text heavily implies, violent outbursts. Daniel, in other words, is equally trauma sufferer and perpetrator. The episode described above regarding the cigarette lighter is one example of this tension, but it is also apparent when Daniel, initially playfully and then dangerously, throws his son up into the air, or in his general behaviour towards his wife. This, as Rasmussen suggests,

> immediately challenge[s] readers' inclination to identify with a text's narrator . . . What kind of husband, he wants us to ask, would speak about his wife in such degrading terms? Is he insinuating that he physically abuses his wife? By describing Phyllis as a "helpless breeder" descended from harem girls and comparing her to a "sand dune," Daniel manages to be sexist, racist, and xenophobic. (204)

Through the novel's complex narrative strategies, Doctorow does more than merely portray an unsympathetic traumatised character. At a deeper level, the novel also interrogates the complex interplays of power relationships in which both Daniel and ourselves, as readers, are situated. The tone of the second-person sequences, for example, posits the reader as both sadistic voyeur and atomised, interpellated subject of state-organised violence. Morgenstern's suggestion that the novel offers us 'a general paradigm for understanding Daniel's troubled relationship to action or agency' (72) is an interesting position in this respect. She argues that Daniel's adult preoccupation with structures of power and the maintenance of agency is related to his childhood sense of incapacity. His 'fascination with sexual violence', she writes, may be understood 'as a reversal of early feelings of powerlessness, feelings that he is depicted as experiencing in an extreme form. Daniel's sadism may be an attempt to overcome, by force, his own liminal status as the subject of (and subject to) the primal scene' (77). While this is borne out by much of Daniel's behaviour in the book, he also appears to fear agency, as in his political stasis in comparison to Susan or the activist, Artie Sternlicht. An aversion to agency in traumatised individuals, especially when they are a perpetrator or in some way culpable, is not atypical, and is revisited in Chapter 5 in relation to Paul Auster's *Man in the Dark*. As in other examples, with Daniel we witness both impulses – the urge to grasp power, and the fear of agency – present but unresolved, within one complex character.

The Book of Daniel clearly offers the reader (and later writers) some important paradigms for the representation of trauma. As a 'repulsive' (Rasmussen 207) narrator-protagonist, Daniel is an iconic perpetrator-sufferer in the midst of traumatic situations in which he is able to exercise limited agency, often to deleterious effect, while also fearing to act. More generally, while the radical strategies of *The Book of Daniel* may have been less universally and less slavishly aped than those of *Beloved*, Doctorow's text provides an important set of formal precedents for a number of later trauma narratives.

CONCLUSION: DANGERS OF THE TRAUMA PARADIGM

In *A Poetics of Postmodernism* Linda Hutcheon mentions the surprising popularity of historiographic metafiction, given the apparent complexity of postmodernist literature. Hutcheon notes how it incorporates and parodies earlier realist forms, and that this is part of what makes it accessible, but also challenging and subversive for the reader (202). A key point to remember is that she is discussing what we might now term a first-generation postmodernism (including *The Book of Daniel*), which employs experimental form as a means not only for the representation of trauma, but also to communicate a strong and committed political critique. This is obviously true of Doctorow, and arguably of all the writers discussed in this chapter. By the time we come to a second- or third-generation postmodernism, however, as in some of the texts discussed in this study, the experimental elements of postmodernism are much more familiar. The power of fragmented and once-subversive formal strategies to shock readers is much diminished, and the related political critique is therefore blunted. A theme underlying much of the discussion in the chapters which follow is what may have been consequently lost in later postmodernism and historiographic metafiction, but also what later writers have done to reinvigorate experimental forms and resist the blunting of their effect upon readers in the representation of trauma.

Criticism has played a part in this blunting of shocking effect. For example, part of the problem of the dulled effect of historiographic metafictions may arise precisely (if inadvertently and indirectly) from its being named by Hutcheon, thus enabling it to become a more readily imitable typology. Similarly, a trauma criticism which has seized on particular aspects of the earliest trauma texts has limited the scope for later writers. Universalising formulaic concepts of trauma and turning PTSD into a monolithic explanatory code has obscured certain elements of trauma explored by writers such as those discussed in this chapter. The appropriation of some of the attributes of paradigmatic texts inevitably weakens what were initially radical effects. We also lose sight of various alternative models of trauma presented in these earlier texts, but subsequently forgotten or marginalised. These include the persistent consciousness of trauma as an alternative to amnesia, the trauma of the perpetrator, and the potentially incremental nature of trauma, only some of which are now re-emerging. The remainder of this book recuperates some of these marginalised and non-formulaic depictions of trauma, and examines ways in which writers in the twenty-first century have sought new ways to represent the phenomenon.

NOTES

1. As with my own 'traumatic metafiction', the term owes an acknowledged debt to and stands in deliberate dialogue with

Linda Hutcheon's 'historiographic metafiction'. As Silbergleid elaborates, 'much as Linda Hutcheon takes historiographic metafiction to be inextricable from historical narratives more generally, autobiographical metafiction takes autobiography as its point of departure; it is vitally connected to and fundamentally distinct from both autobiographical fiction and metafiction' (137).

2. These terms are drawn from Gérard Genette's theories of narrative. In singulative narration there is an equivalence between the number of times an event happens and the frequency of its narration. In iterative narration an event that happened more than once is condensed into a single instance. Thus iterative narration is usually employed to provide background to the main narrative, showing not so much 'what *happened* but what *used to happen*' (Genette, *Narrative Discourse* 117, original emphasis).

CHAPTER 2

Traumatic Metafiction and Ontological Crisis

It is therefore not astonishing if that which man himself semi-consciously projected into things from his own being now begins again to terrify him in those very things, or that he is not always capable of exorcising the spirits which were created out of his own head from that very head. This inability thus easily produces the feeling of being threatened by something unknown and incomprehensible that is just as enigmatic to the individual as his own psyche usually is as well. (Ernst Jentsch, 'On the Psychology of the Uncanny' 13–14)

The modernists and early postmodernists . . . broke most of the rules for us, but we tend to forget what they were forced to remember: the rule-breaking has got to be for the *sake* of something. (David Foster Wallace, 'Interview' 132)

At the time of writing, the David Foster Wallace quotation in the epigraph is twenty years old, yet a number of his concerns are still highly pertinent. In the wake of those true pioneers in the avant-garde of literary experimentation, bemoans Wallace, 'always come the crank-turners, the little gray people who take the machines others have built and just turn the crank, and little pellets of meta-fiction come out the other end' (135). As arguments throughout this study suggest, I have considerable sympathy for Wallace's perspective; the bold experiments of postmodernism have indeed frequently become approved formulaic markers of trauma genre literature. The following extends the examination of links between postmodernism and the representation of trauma begun in Chapter 1, focusing in particular on Mark Z. Danielewski's 2000 novel, *House of Leaves*. In part, this exploration is carried out in the spirit of Wallace's withering assessment: if those writers considered in Chapter 1 were amongst the pioneers, does this necessarily mean that later postmodernist trauma writers such as Danielewski are simply 'crank-turners'? In this sense, we need to ask whether *House of Leaves* represents just another programmatic work of ersatz postmodernism, or whether it adds something original and disconcerting to existing models.

The complex narrative of *House of Leaves* presents the discovery of a manuscript by a young Los Angeles resident named Johnny Truant. The manuscript, entitled 'The Navidson Record' and written by a mysterious, recently deceased blind man named Zampanò, is a fictional account of a film made by one Will Navidson, depicting the Navidson family's experiences in their new house in Virginia.[1] The house's internal dimensions slowly reveal themselves to be unstable: first they exceed those of the exterior, then a hallway appears, and then a dark basement of seemingly infinite dimensions. Explorations of this basement are carried out, resulting in a number of deaths, including that of Will's brother Tom. Zampanò's manuscript is replete with lengthy erudite and digressive footnotes, to which Johnny adds a number of his own as he edits Zampanò's work. The book also contains numerous appendices, including a series of letters that purport to have been sent to Johnny by his mother, Pelafina, from a mental hospital.

In some ways, it is not difficult to conceive of *House of Leaves* as precisely the type of postmodernism at which Wallace took aim. The novel owes, as this chapter explores, a clear debt to Jorge Luis Borges, one of the founders of literary postmodernism. Amongst other things, *House of Leaves* borrows from Borges a pseudo-academic architecture of extensive footnotes, the detailed description of fictional texts, and the shady presence of an undetermined number of 'Eds.' occasionally given voice in the footnotes. If *House of Leaves* is not exactly the novel Borges never wrote, one can nevertheless trace a lineage from Borges to the decadent, ecstatic, sublime, excessive culmination (or death throe) of postmodernism that is Danielewski's novel.

Notwithstanding this influence, there are a number of elements in *House of Leaves* which significantly extend earlier combinations of postmodernist form and trauma such as those discussed in the previous chapter. This chapter argues firstly that Danielewski stretches the possibilities of narrative discourse so far in *House of Leaves* that new links are developed between literary postmodernism and trauma. With its overlapping layers of narratives, Danielewski's labyrinthine novel interrogates the possibility of narrating trauma. To this extent, *House of Leaves* may be catagorised as an innovative work of traumatic metafiction, rather than a trauma genre work. In some ways, this novel pursues a development of forms found prototypically in some of the works discussed in Chapter 1, such as the use of inscribed narration in O'Brien and Doctorow. As we shall see, Danielewski complicates the effect of inscribed narration in ways that complement the particular types of traumatic experience he is attempting to represent in *House of Leaves*. Some illustrations of this complexity should serve to underline certain innovations in this novel's stretching of form. Many critics writing on *House of Leaves* have suggested that its strikingly experimental architecture transcends the traditional form of the novel. In particular, Katherine Hayles and Mark Hansen argue that the novel represents a new media, a 'remediation,' as the (fictional) film, *The Navidson Record*, is transformed through layers of embedded narration into a text that resembles hypertext. Martin Brick notes that '[h]ypertext, like Danielewski's narrative and his mysterious house, relies upon an invisible architect'. In fact, this is a slightly reductive reading, while even the architecture analogy is flimsy; one reason that the narrative strategies of *House of Leaves* are unusual – as we shall see – is precisely because of their visibility. Brick's resultant reading of the novel's editor-narrator, Johnny Truant, asserts that 'Truant establishes a conflicting relationship with the text and with the reader,' which may be true, but considerably diminishes the complexity of Danielewski's narrative architecture.

Secondly, and more radically, while postmodernist literary form, as the previous chapter suggests, has long been used as a means of representing trauma's effects, *House of Leaves* develops a strong relationship between trauma and postmodernist themes and perspectives. Of the writers considered in the previous chapter, such a link is at best only tentatively explored in writings by Vonnegut, Doctorow, and O'Brien. By contrast, the type of trauma found in *House of Leaves* is frequently borne of the kind of ontological unsettlement which might be identified as a key component of the postmodern condition of radical uncertainty. This chapter argues that the postmodern condition is thus found to be at the centre of the experience of trauma in Danielewski's novel. Before this we turn to Danielewski's use and development of the inscribed narrator in *House of Leaves*.

TRAUMATIC METAFICTION AND THE INSCRIBED NARRATOR

In texts by Vonnegut and O'Brien discussed in the previous chapter the figure of the narrator – to a varying and often minimal degree distinguishable from the author – is carefully inscribed into the narrative, to the extent that the production of the text is overtly foregrounded. What was termed there the inscribed narrator is a key component of traumatic metafiction, but it is developed considerably in *House of Leaves*. Danielewski carefully positions the narrating act as a key subject of investigation through his emphasising of Johnny as, in multiple ways, a symbolic writer figure. Johnny bears inscriptions himself, being scarred both psychically and physically following his childhood scalding at the hands of his mother, and, like many other characters in the book, bears tattoos. Johnny's job in a tattoo parlour is doubly appropriate, since he is an assistant, mirroring his second-fiddle role as editor of Zampanò's work. In both instances, he is not himself an artist-inscriber, but assists in acts of inscription. Just so, Johnny's boss at one point suggests he should 'Take up typing' (51) rather than aspire to be an artist, which is a suggestive distinction in terms of his position regarding Zampanò's text. Moreover, Johnny at one significant point hallucinates that he has accidentally covered himself in tattooists' ink (69–72), not only mimicking his childhood scalding in hot oil, but also temporarily becoming himself a text.

As described in the previous chapter, inscribed narration (re)introduces a generally omitted simulation of physical writing into the narrating act. Hayles, echoing Gérard Genette, notes that there is generally no indication of how 'oral narrations are transcribed into writing. However visible the mediations of consciousness (and unconsciousness), the technologies of inscription are invisible, their effects erased from the narrative world' (784). Similar to works by O'Brien and Doctorow discussed in the previous chapter, *House of Leaves* is precisely one of those rare novels – albeit increasingly common in the literature of trauma – that places at centre stage the transcription of narration into writing. Inscribed narration serves a number of purposes in traumatic metafiction. The foregrounding of the inscription of writing in *House of Leaves* makes the textual representation of trauma a performative act. The manifold difficulties of constructing a written narrative about trauma become a central subject for this novel, in much the same way as Linda Hutcheon perceives historical narrative to be problematised in historiographic metafictions. In traumatic metafictions such as *House of Leaves*, the representation of trauma, long held to be almost insurmountably difficult by theorists of the genre, is dramatised alongside the traumatic incidents and their aftermath.

This process is achieved in large part through the construction of a performance of narrating within the narrative itself. *House of Leaves*, building on earlier trauma texts, suggests that writers increasingly find it necessary to depict both how their narrators carry out the physical task of inscription, and how long this process takes. It is, of course, necessary to investigate more deeply why this particular narrative strategy has become so prevalent a marker of traumatic metafiction. As suggested above, traumatic metafiction shares certain characteristics – in both intention and procedure – with historiographical metafiction, aiming to foreground the difficulty of representing trauma and the resultant aporias. In other words, inscribed narration – at least until it, like other experimental techniques, becomes over-familiar – offers a potential solution to the apparent impasse regarding the unrepresentability of trauma. In traumatic metafiction the narration of trauma becomes a genuinely experimental act rather than an exercise in proving certain tenets of existing theory. The constant doubts expressed by Johnny (as when commenting on inconsistencies in Zampanò's account, '[m]aybe it's a mistake. Maybe there's some underlying logic . . . Your guess is as good as mine' [57]) and the numerous contradictions and paradoxes in the diegetic layers of *House of Leaves* constitute evolving and contingent commentaries on the trauma narratives with which these narrating acts are imbricated.

Again, the question arises of how, if at all, Danielewski's representation of trauma is different, either from earlier traumatic metafictions or from contemporary works of the formulaic trauma genre. There are a number of answers here that we shall consider in a moment – for example, *House of Leaves* employs a number of unsettling effects in more radical and sustained ways than imitative trauma texts – but first it should be briefly acknowledged that certain forms are indeed familiar from earlier texts. Johnny's self-confessed procrastination, making up entertaining false stories to cover his past misadventures since they 'help me look away' are, as even he admits, 'nothing new. We all create stories to protect ourselves' (20). To this extent, Johnny's procrastination is indeed a practice familiar from texts such as *Beloved*, and it takes him until around halfway through his narrative before he finally broaches 'the story I've been meaning to tell all along, one that still haunts me today' (265). A number of critics have commented on the general narrative structure of *House of Leaves*, insisting that the novel follows a circular form. Hayles, for example, argues that the novel's unusual form 'suggests that the appropriate model for subjectivity is a communication circuit' (803). If this were so, this form again would recall the circling procrastination of trauma texts discussed in Chapter 1. While much of the narration in *House of Leaves* is arguably circular in structure, however, a better model is actually provided in the resonant imagery of the spiral staircase located in the house's void. This model retains the circuitous character of narrated events in *House of Leaves* but also suggests a movement downward, or the combination of circularity and linearity which more accurately describes the novel's narrative. The unstable dimensions of the spiral staircase, moreover, prone as it is to stretching to near-infinity, are analogous to the book's frustrating efforts to proffer and then withhold answers (such as the abrupt break in the narrative thread of Karen's story between the end of Chapter XVIII and the start of Chapter XXII). In a book where form so self-consciously complements theme, the expanding spiral staircase structure rather than simple circularity provides a better analogy for the book's exploration of trauma. Danielewski thus not only employs a structure of gradual circling towards trauma familiar from writers such as Heller, Morrison and O'Brien, but also self-consciously represents this structure through one of the novel's most memorable symbols. Thus while influenced by earlier experiments in postmodernist trauma narrative, Danielewski's usage represents at least an extension of such techniques.

Distinct evocations of *Nachträglichkeit* or belatedness in Johnny's eventual admission of memories of his mother might similarly be taken as signalling some derivativeness in the novel's treatment of trauma. Towards the end of Johnny's narrative he begins to acknowledge the influence of his mother's behaviour upon the story he has shaped throughout the novel: 'I cannot tell you why I didn't see her until now. And it wasn't a scent that brought her back either or the wistful edges of some found object or any other on-the-road revelation. It was my own hand that did this' (502). As with the self-consciousness mentioned above, however, the language here hints at a knowing use and even satirising of the kind of popular trauma discourse which would recall the past based on 'the wistful edges of some found object'. Johnny's abrupt switch to third person when describing the traumatic circumstances of his father's death (37) is another narrative strategy familiar from earlier texts. This passage evokes conventional elements of the persistent effects of childhood trauma, and does so using a distanced voice which suggests the gap Johnny wishes to place between himself and the incident. Both incident and discursive means might be considered surprisingly conventional for such an ostensibly innovative text, but the overtness of the usage here – as with the examples in O'Brien's work discussed in the previous chapter – perhaps again signals parodic intent. Further familiar tropes are used to describe Johnny's initial encounter with the insidiously affecting world of Zampanò. 'Ever see yourself doing something in the past and no matter how many times you remember it you still want to scream stop, somehow redirect the action, reorder the present' (xiv), Johnny asks, recalling the fantasies of reversal found in *Slaughterhouse-Five* and the theoretical writings of Judith Herman (see Chapter 1). Johnny continues, expressing a sense of being absent at the source of the memory of trauma: '[n]ow I shudder,' he states as he recalls the same incident, '[b]ack then, I think I was elsewhere' (xv). This dissociation too may be taken as evoking some familiar tropes of the representation of trauma.

The sheer number of ways in which *House of Leaves* apparently draws on existing literary and theoretical models of trauma may be taken in two ways. Either it suggests that the novel is a highly derivative work of generic trauma discourse, or that Danielewski's usage of recognisable tropes is so excessive, so overt and – like so much of *House of Leaves* – self-conscious, that it is taken into the realm of parody. Before we return to the deeper significance of the novel's employment of inscribed narration, a short digression analysing a couple of instances may serve to demonstrate that Danielewski's employment of trauma discourse is broadly parodic in intent. Such parody is important, as it comprises a significant component of traumatic metafiction's wider project of unsettlement and its concomitant challenge to conventional trauma narratives.

Perhaps the best example is found in one of Zampanò's footnotes concerning the tale of the Minotaur. Ilana Shiloh notes the prevalence of stories of parents abusing children in *House of Leaves*: 'Zampanò keeps telling the same story, and then crossing it out; Johnny keeps telling different versions of the same story – his childhood traumas – progressively getting nearer to what must actually have happened' (138). For Shiloh, that this is the hidden trauma informing Zampanò's narrative (to the extent that it is separate from Johnny's) is revealed in part by the way in which all passages discussing the Minotaur have been struck through by Zampanò. As far as Shiloh is concerned, evidence for this is found in footnote 123 (or, to be strictly accurate, ~~123~~), a passage claiming to tell the true story of the Minotaur. What Shiloh does not mention is that this footnote is subject to one of Danielewski's many eccentric choices of layout, being rendered – if the reader ignores the page break – in the distinct shape of a key (110–11).

Such an overtly foregrounded indicator that this section provides the 'key' for unlocking Zampanò's trauma may very well be taken as parodic of the kind of popular trauma discourse with its origins in psychoanalysis which insists on opening up the sufferer's past. This reading is only reinforced by the fact that the entire text comprising the key footnote is struck through.

Even more explicitly parodic of contemporary trauma discourse is the 'Haven-Slocum Theory,' one of three (fictional) competing psychological theories discussed by Zampanò that attempt to explain the traumatic after effects of the events in the Navidson house. Zampanò's citing of the theory includes passages which are strikingly similar to dominant trauma theory, not least the offering of interpretations of three of Navidson's dreams. These interpretations accurately skewer particular characteristics of trauma criticism. The first illustrates the potential for formulaic reductiveness in psychoanalysis, ending with the pat interpretation that 'in order for Navidson to properly escape the house he must first reach an understanding about his own life' (399). Zampanò's summary of the second interpretation – purportedly condensing a tract that is 'impossible to locate and reportedly well over two hundred pages long' (399) – adroitly parodies the flights of fancy involved in deconstructive-psychoanalytic trauma theory (399–402). The final interpretation, of what is 'by far [the] most terrifying' dream (402), actually consists only of the note, '[2 pages missing]' (403), which may be taken to indicate the emptiness of this type of discourse. Together, the more explicit parodies of trauma discourse represented by Zampanò's 'key' footnote and the Haven-Slocum theory suggest that even Danielewski's inclusion of apparently more conventional representational practices is actually slyly parodic in its determinedly literal character.

To return to Danielewski's employment of inscribed narration, there are three ways in which this goes beyond a more conventional kind of usage, and these are related to the more unusual types of trauma the characters – in particular Johnny – experience. In this respect, the use of inscribed narration in *House of Leaves* is especially concerned with insidious (rather than sudden) trauma, trauma that is not worked through or resolved, and (to a lesser extent) perpetrator trauma. In terms of the first of these, as suggested above, authors of traumatic metafictions use inscribed narration partly in order to introduce temporality to the narrating instance. Genette correctly notes that narrating is conventionally 'considered to have no duration; or more exactly, everything takes place as if the question of its duration had no relevance', and that this absence of temporal dimension is perhaps one of the most powerful elements of narrating, 'because it passes unnoticed, so to speak' (71). The fact that Johnny's narrating instance has duration is both unusual and significant in terms of the text's representation of trauma. The reader is regularly reminded of this unusual dimension: 'Three months have gone by' (20), for example, by the time we get to Johnny's editing of Zampanò's third chapter. The temporal element in inscribed narration here is a direct challenge to the general tenet of trauma theory, especially as popularised through the concept of PTSD and through Caruth's work, that trauma is necessarily sudden and violent in impact. Since we are present alongside Johnny's narrating act – through his footnotes – we are able to witness the gradually traumatising effect of his unsettling encounter with Zampanò's manuscript. It is thus precisely this innovation in form which enables a critique of the widely accepted allegedly instantaneous facet of PTSD.

It is also significant that the inscription of the narration reveals that the time period of Johnny's discourse is circular (here slightly violating the narrative trajectory of the descending spiral described above) in that Johnny's introduction is revealed to have been written after the bulk of his notes on Zampanò's text. Passages narrated by Johnny towards the end of the novel bear the same date as his introduction, and reveal him to be suffering from trauma symptoms which bring on extreme panic attacks. Although to an extent this evokes a typical functioning of trauma, in suggesting that Johnny is locked into repetitive patterns of behaviour, at a deeper level this circularity presents a further challenge to conventional narrative trajectories concerning the therapeutic working through of trauma. A two-page series of diary entries (507–8) directly lampoons this notion, as Johnny first claims to have been cured of his breakdown through the intervention of two doctor friends, and then reveals that he 'just made all that up . . . And if you bought that Yellow-Tablet-Of-Shine stuff, well then you're fucking worse off than I am' (509). This direct parody of recovery from trauma is reinforced at a deeper level as powerful disruptions to the narrating process – including the breaking of narrative frames, paradoxical elisions and disjunctions in the narratives of Navidson and Zampanò, and the frequently circular digressions entailed by the labyrinthine footnotes – suggest that this is a narrating instance unlikely to reach a resolution or conclusion. These powerfully decentring narrative structures undermine any sense that the narrating act provides Johnny with a conventionally therapeutic sense of closure or recovery. This destabilising of the narrating process therefore signals that in *House of Leaves* we encounter a failed – or at the very least minimal – instance of working through, a proposition reinforced by the unresolved traumatised state in which Johnny remains even at the end of his narrating act. Again, texts employing a genuinely experimental form alongside a more sceptical perspective enable a challenge to dominant models, in this case of the comforting notion that trauma is followed by recovery.

Finally, Danielewski's use of inscribed narration also has some significance in terms of a representation of perpetrator trauma. Johnny, for all his faults, is presented to the reader broadly sympathetically throughout the novel. His introduction includes an obscure reference to blood 'still caked around my fingers' (xix), and it is only revealed nearly 500 pages later how this came about. Crucially, because this part of the narrative comprises dated diary entries, we learn that Johnny wrote the introduction shortly after committing murder or serious assault – although even this is open to question, because he is extremely prone to hallucinations at this point (497–8). As we shall see when we consider Johnny's agency in shaping Zampanò's narrative, the issue of whether he is cast as a perpetrator is significant in terms of how it affects his experience of trauma, and therefore the narratives that he constructs. The temporal dimension introduced through Johnny's inscribed narration is again important here, both in terms of adding new information about his possible criminal acts and in suggesting possible links between Johnny's part-perpetrator status and his insidious experience of trauma (a phenomenon discussed further in Chapter 4).

TRAUMATIC METAFICTION: EFFECT ON THE READER

Inscribed narration is important in *House of Leaves* in terms of insidious trauma, the depiction of a failed narrative of recovery, and issues concerning perpetrator trauma, but it is necessary to ask what else besides this formal device marks out traumatic metafiction. The effects discussed in this section in relation to the metafictional representation of trauma retain some power to unsettle the reader. Just as historiographic metafiction employed similar techniques in order to lay bare the artificiality of historical (and indeed all) narrative, so traumatic metafictions such as *House of Leaves* provoke an ontological unsettlement in the reader that questions the possibility and purposes of representing trauma in prose. This is not to insist either that trauma must be represented in such a fashion or that it can thus be transmitted to the reader of such texts, since this risks instilling the kind of programmatic model criticised in the introduction. But such unsettlement as that found in traumatic metafiction may produce the beginnings of a disquieting sense of the uncanny, especially as barriers between layers of reality are dismantled, as in *House of Leaves*. This ontological unsettlement in contemporary trauma texts is worth considering for a moment, in terms of its *modus operandi* and its potential effects. The final parts of this chapter consider examples of this in relation to *House of Leaves*, but first it is worth considering a couple of post-9/11 fictions – Jess Walter's *The Zero* (2006) and Laird Hunt's *The Exquisite* (2006) – both to show how trends in traumatic metafiction have continued beyond Danielewski's novel, and to demonstrate how traumatic metafictions might operate without the use of inscribed narration.

The Zero is focalised through a New York City policeman, Brian Remy, traumatised by his experiences of 9/11 and the subsequent cleanup, and begins with his attempted suicide. Remy suffers telling physical symptoms throughout the narrative, most notably connected with gradually deteriorating vision. Even more significantly, he experiences psychic disturbance, a constant 'loose string between cause and effect' (4) because he has blank spells, 'gaps in his memory, or perhaps his life, a series of skips – long shredded tears, empty spaces where explanations for the most basic things used to be' (5). Reflecting Remy's state of mind, the narrative comprises a series of scenes characterised by profoundly unsettling leaps forward in chronology and punctuated by jarring ellipses covering variable and frequently sizeable periods of time. The ellipses have the effect of underlining Remy's clearly profound experience of trauma, but also undermine the reader's certainty with regard to what is happening; the ellipses are not, as conventionally, completed by later analepses.[2] Secondly, the ellipses obscure the degree to which Remy is a victim or a perpetrator. While he is the unwitting sufferer of numerous circumstances in the wake of 9/11, Remy also becomes involved in a number of dubious federal operations, some of which involve acts of violence, torture and possibly murder of those suspected of what the authorities deem post-9/11 to be terrorism. Both Remy's acquiescence in agreeing to take part in these operations, and the violent acts themselves, however, are amongst those events that must be inferred by the reader, as they are prey to Remy's blanks in consciousness. Because of the narrative ellipses, the reader is never fully apprised of the degree of Remy's agency. Indeed, such is Remy's confusion resulting from the gaps in his memory that it seems more likely that he has drifted unwittingly into his position as perpetrator. In this sense, the unsettling ellipses underline not only the protagonist's disconnected post-traumatic state, but also wider political points regarding the invisibility of American 'counter-terrorism' operations post-9/11, and the way in which the American mainstream failed to discuss the ethics of such measures. Clearly the answer as to whether Remy is a trauma sufferer or perpetrator lies, as so often, in the grey zone in between, but it is unsettling for the reader just how many violent acts in the name of 'American security' he is apparently carrying out and traumatised by. This unsettlement is dependent at a fundamental level on Walter's metafictional use of strikingly disconcerting narrative structures to reproduce the protagonist's traumatised confusion.

The Exquisite is similarly, if tangentially, a post-9/11 fiction. Heavily postmodernist, it paradoxically contains two parallel, apparently mutually exclusive but also overlapping narratives. Protagonist Henry has, it seems, been the victim of a traffic accident, with possibly lasting traumatic effects. The narrative divides at this point into scenes set as he recovers in hospital and another narrative set outside. In the latter, Henry becomes involved in an underground organisation run by the sinister Mr. Kindt (who bears a passing resemblance to Danielewski's Zampanò), which carries out a series of what may be either real or simulated 'murders'. Again the effect of the metafictional structure – here the juxtaposition of the competing narratives – is to undermine the reader's certainty. The resultant unsettlement works to illustrate certain deeply decentring effects of trauma as Henry, torn between competing life narratives, loses virtually all sense of coherent subjectivity. As with *The Zero*, such profound and overt ontological unsettlement has the further effect of blunting the reader's attempts to determine the protagonist's culpability: is Henry a victim or a perpetrator? This blurring of victim/perpetrator status in *The Exquisite* thereby similarly alludes to America's ambiguous post-9/11 conception of itself, contested across the political and cultural arena, an issue which is explored more fully in the next chapter. As a traumatic metafiction *House of Leaves* employs some similar effects as a way of destabilising meaning, and the following sections examine this profound ontological unsettlement more fully in relation to this novel's engagement with postmodernist perspectives.

TRAUMAS OF ONTOLOGICAL CRISIS I: JOHNNY'S TRAUMA

One key characteristic which marks *House of Leaves* off from the trauma texts discussed in Chapter 1 is that it not only employs postmodernist literary techniques as a means to illustrate the effects of trauma, but also explores concrete thematic links between postmodernism and trauma. While a postmodernist aesthetic is arguably overfamiliar by the time Danielewski publishes *House of Leaves* (and indeed by 1993 when Wallace makes his statement against the 'crank-turners'), this engagement with the trauma of the postmodern condition is innovative. The following suggests that one of the key experiences of characters in *House of Leaves* is an ontologically-based trauma similar to that depicted in *The Exquisite* and, especially, *The Zero*. Given that the undermining of ontological foundations is a key part of postmodernism and that *House of Leaves* may be read as a culmination of literary postmodernism, this connection is doubly appropriate. Blurred ontology is significant in the text both as a cause and result of trauma, as evidenced throughout, but particularly through the character of Johnny and his increasingly eroded foundations for identity. The text's insecure diegetic layers and the resultant ontological uncertainty for both characters and readers are bound in a strong interdependent relationship with Johnny's role as unreliable – indeed, unstable – narrator. The way in which the narrative experimentation produces Johnny, the embedded, inscribed but also traumatised narrator, whose thematic interest so often centres on trauma itself, has led a number of critics to produce readings which suggest that the various embedded narratives in *House of Leaves* are either (merely) an expression of Johnny's trauma, or a prompt for the reawakening of Johnny's childhood traumas. Before exploring the broader theme of ontological crisis in this novel, it is necessary to evaluate some of these interpretations.

There are clearly a number of episodes in the novel for which such a reading is plausible. For example, a lengthy use of stream-of-consciousness to gesture towards what Johnny describes as 'this unread trauma' (49) culminates in him stating, '[i]nside me, a long dark hallway' (49). This is anything but the only allusion linking Johnny's traumatic past with the narrative he edits (or constructs) regarding the uncanny experiences of Navidson. Danielewski is aware enough of the readings this kind of linkage might produce to slyly include in his simulated academic discourse a reading of the house as a kind of objective correlative to Johnny's (or Navidson's) trauma. This is apparently excerpted from what Zampanò terms a 'stupendous study of space' by one 'Ruby Dahl,' who argues that 'the house, the halls, and the rooms all become the self – collapsing, expanding, tilting, closing, but always in perfect relation to the mental state of the individual' (165). Again, Danielewski is satirising academic analysis, but the point is that these interpretations lead back to Johnny, and an exploration of his trauma.

Fittingly, a number of real critics have also suggested a strong relationship between 'The Navidson Record' and Johnny's past, proposing ways in which one influences the other. 'The action of gathering and critiquing Zampanò's writings leads [Johnny] Truant to evaluate his life and begin, unintentionally, to approach the repressed memories of Pelafina,' Katharine Cox argues, for example, suggesting that the Navidson family's trauma represents 'an analogy for the tortured and mysterious story of Truant and Pelafina; they too mask a secret that is confronted and finally resolved in the space of the labyrinth' (6). This is a fairly standard trauma reading for such an unconventional novel, reducing it to the kind of formulaic text which simulates *Nachträglichkeit* by the withholding and eventual revelation of the central character's hidden trauma. Consequently, the parallels between Johnny's past and Zampanò's narrative lead Cox to overstate Johnny's role in constructing the story of Navidson. Again, this produces a reductive and broadly conventional repression-based reading of the relationship between the narrative layers: 'the labyrinth is conjured unknowingly by Truant as a mechanism to reinvestigate his mother and to recover his past. The eruption of the labyrinth from within the Navidsons' house is a physical embodiment of the terrible pain experienced by Truant at the loss of his mother from within the domestic environment' (7). If this sounds uncannily like the fictional reading of 'Ruby Dahl' cited above, with the Navidson house as symbol for Johnny's trauma, then this is followed by a suggestion that *House of Leaves* similarly encapsulates a conventional recovery narrative: 'Pelafina's exclusion from the family home ensnares Truant in a labyrinth of repressed memories which, through contact with the book, forces Truant to retrace his history, to enter the labyrinth and to rediscover his heritage' (7). While this is an interesting reading, it is based on familiar understandings of literary representations of trauma and recovery, and thus reduces the text in a way that too neatly explains away elements which are more complex and undecidable. Moreover, Cox's drawing upon conventional trauma theory helps to construct a unidirectional dynamic of influence – Zampanò's 'Navidson Record' text to Johnny – whereas in fact the relationship is, as we shall see, considerably more complex.

Other critics, assigning Johnny a much more active role in the construction of Zampanò's narrative, see the influence flowing more in the other direction, and have suggested that Johnny's childhood traumas directly affect the form of 'The Navidson Record'. Sinda Gregory and Larry McCaffery, in an interview with Danielewski, argue that the text of *House of Leaves* becomes a 'springboard allowing Johnny to explore the darkest regions of his own past' (131). They suggest that Pelafina's letter to Johnny dated January 3 1988 (in Appendix II. E) is significant, as the type descends into a muddled series of overprinted reproductions of 'forgiveme' [sic] (*House of Leaves* 627), which clearly only simulate, at best, the original, handwritten letter. Gregory notes that the reader is thus 'faced with the possibility that nothing here is "authentic," and all the texts . . . have been transformed somehow, whether by Johnny or somebody else' (121). This is a provocative proposal, perfectly correct on one level, but 'transformed' unfortunately suggests there is some buried level of truth or reality, with metaphysical presence, probably originating in either Johnny or Zampanò. The reality of this multiply and intertextually authored text is more complex, however, as the various competing narratives – Johnny's, Zampanò's etc. – bleed into one another. So while Johnny narrates a situation wherein Zampanò's narrative is affecting him, we need to be alert to how it (also) functions in the other direction (as in Vladimir Nabokov's *Pale Fire*). This reading is supported by Danielewski himself in the same interview, when he guardedly refuses the notion of authenticity proposed by Gregory and McCaffery: 'there is no sacred text here. That notion of authenticity . . . is constantly refuted' (121). If there is no authentic text by Zampanò which conveniently exists in order to unlock Johnny's childhood trauma (as in Cox's reading), neither do Johnny's past traumas simply inspire him to create Zampanò and 'The Navidson Record'. As Johnny admits, even though '[i]t's almost as if I believe questions about the house will eventually return answers about myself' (297), in reality, 'it's not really all that simple' (19), with the major ontological layers in the book merging and feeding off one another in multidirectional ways.

In order to illustrate the complexity of the interdependence between these different narrative levels it would be useful to examine further the unstable bleed between them. For example, Johnny's fragmented self, the dilapidated state of Zampanò's manuscript, and the narrative it contains are often symbolically linked, as when Johnny explains that ash (recalling the grey walls of the infinite hallway) 'landed on the following pages, in some places burning away small holes . . . small flakes leisurely kissing away tiny bits of meaning' (323). The symbolic resonance of this is reinforced a few pages later, as Johnny describes his 'crumbling biology, tiny flakes of unknown chemical origin already burning holes through the fabric of my mind, dismantling memories' (325–6). These two passages, in close proximity, contain symbolism so close that the allusive link must be intentional. As usual, however, it is unclear whether the connection is entirely Johnny's creation or if he is inspired to make a link by reading about the initial incident with the ash in Zampanò's manuscript.

Further links between Navidson's experiences and Johnny's are suggested towards the end of Navidson's episode lost in the blackness of the hallway when he experiences extreme time dilation and consequent disorientation. Again in close proximity, Johnny's final series of journal entries in the following chapter is headed (after reporting his friend Lude's death), 'October 25, 1998 (An hour??? later)', and goes on to describe a 'sudden vertigo of loss, when looking down, or is it really looking back?, leaves me experiencing all of it at once, which is way too much' (491). In other words, Johnny experiences psychological symptoms which perfectly correlate with what Navidson has just been described as physically undergoing in the black of the house. The direction of influence is unclear here, but at the very least, the reader cannot avoid the impression that Johnny is more than merely transcribing Zampanò's manuscript. A little later Johnny describes how he is tempted to set fire to the manuscript, just as Navidson has just burned his copy of 'House of Leaves'. Johnny holds the matches 'a quarter of an inch from the paper' but is unable to 'close that fraction of space. One quarter of an inch' (493). The distance is significant, being the same distance by which the interior space of Navidson's house exceeds its exterior, and so again suggests a link between the diegetic levels. Ultimately, even Johnny is not clear regarding the primary direction of influence, as the twin parasitic–vampiric relationship he endures with 'The Navidson Record' suggests. On the one hand Zampanò's manuscript is 'bloodless and still but not at all dead, calling me to it, needing me now like a child, depending on me despite its age. After all, I'm its source, the one who feeds it, nurses it back to health' (326). On the other, Johnny is 'overcome by the strangest feeling that I've gotten it all turned around, by which I mean to say . . . without it I would perish' (326, original emphasis). This is, perhaps, the clearest statement that Johnny's story and Zampanò's manuscript share a mutual dependence, if not always a healthy one, given the levels of psychological hurt that are reinforced.

Finally with regard to the significance of Johnny's individual traumas, as Ilana Shiloh notes, 'perhaps the most significant overlap of Johnny's life story with the stories he is studying can be found toward the end of the novel, when his childhood traumas begin to resurface,' and where the 'language and imagery of Johnny's story echo the language and imagery of *The Navidson Record*' (127). As the discussion above suggests, this echoing and re-echoing is perhaps more prevalent than Shiloh notes, but the specific episodes in Chapter XXI that she discusses, which draw a parallel between the growl/roar heard in the void of Navidson's house and that made by Johnny's father during his wife's breakdown, are indeed significant. This episode marks perhaps the strongest instance of Johnny's past being directly reflected in the Navidson story. Relating the story of his father's reaction to his mother's scalding Johnny's arms Johnny recalls, 'the way my father had *growled*, *roared* really, though not a roar, when he'd beheld my burning arms, an ear shattering, nearly inhuman shout, unleashed to protect me, to stop her and cover me, which I realize now I have not remembered' (506, emphasis added). Initially this reads as if Johnny has been prey to *Nachträglichkeit*, the traumatic memory being hidden beneath the narrative Johnny constructs. But once recalled the memory is decidedly not literal (as dominant trauma theory would suggest) as Johnny remains uncertain regarding its veracity which, although it is 'too vivid to just pawn off on the decibels of my imagination', remains opaque in origin: 'I must have heard it – or something like it – not then but later, though when? And suddenly I find something, *hiding down some hall in my head*, though not my head but *a house*' (506, emphases added). The phrasing is of course crucial, explicitly linking his mother's breakdown, which his father protects him from, with 'a roar to erase all recollection' (506), with the architecture of Navidson's house and its hidden hallways. This would seem to indicate clearly that Johnny has, at the very least, strongly influenced the narrative of 'The Navidson Record' to reflect his past. And yet, as we should by now expect, Danielewski is too aware of trauma discourse to offer us a simplistic key to unlock Johnny's past – recall the parodic typographically-shaped key to Zampanò's traumas – and he therefore undermines the link between the roaring sounds as an explanation. A few pages later Johnny's apparently recovered memory is abruptly dismissed:

> She hadn't tried to strangle me and my father had never made a sound.
> I can see this now. I can hear it too. Perfectly. (517)

On this occasion Johnny remembers 'the roar, the one I've been remembering, in the end not a roar, but the saddest call of all' (517) instead as his mother, as she is led away to the mental institution. The roar becomes a plaintive call, as Pelafina is instantly transformed from monstrous perpetrator – scalding and attempting to strangle her child – to victim. Johnny's traumatic memories are unreliable and thus undecidable, therefore undermining the notion that Johnny's past informs the Zampanò narrative – or vice versa – in any straightforward sense. We should be beginning to appreciate that the kind of trauma represented in *House of Leaves* is broader and much more pervasive than just a conventional exploration of Johnny's childhood trauma evoked by contact with Navidson's narrative. As the following section examines in more detail, trauma in Danielewski's novel is deeply bound up with its status as a postmodernist text.

TRAUMAS OF ONTOLOGICAL CRISIS II: POSTMODERNISM

Following the disastrous exploration of the house's huge void led by Holloway Roberts, one party member, Kirby 'Wax' Hook, on returning delirious and wounded to safety, begs Navidson's children for water. More precisely, he is quoted as demanding '"What. I need what-er"' (317). One must recognise that this is a deliberate insertion of Zampanò's (or emendation of Johnny's) since *The Navidson Record* is a film which Zampanò claims merely to be transcribing (although the film is actually fictional, constructed by Zampanò). Regardless of the precise way in which this utterance came into being, either Zampanò or Johnny choose to interpret Wax's words not as 'water' but as 'what-er'. This is significant for the following section, since it suggests that Wax's immediate reaction to the void is to pose ontological questions: 'what-er' perfectly summarises the ontological uncertainty encountered in Navidson's house: '*what* is in the hallway (or hollow-way)?' '*er. . .*'. Although this risks sounding like one of Zampanò's quoted critics from the novel's parody of overzealous academic discourse, in an interview with Sophie Cottrell, Danielewski himself crucially locates ontological crisis as a key part of traumatic experience: '[a]t the heart of any terror is the fear of losing what we find meaningful . . . the fear that our life and our loves will be rendered inconsequential.' This is an illuminating statement, and this section explores these thematic links between trauma and postmodernism, specifically the crisis in ontology at the heart of both. The unsettling perspective of postmodernism is shown to be profoundly traumatic since it entails the destabilisation of the Enlightenment's attempt to provide foundations for knowledge. *House of Leaves* is an unusual postmodernist trauma text because of its engagement with this key perspective of postmodernism rather than merely its aesthetic.

Mark Hansen suggests that *House of Leaves* is characterised by 'ontological indifference' (601) rather than a concerted investigation into the nature of being. In other words, the layers of mediated discourse actually produce so many paradoxes that it becomes pointless to try to make sense of them: 'the novel insistently stages the futility of any effort to anchor the events it recounts in a stable recorded form' (602). Hansen's terminology is useful in drawing attention to the ontological questions at the centre of *House of Leaves*, but his refusal to pursue the text's strategies beyond a certain point leaves room for further investigation. As we have seen in discussing Johnny's role in the construction of the narrative, this ontological crisis is produced in part through a profound instability in layers, as Johnny's past life bleeds through into the other diegetic levels, while his encounter with Zampanò's manuscript apparently affects his present. Just as the interior of this house demonstrates an inability to be contained, through its violation of the laws of physics, neither will any of the narrative layers in this novel remain separate, since trauma is freely transmitted between them. This extends into a deconstruction of distinctions between the real and the fictional, as we shall see when we discuss the novel's relationship with the work of Borges below.

As suggested at the end of the previous section, one key trope through which the narrative layers overlap concerns the recurring roar or growl, a feature of the house's void and, variously attributed, traceable in Johnny's past. An even more striking blurring of the novel's diegetic and thus ontological layers is found in the recurring figure of five-and-a-half, which permeates the novel's various trauma-inducing incidents. This is signalled most clearly by Navidson's short excerpt, 'The Five and a Half Minute Hallway', which precedes the release of the full-length version of *The Navidson Record*, but the figure recurs uncannily in various guises. The footnote between 85 and 86 is rendered as '$5\frac{1}{2}$' and refers to the possible, but characteristically obscure, origins of the 'Five and a Half Minute Hallway' (81). Similarly, a short film by Navidson's wife, Karen, entitled 'A Brief History of Who I Love', and which explores her traumatised state having escaped the house, is also revealed to comprise '8,160 frames' (368), that is, almost exactly five and a half minutes. This is echoed at a point of extreme stress in *The Navidson Record*, when after Navidson burns his copy of *House of Leaves* while in the void, 'nearly six minutes of screen time is black' (468). Revealingly, the figure crosses over into Johnny's narrative, and similarly evokes traumatic incidents. 'The Five and a Half Minute Hallway' is described as including, for example, a shot of '[b]lood on the kitchen floor' (5), a kitchen being the site, of course, of Johnny's traumatising childhood injury. Much later, shortly after the long-deferred revelation of how Johnny's mother inflicted this injury on him while suffering a nervous breakdown, Johnny reveals that he subsequently blacked out in his consciousness the 'details of those five and a half minutes' (517). As with other examples of porous narrative layers in *House of*

Leaves, the figure of five and a half, occurring in so many guises in the Navidson narrative and in Johnny's footnotes, suggests either (and irresolvably) that he has altered Zampanò's manuscript in order to insert it, reflecting his own traumatised obsession, or that its appearance in the manuscript provokes recall of his childhood trauma. The repetition of five and a half across the diverse narrative layers works similarly, if a little more subtly, to the rendering of the word 'house' in blue, to make shorthand links for the reader between various traumatic incidents.[3] More importantly, it begins to draw attention to the connection between ontological doubt and trauma throughout *House of Leaves*.

The epigraph from Ernst Jentsch that heads this chapter is relevant here, since it begins with the description of a subject terrified by that which he 'himself semiconsciously projected into things' – that is, just like Johnny in *House of Leaves* – before linking this to the threat of 'something unknown and incomprehensible' (14), a phenomenon akin to the trauma of postmodernist ontological crisis that lies at the heart of Danielewski's project. The similarity between Jentsch's statement and patterns found in *House of Leaves* is almost uncanny, and it is on this concept that we should now focus, since an effect of the uncanny is crucial to much of this novel's ontological unsettlement. Helpfully, Jentsch himself discusses the uncanny: 'the word suggests that a *lack of orientation* is bound up with the impression of the uncanniness of a thing or incident' (8, original emphasis). This is apposite since the uncanny clearly, in *House of Leaves*, begins its manifestation through a return to etymological roots in the unheimlich, based as the novel is on an uncanny or unhomely house, in which people quite literally lack orientation, both physically and metaphorically.

Initially the uncanny in *House of Leaves* is manifested through the disjunction between the qualities of its world and the conventional unsaid of realist novels. These include those elements such as physical laws which a reader would normally assume regarding the operation of the fictional world without even thinking about them, but which in *House of Leaves* do not function in normal ways. These anomalies begin to impinge upon the fictional world, and produce a range of unnerving effects that together comprise a profound sense of the uncanny for both readers and characters. This

is detectable in Billy Reston's outraged sensibilities on encountering the Navidson house's violation of the laws of physics, which
he describes as 'a goddamn spatial rape' (55). The undermining
of ontological and discursive certainties that so disturbs Johnny
assumes literal form in the behaviour of the house: the intrusion of
the terrifying hallway-void mirrors the general structure of inde-
terminately overlapping realities which is central to the book's disquieting effect. While Reston et al. are unsettled by the emergence
of what is marginal, assumed, and unsaid in conventional realist
discourse – that is, that houses are stable entities with solid and
unchanging dimensions – the reader may be similarly unnerved
by the 'goddamn spatial rape' of the dimensions of a physical book
(in Danielewski's numerous violations of conventional page layout)
and narrative (in the indeterminate bleeding between initially separate discursive layers). In this sense what in the diegetic frames of
the text – such as they are – is a breach of the laws of physics is for
the reader a violation of the principle of minimum departure, that
is, that the fictional world should behave as ours does. As readers
who can no longer assume the stability of the generally unnarrated
but normative situation – that the laws of physics in the fictional
text will be the same as those of our world – we are encountering,
precisely, the uncanny. And just as the house's physical architecture is rendered unstable, so Danielewski demonstrates postmodernism's traumatic undermining of the foundations of knowledge.

Unsurprisingly, given his autodidact erudition, Zampanò
addresses the uncanny in one of his etymological footnotes which,
moreover, unconsciously evokes the characteristic manifestation
of the uncanny as ontological crisis in *House of Leaves*. Zampanò
describes the uncanny as 'that which is <u>not</u> <u>full</u> of <u>know</u>ing or
conversely <u>full</u> of <u>not</u> <u>know</u>ing', thus 'that which is *uncanny* may
be defined as empty of knowledge and knowing or at the same
time surfeit with the absence of knowledge and knowing' (359,
original emphasis). In *The Uncanny*, Nicholas Royle's monograph
on Freud's namesake essay, Royle cites Freud's assertion that 'an
uncanny effect is often and easily produced when the distinction
between imagination and reality is effaced' (13). Together, these
two facets of the uncanny – its paradoxical plenitude of ontological
uncertainty and its elision of fact and fiction – are key elements in

the relationship between trauma and postmodernism in *House of Leaves*. As we shall see, an important part of this novel's engagement with the perspectives of postmodernism concerns the diegetic and ontological confusion introduced through its indeterminate mixture of fiction and non-fiction (especially in the footnotes) and the resultant challenge to the foundations of knowledge. Again, postmodernism's undermining of previously cherished certainties produces a trauma of ontological crisis in the characters, Johnny and Navidson especially.

The multiple encounters with the uncanny – and the resultant ontological traumas of Johnny, Navidson et al. in *House of Leaves* – also consist in the continually breached border between fiction and fact. The frame between our world and those fictional worlds apparently diegetically beneath is ultimately shown to be vertiginously porous. Johnny's introduction describes the onset of his ontological crisis, although the use of second-person address universalises the experience by implicating the reader as well:

> it doesn't happen immediately. You'll finish and that will be that, until a moment will come, maybe in a month, maybe a year, maybe even several years . . . Out of the blue, beyond any cause you can trace, you'll suddenly realize things are not how you perceived them to be at all.[4] For some reason, you will no longer be the person you believed you once were. You'll detect slow and subtle shifts going on all around you, more importantly shifts in you. Worse, you'll realize it's always been shifting. (xxii–xxiii)

This suggests that the ontological terror of the postmodern condition is not only universal but also insidious, underlining the appropriateness of the introduction of temporality through the employment of inscribed narration discussed above.

Nicoline Timmer seems to agree that a key source of trauma in *House of Leaves* is the ontological terror of something neither fully seen nor comprehended: 'faced with what resists interpretation, what defies the capacity to understand intellectually, the human figures in this novel resort to another form of "understanding" needed to fill this gap in meaning-making: all their senses are on high alert' (274). In other words, the psychological crisis borne of ontological terror is manifested in part through hyperarousal. This hyperarousal is coupled with flashbacks, another conventionally identified key symptom of trauma. 'You'll stand aside as a great complexity intrudes,' Johnny continues, '[a]nd then the nightmares will begin' (xxiii). Trauma, as described here by Johnny, consists of a series of unsettling phenomena which trigger feelings that things to which one was accustomed have altered disconcertingly. In effect, this elaborates what we have previously discussed in terms of the emergence of the uncanny ontological crisis in this novel through violation of the principle of minimum departure. Perhaps more significantly, though, the prevailing usage of second-person voice in this passage suggests the concept of transmissibility. The reader, so Johnny asserts, not only recognises but may actually experience the traumas embedded in the novel's various narratives, undergoing the same kind of uncanny ontological crisis of perception in everyday objects, which no longer match up to memory. Transmissibility of traumatic affect into the second-hand witness (in this case the reader) is a controversial element in contemporary trauma theory and one regarding which this study is otherwise sceptical (see the introduction). But we shall return to this idea below, with regard to the proposition that the fully postmodernist undermining of ontological certainties in *House of Leaves* may indeed be transmissible in part because it is something with which western readers are already familiar.

Johnny's indeterminate narrator-writer-editor role in *House of Leaves* may actually be partly responsible for the novel's production of ontological crisis. Uncertainty regarding the extent of Johnny's interventions, for example, is one reason the narrative layers are so prone to merge, and this is compounded as Johnny admits in his introduction to mistakes even in his transcription role, never mind deliberate inventions: 'Add to this my own mistakes (and there's no doubt I'm responsible for plenty) as well as those errors Zampanò made which I failed to notice or correct, and you'll see why there's suddenly a whole lot here not to take too seriously' (xx). Johnny, here and elsewhere, dismisses the effect of these inaccuracies, but his blasé attempts to downplay their significance in fact have the counter effect of alerting the reader to the ontological unease they cause. One such effect relates to the precise status of 'The Navidson Record'. This is an elaborate narrative, replete with factitious quotations from academics and an extensive – if eccentrically rendered – architecture of footnotes, but it is a fictional phenomenon; even in Johnny's world it is the creation of Zampanò (so long as we accept that Johnny fulfils an editorial rather than an authorial role). Nevertheless, as the narrative progresses it begins to assume factual status as the novel's diegetic layers overlap and merge. Navidson and others read a 'House of Leaves' manuscript, for example, and Johnny encounters the 'first edition' of House of Leaves allegedly edited by him (513).

This reference to the elaborate world of Zampanò's simulated academic discourse should alert us to the heavy influence on *House of Leaves* of Borges. The intertextual links with Borges constitute a significant connection between the postmodernist form and concerns of *House of Leaves* and its preoccupation with the trauma of ontological crisis. These links are not kept covert by Danielewski; in one footnote Zampanò explicitly acknowledges Borges (et al.) as an influence on *The Navidson Record* – therefore constituting Danielewski's implicit recognition of his own debt (133) – and a photograph of Borges is visible in one of Johnny's collages (Appendix II. C, 582). In the picture Borges has one eye closed, perhaps linking him to Navidson, who loses an eye to frostbite, and since he is also clearly linked to Zampanò we might take Borges in part as binding together the various levels of authorship.[5]

As well as Borges, Zampanò's blindness functions intertextually to the extent that he calls to mind other real and fictional 'blind seers' such as Milton, Tiresias, and Homer, the latter of whom, like Zampanò, has been undermined as a single, authoritative voice. It is intertextual allusions such as these that represent a partial means of undermining Zampanò's narrating voice, since the notion of authorship inevitably becomes more plural. The links between Zampanò, Borges, and the other writers mentioned above again reflect postmodernist concerns in serving to make authorship in *House of Leaves* (in the Barthesian sense) intertextual. *House of Leaves* quotes Barthes (even if his name is misspelt [146]), which is appropriate not only because he is one of its 'intertextual authors,' but also since Barthes describes the dislodgement of the 'author-God' from a position of power, which is precisely what the complex narrative strategies of *House of Leaves* enact. The numerous sources drawn on by Zampanò – both real and fictional – in his apparently authenticating footnotes, and the lack of stable frames between narrative levels experienced by Johnny, shift authority away from any originating source of discourse and towards the interpretive capacity of the reader.

House of Leaves may be understood in this sense as exploring the consequences of the insistence in postmodernism and post-structuralism on the death of narrative authority, which partly explains the extreme reaction of Johnny to the diminution of ontological certainties from his world. This stripping away, whereby Johnny becomes precisely Barthes's scriptor, assembling a text from a variety of intertextual sources, unsettlingly enacts for him the death of both his and Zampanò's authority. As we can see, then, for most of these characters – and certainly for Johnny – it is this postmodernist ontological crisis of existence and authority that produces, or at the very least reawakens, traumatised responses. Once more this is a synecdoche for the traumatic effect of postmodernism's more general stripping away of foundational certainties.

Crucially, allusions to Borges, one of the most important founders of literary postmodernism, are heavily imbricated with Danielewski's focus on ontological trauma. For example, the section discussed above, where Johnny expresses a fear of an intangible but menacing presence, of something uncanny on the edge of his reality which is a consequence of his involvement with Zampanò's manuscript, proceeds through expressing a prevalent sense of profound ontological unsettlement:

A moment comes where suddenly everything seems impossibly far and confused, my sense of self derealized and depersonalized, the disorientation so severe I actually believe – and let me tell you it is an intensely strange instance of belief – that this terrible sense of relatedness to Zampanò's work implies something that just can't be, namely that this thing has created me; not me unto it, but now it unto me, where I am nothing more than the matter of some other voice . . . forcing me to face the most terrible suspicion of all, that all of

this has just been made up and what's worse, not made up by me or even for that matter Zampanò.
Though by whom I have no idea. (326)

Johnny's subject position and foundations for knowledge – never particularly secure in any case – are shown to have been severely shaken by his encounter with Zampanò's manuscript. This is again linked to wider postmodernist concerns, since the manuscript is a perfect example of a simulacrum, in its knowing pastiche of academic discourse. His tentatively offered solution to the crisis at this point is to 'finish what Zampanò himself failed to finish. Re-inter this thing in a tomb binding. Make it only a book' (327). In other words, Johnny wishes to banish this return of the repressed, a repressed which signals his diminishing sense of his own authority, certainty, and thus subjectivity.

As important as this, the passage contains further direct allusions to the stories of Borges. Johnny's fear 'that all of this has just been made up' and that 'this thing has created me' echoes a number of postmodernist narratives where characters become aware of 'their master's voice' (McHale 121) and thus their own fictionality. Specifically, this recalls the climax of Borges's 'The Circular Ruins', whose protagonist, 'with humiliation, with terror', experiences exactly the same sense of ontological crisis, ultimately realising that 'he, too, was but appearance, that another man was dreaming him' (*Complete Fictions* 100). Johnny's final sentence in this passage – 'Though by whom I have no idea' – similarly recalls another ontological crisis in the work of Borges, this time expressed by the narrator at the end of 'Borges and I' ('I am not sure which of us it is that's writing this page' [*Complete Fictions* 324]). This calls attention to language's inevitably incomplete and uncertain capture of a subject position, an unsettling postmodernist concern revisited relentlessly through the indeterminate overlaps between Johnny's and Zampanò's narratives in *House of Leaves*.

Further links between Borges's work and the uncanny ontology of Danielewski's novel emerge in the episodes cited previously: firstly when Navidson reads something called *House of Leaves* (465), and secondly when Johnny meets a rock band whose members have in their possession 'a big brick of tattered paper' that turns out to be a first edition of *House of Leaves* that includes Johnny's own notes and introduction (513). These episodes call to mind Borges's 'Tlön, Uqbar, Orbis Tertius' and its encyclopaedia of a fictional world, Tlön, whose described objects, hrönir, begin disturbingly to penetrate the real world of the story. This infiltration of hrönir precipitates an ontological crisis: 'Almost immediately, reality "caved in" at more than one point' (81). In *House of Leaves*, just as in 'Tlön', a central issue is the crisis engendered in one's personal existence once apparently fictional worlds begin to enter ours. In other words, this is again a trauma borne of the ontological instability inspired by the insights of a postmodernist perspective, one which dismantles the boundaries between fiction and the real.

Lost in the impenetrable black of the void in his unheimlich house, Navidson is only able to read 'House of Leaves' by setting light to each page after he has completed it in order to read the next. Finally – and in a knowingly Derridean locution – 'the book is gone leaving nothing behind but invisible traces already dismantled in the dark' (467). *House of Leaves* then, or 'House of Leaves', is ultimately a postmodernist text which leaves us – traumatised? – in ontological darkness. In this, the text marks a true meeting – indeed the ultimate, the culmination – of postmodernism and trauma. We experience, even as readers, the unsettlement of ontological uncertainty, Borges writ large. If this is the final extreme gasp of the postmodernist aesthetic, unlike the texts discussed in Chapter 1 and their later imitators we are neither concerned merely with form nor witnessing writers using postmodernist means to represent trauma's effects. Instead, in *House of Leaves* the very project of postmodernism – its challenge to the foundations of Enlightenment thought and its dismantling of ontological certainty – is examined, and its consequences are found to be fundamentally traumatic.

This is part of the reason that I am more willing to grant the representation of trauma in *House of Leaves* an element of transmissibility. The kind of trauma with which this novel is preoccupied is intrinsically more transmissible than, say, the gothic horror of the house or Johnny's past. The twenty-first-century reader's familiarity with postmodernism's dismantling of once-invaluable certainties means that we encounter, on a smaller scale, the kind of ontological unsettlement depicted through this novel's chaotic form and collapsing narrative layers on a regular basis. In a pleasing circularity, the novel thus stages an encounter with the ontological abyss that is itself uncanny in its strange familiarity. We should finish, appropriately, on one of Zampanò's footnotes, clumsily transcribed – it would appear – by Johnny. According to Johnny, this section of Zampanò's manuscript has been damaged when ash (from the ashy deposits within the House on Ash Tree Lane?) has fallen upon it and burned through the pages. Thus footnote 290 'consists' of several lines of blank white space enclosed in square brackets, followed by 'o' – that is nullity, which is all that remains (334). The brackets, in other words, are as empty as the terrifying and uncanny hallways lurking in Navidson's house. Here we can perceive a transmission to the reader of ontological unease, expressed through a zero following a void which we try to fill.

NOTES

1. 'The Navidson Record' in the following refers to Zampanò's manuscript, whereas *The Navidson Record* denotes the fictional film.
2. Completing analepses, as defined by Genette, are flashbacks which fill in details omitted at an earlier point in the narrative.
3. In the full-colour version of *House of Leaves*, the word 'house' is highlighted throughout by being printed in blue ink.
4. Danielewski's repeated use of the phrase 'out of the blue' (in particular in Johnny's narrative) merits some comment, not least because it evokes trauma's alleged sudden impact and connects with the repeated rendering of the word 'house' in blue. There have been a number of ingenious interpretations of the blue rendering of the house, including that it mimics a hypertext link (see, for example, Hayles), or that the colour constructs a traumatised 'house of blues' (see Little). Equally significant is the simple way in which the blue 'house' strikes the reader again and again, mimicking the trauma symptom of repetition. The blue rendering of 'house' becomes mantra-like, in a sense

codifying trauma. The separation of 'house' through colour from the rest of the text creates an effect of the uncanny in the reader. In some ways this revisits, albeit in less subtle form, the kind of traumatic shorthand codifications used by Vonnegut or, especially, Henry Roth (see Chapter 1).

5. My thanks to Conor Dawson for making this suggestion. Zampanò in *House of Leaves* seems to be as deliberate an allusion to Borges as Jorge in Umberto Eco's *The Name of the Rose*. Like Borges, Zampanò possesses a Latinate name, suffers from blindness, and is a creator of fictional worlds and a summariser of others' (fictional) work. Similar to some of Borges's narrators, Zampanò is bookish, occasionally slightly pompous, and delights in his classical erudition in a similar way to the narrator of 'Pierre Menard, Author of the *Quixote*'. Menard appears in Zampanò's narrative, treated as an actual person, that is, on the same diegetic plane as Zampanò (42). This not only further complicates the novel's ontological unsettlement, but also strengthens the thematic link with Borges, who is similarly embodied as a character-narrator within a number of his stories.

CHAPTER 3

9/11, Collective Trauma, and Postmodernist Responses

As the previous chapter suggested, postmodernist literary techniques at their most formulaic are no longer likely to shock readers. Indeed, it might be argued that far from presenting a challenge to readers and viewers, such is the successful absorption of a postmodernist aesthetic into mass culture that it instead encourages a conservative retreat into the familiar and reassuring. Some critics have directly linked postmodernism's alleged demise with 9/11, David Wyatt arguing that on that day 'any reign of irony ended' (139), replaced instead by 'a return to feeling, an upwelling of unironized emotion that writing has attempted to honor, represent, and contain' (140). On the other hand, some have maintained that elements of postmodernism remain all the more relevant post-9/11. 'Ground Zero Literature' as Birgit Däwes labels it, 'does not necessarily abandon the principles of relativity, pluralism, and self-reflexiveness which postmodernism cherished' (522). The following chapter analyses two postmodernist responses to the events of 11 September 2001, Art Spiegelman's *In the Shadow of No Towers* (2004) and Jonathan Safran Foer's *Extremely Loud and Incredibly Close* (2005). Part of the purpose is to assess the relative effectiveness and appropriateness of experimental techniques and postmodernist perspectives employed by each author in order to broach the trauma of 9/11. The chapter begins by contrasting two conceptual alternatives on 9/11: whether it should stand as an exceptional limit event, outside understanding; or whether it can be contextualised as part of a continuing world political narrative, with particular reference to American foreign policy. The issue of collective trauma – its manufacture and its uses – is particularly relevant here, and its appearance in these two texts is also debated. It is worth noting that Foer's novel is precisely one of those accused of employing some of the more tired tropes of postmodernism. Walter Kirn, reviewing *Extremely Loud* in *The New York Times*, questions whether Foer should even be considered experimental, since his 'signature high jinks, distortions and addenda first came to market many decades back and now represent a popular mode that's no more controversial than pre-ripped bluejeans.' This recalls David Foster Wallace's remarks regarding the 'crank-turners' of second-generation postmodernism discussed in the previous chapter. The notion that postmodernist literary techniques that were once used to shock the reader and bear political critique have now become cosily recognisable is mirrored in another dismissive review, by Harry Siegel, wherein he claims that the flipbook which ends the novel 'serves no purpose but to remind us . . . what a daring young author this Foer is,' and that in his choice of subject, Foer 'snatches 9/11 to invest his conceit with gravitas, thus crossing the line that separates the risible from the villainous'. Even assuming we accept that anti-realist narrative devices are necessary for the presentation of trauma, the critical controversy briefly outlined here suggests that the postmodernist techniques employed by Foer are no longer sufficiently disruptive for dealing with a trauma on the scale of 9/11.

This sense that what was once avant-garde now feels antiquated may be directly related to the contemporary literature of trauma. As argued in the introduction, a number of American writers – Foer amongst them – have been swayed by the assertion of dominant contemporary theories that trauma cannot be represented using conventional language. To this end, they have typically drawn on postmodernist techniques discussed in Chapter 1, such as fragmentation, in order to broach the subject. Rather than defamiliarise the subject of trauma, however, such practices have developed into a usable framework, what Roger Luckhurst denotes as 'an implicit aesthetic for the trauma novel' (87). Tellingly, Foer is one of the principal authors identified by Luckhurst as reproducing this aesthetic: 'New careers in trauma fiction are still being forged: Jonathan Safran Foer's tragi-comedies of the Holocaust, *Everything is Illuminated* . . . and 9/11, *Extremely Loud and Incredibly Close* . . . show every sign of becoming canonical' (87). Foer thus provides one of the clearest examples of an author working too closely alongside the 'popular academic script' (Radstone, 'War' 118) of contemporary trauma theory. As suggested later in this chapter, many critics are then guilty of finding in his work a hardly surprising validation of their own theories of trauma.

Reviews of Spiegelman's *In the Shadow of No Towers* were also mixed, some reviewers reproving him for alleged solipsism, although stopping well short of the damning accusations of self-indulgence and insincerity levelled at Foer. Spiegelman's formal experimentation is less reliant on existing postmodernist models, and therefore not open to this particular criticism. Much of the experimentation in *In the Shadow* draws on and develops ideas found in Spiegelman's earlier work, including *Maus* and a number of the strips collected together in *Breakdowns*. As Scott McCloud notes, the focus in Spiegelman's art before *In the Shadow* has veered markedly between form and content, which is partly why 'the unassuming "report" style of his landmark biography *Maus*' (181) came as such a surprise. If Spiegelman's earlier work was preoccupied with formal experimentation, and *Maus* more focused on content, it is reasonable to interpret *In the Shadow of No Towers* as a synthesis of the two. There is clearly, for example, in the formal experimentation, a committed rumination on art and form; but there is also a sincere drive to explore the theme of 9/11 and America's response. Spiegelman's 9/11 text may be driven by an urgent need to explore the events' meaning – both personally and geopolitically – but its success lies equally in the necessary experiments Spiegelman carries out in terms of comics and literary form. As we shall see, *In the Shadow* is constructed upon the synthesis of what initially appear to be irreconcilable oppositions. Besides the realist content/anti-realist form mentioned above, for example, or the apparent oxymoron in its title, productive tensions between the eternal and the ephemeral, the individual and collective, and fragmentation and coherence, are key to Spiegelman's exploration of trauma as – another opposition – shattering but narratable.

THE HISTORICISTS VERSUS THE DECONTEXTUALISTS

We turn firstly to another key opposition at the heart of *In the Shadow* and, more generally, debates about 9/11. This is perhaps best conceived as a broad spectrum of responses between commentators who contextualise the events in a historical and political narrative, and those who refuse understanding of what they see as an abhorrent limit event. I refer to these, respectively, as the historicising and decontextualising tendencies. The historicist position envisions 9/11 as one event in a geopolitical narrative, even an unremarkable event compared to the suffering endured in many other parts of the world. The decontextualising position, by contrast, understands 9/11 as a major world event, something indeed 'outside the range of human experience' and a cause of widespread and lasting trauma.

Slavoj Žižek and Judith Butler are amongst those historicists who stress the need to comprehend the events of 9/11 in their wider context. Žižek asks, for example,

[w]hy should the World Trade Center catastrophe be in any way privileged over, say, the mass slaughter of Hutus by Tutsis [sic] in Rwanda in 1994? . . . the list of countries where the mass suffering was and is incomparably greater than the suffering in New York, but which do not have the luck to be elevated by the media into the sublime victim of Absolute Evil, is long, and that is the point: if we insist on the use of this term, these are all "Absolute Evils". (137)

Butler's *Precarious Life* records her outrage that representation of 9/11 as a limit event establishes a 'hierarchy of grief' (32) in the US, and suggests that only citizens of the West are included in 'what counts as a livable life and a grievable death' (xiv–xv). As she observes, this hierarchy helped to set the terms for the lawless retributive action subsequently undertaken by the Bush administration. David Holloway notes a broad decontextualising tendency of American commentators, which accepts official and mass media renderings of 9/11 as a unique event signalling a break with the past. He insists that 'Catastrophic though they were, the

9/11 attacks were just one incident in a much bigger, transnational Islamist insurgency' (1). In fact, Holloway continues, 'wherever one looked in the post-9/11 era what was most striking was the absence of clean breaks' (4). Kristiaan Versluys's response is typical of the decontextualists, finding 9/11 to be 'unpossessable . . . a limit event that shatters the symbolic resources of the culture and defeats the normal processes of meaning making and semiosis' (1). The title of Versluys's study, *Out of the Blue*, is interesting, not only given the discussion of this phrase in the previous chapter (see note 4), but also since it proclaims the events as unforeseen and exceptional right from the outset. There is much at stake here, especially since Versluys's study conforms strongly to dominant tenets in trauma theory. This suggests that Caruthian theory and PTSD, with a shared understanding of trauma as sudden and incomprehensible, provides a strong basis for decontextualised interpretations of 9/11. Given the subsequent political uses of the decontextualising tendency – as Holloway suggests, '9/11 was long in the making . . . however much it suited politicians to claim that the attacks came *out of the blue*' (2–4, emphasis added) – one could argue that trauma theory is indirectly complicit with US actions following 9/11. Once history is elided and the events of 9/11 are popularly accepted as arriving 'out of the blue', agency is diminished, since 'our narrative memory must then inevitably proceed from the perspective of victimhood' (Saal 467). As we shall see below, the mass media's decontextualisation of 9/11 was an essential element in constructing a sense of collective trauma that was in turn crucial in garnering support for the Bush administration's forays into Afghanistan and Iraq. In other words, trauma theory sets an ideal foundation for tendencies which, in these circumstances, enabled a sense of victimhood and false innocence to take root and deflect attention from America's complicity in actions both before and after 9/11. In this sense trauma theory is not only depoliticising, as critics such as Anne Rothe have claimed, but actively aiding the political right.

We return to this notion at the end of this chapter, but should remind ourselves that in recognising this spectrum of responses to 9/11, from historicising to decontexualising, it should be noted that the overwhelming weight of representation and commentary is attached to the latter, with the more relativist view tending to be marginalised. The official and mass media conception was to depict 9/11 as outrageous and outside normal processes of comprehension. As Holloway suggests, 'the idea that 9/11 was a moment when "everything changed" quickly became established in official discourse, where it played directly to partisan political agendas in Washington' that sought to strengthen American influence and commercial interests overseas (4). To reiterate, what is particularly relevant for this study is that the dominant Caruthian model of trauma is attached to the decontextualising tendency, and therefore becomes implicated with the consequences of this ideology. As Michael Rothberg argues, to 'focus on trauma solely as a structure of reception might . . . actually end up unwittingly reinforcing the repressive liberal-conservative consensus in the United States that attempting to explain the events amounts to explaining them away or excusing them' ('No Poetry' 150). The Caruthian model of trauma, with its focus on incomprehensible effect rather than overwhelming event, therefore implicitly supported an establishment wishing to decontextualise an event such as 9/11 and use it for other ends.

Given the genuinely overwhelming nature of events as they occurred, however, it would be unfair to condemn every reaction to 9/11 which neglected to place the events in their historical context. A number of pieces published shortly after 9/11 attempt to convey the immediate terror of the attacks, and are consequently little concerned with their cause. Don DeLillo's 'In the Ruins of the Future', from December 2001, emphasises how events were sudden and 'so vast and terrible that it was outside imagining even as it happened', thus producing traumatic shock. Where DeLillo does consider context the article is unconvincing: 'This catastrophic event changes the way we think and act, moment to moment, week to week, for unknown weeks and months to come, and steely years.' This contrasts with David Simpson, who begins his monograph by asking whether 9/11 really changed the world. If not, 'then who has an interest in claiming that it has?' (1). This is a telling question, correctly implying that those who insist on a decontextualised interpretation of 9/11 betray the kind of western bias further evident when DeLillo claims that the attack was caused by 'the high gloss of our modernity. It was the thrust of our technology. It was our perceived godlessness. It was the blunt force of our foreign policy.' While this final, euphemistic sentence is alone in broaching any kind of historical context, it is nevertheless naïve. As Holloway observes, '[t]he suggestion that suicide bombers attacked the World Trade Center because of "who we are", rather than because of the policy-making of US political administrations since the 1950s, made it easier for citizens to live with the realities of war' (10). Importantly, it is decontextualising rhetoric such as DeLillo's, with 'little consideration of the roots of such hatred and violence' (Ryan 20), which makes possible the specious arguments about America's innocence.

Another common reaction of the decontextualists was to refuse to understand the events of 9/11. Echoing Claude Lanzmann regarding the Holocaust, Jenny Edkins advocated a refusal to place the events in context, instead suggesting 'that we try desperately to hold on with all our might to the feeling of utter astonishment, incredulity and disbelief that was many people's first reaction . . . we shouldn't accept what happened. We should refuse to admit it to the everyday world of things that exist' ('Absence'). This viewpoint is echoed in diverse forms, including commentaries by Ann Kaplan and Dori Laub, documentaries that employ montages of footage of the day (for example, Greg Jacobs's and Jon Siskel's *9/11: 102 Minutes that Changed America*), and Oliver Stone's *World Trade Center*. Again, the determined focus on the events of the day and a refusal to comprehend them is an understandable but, as we shall see, dangerous reaction in terms of the potential political uses of such a perspective.

Efforts to address both perspectives – historicising and decontextualising – are discernible in the works by Foer and Spiegelman. Foer incorporates into his novel accounts of the bombings of Dresden and Hiroshima during World War Two, as an apparent attempt to cast 9/11 in a relative light and diminish its exceptional significance. Francisco Collado-Rodriguez suggests that clear equivalences thus result: '[t]he two events, distant in time and presented fragmentarily by the two traumatized narrators, coincide in many respects' (58), and thus 9/11, Dresden and Hiroshima are all cast as morally reprehensible. Matthew Mullins similarly comments on Foer's resistance of an unquestioning adoption of victim status, observing that *Extremely Loud* considers these two previous bombings in order 'to complicate a seemingly simplistic view of what it means to be the victim of trauma in the wake of 9/11' (315). Mullins argues that the novel is transnational to the extent that traumatic grief is not allowed to be restricted – as official and mass media discourse suggested it should be – to America. Other critics have suggested that Foer's comparison of 9/11 to other acts of mass violence is less successful. Ilka Saal finds that the attempt to construct dialogues between mass traumatic events is largely stymied by the novel's finally overwhelming focus on Oskar: 'Foer's deployment of Dresden as the primary trauma analogy ultimately appropriates these older traumata for a unilateral framing of 9/11' (463). The most serious implicit accusation here is that Foer is instrumental in his approach to Dresden, not in fact opening a dialogue, but using it to underscore the magnitude of 9/11. Even Holloway, who generally approves the novel, concedes that '[a]lmost everything about Foer's novel drove the attention of the reader inward, into the private agonies of the traumatised self and away from any meaningful contextualising of 9/11 in public or historical space' (114).

If this suggests that Foer's novel is more successful in capturing the immediate terror of 9/11 than its historical context, then Spiegelman's comic book account is perhaps the 9/11 text that best captures elements of both ends of the historicist-decontextualising spectrum. Again, this is in accord with my general reading of *In the Shadow of No Towers* as successfully synthesising numerous apparent oxymora. *In the Shadow* certainly evokes the sheer terror, panic and traumatic detachment caused by the attacks. But it also comprises – indeed evolves into – a political re-engagement and critique, and a reconsideration of how the US should (have) react(ed). The opening frame of the text effectively delineates the twin ends of the historicising-decontextualising spectrum. The first text we encounter runs thus: 'SYNOPSIS: In our last episode, as you might remember, the world ended' (1). Of course, there is no actual previous episode of the strip, only of Spiegelman's and our reality, albeit, as suggested here by the deliberately hyperbolic language, a heavily mediated reality. So while the phrase implies continuity, that the events to be depicted in the text are part of a larger geopolitical narrative, this episode is also outrageous, unprecedented, and seemingly beyond context: 'the world ended'. Thus, right from the beginning, Spiegelman suggests that his text will pay attention to both possible interpretations of 9/11, as exceptional and as part of a historical narrative.

Although the text successfully combines both interpretations at its start, the first half of *In the Shadow* (up to and including Plate 4) is more concerned with conveying the immediate terror of 9/11. The narration quoted above continues in the next frame, where Spiegelman describes how '[m]y wife, my daughter and I are rushing from the bomb site. We hear a roar, like a waterfall, and look back. The air smells of death –' (1). Spiegelman's use of continuous present tense here not only effectively evokes the insistent presence of the traumatic memories (rather than any inaccessible quality), but also, combined with the brief, breathless sentences, communicates immediate and instantaneous impressions. His priority in *In the Shadow* later shifts toward the political, as he develops a counter-narrative disputing the mass media rendering of 9/11 and critiques the Bush administration's violent response. This project consequently shifts the work away from a conventional representation of trauma as overwhelming and incomprehensible. Spiegelman uses the images in his work to refocus on the political context of 9/11 and its aftermath, or as Katalin Orbán suggests, 'to reorient the reader from the "awesome" sublime to a more contingent history that does not transcend material bodies and traces' (58). The following section develops this exploration of the contrasting historicising and decontextualising readings of 9/11, examining how these are manifested in the construction of a sense of collective trauma, and how this is articulated in Foer's and Spiegelman's texts.

MEDIATION AND COLLECTIVE TRAUMA

The notion of a universal collective trauma engulfing America is addressed in a number of post-9/11 literary texts. In Ken Kalfus's blackly comic novel *A Disorder Peculiar to the Country* Joyce, the central female character, is notably sceptical about the sense of collective trauma allegedly affecting even those who did not directly experience or witness the attacks:

> *Every* American felt that he had been personally attacked by the terrorists, and that was the patriotic thing of course, but patriotic metaphors aside, wasn't the belief a bit delusional? There was a difference between being killed and not being killed. Was everyone walking around America thinking they had been intimately, self-importantly, involved in the destruction of the World Trade Center? (78, original emphasis)

The mediation of 9/11 – including the media's selective and incessant repetition of images in the days following the attacks – is heavily interwoven with this sense that 'everyone walking around America' was suffering from collective trauma.

While collective trauma is a term much used in contemporary trauma theory, it tends to be employed unquestioningly, as if this complex and nebulous phenomenon arises quite naturally following large-scale events such as 9/11. But if trauma manifests itself in so many diverse ways and in response to such unpredictable stimuli, can it ever become a collective experience in more than the very loosest sense? It is worth asking whether this is another reason for the attempt of dominant theory to impose a monolithic model of trauma causation and symptoms, disregarding their actual diversity, particularly across different cultures. In 'Reconceiving Binaries: the Limits of Memory', Susannah Radstone laments precisely this vague and metaphorical character of collective trauma, which gains credence principally through 'the extension and application of terms associated with personal memory to domains beyond the personal. This "personalization" has the effect of hardening into literality what might better be regarded as a series of compelling metaphors – the "traumatization" of a nation, for instance, or the "healing" of a culture' (137). This is a persuasive observation – not least in the context of 9/11 – which leads us to conclude that the idea of collective trauma is much more culturally based than generally recognised and also highly dependent on mass mediation. This may be considered alongside Jeffrey Alexander's argument that collective trauma needs to be rethought as a cultural application or diagnosis, something assigned rather than a naturally occurring phenomenon: '[w]hether or not the structures of meaning are destabilized and shocked is not the result of an event but the effect of a sociocultural process. It is the result of an exercise of human agency' (10). Moreover, Alexander observes that '[t]his cultural process is deeply affected by power structures' (10), a significant point when we consider the uses to which the supposed sense of collective trauma following 9/11 was put. A deeper point here is that a sense of collective trauma cannot occur without mediation, as Alexander points out: '[m]ediated mass communication allows traumas to be expressively dramatized and permits some of the competing interpretations to gain enormous and persuasive power over others' (Alexander 18).

In the Shadow of No Towers engages most clearly with the issue of mediation when Spiegelman uses his text as a sincere attempt to unpick his own first-hand experience of the tragedy from those memories acquired through exposure to the blanket mass media coverage. In the short prefatory essay, entitled 'The Sky Is Falling',[1] Spiegelman explains an important impulse behind the strips: 'I wanted to sort out the fragments of what I'd experienced from the media images that threatened to engulf what I actually saw, and the collagelike nature of a newspaper page encouraged my impulse to juxtapose my fragmentary thoughts in different styles.' To this extent, the eclectic form of *In the Shadow* emerges organically from Spiegelman's attempt to address the problem of mediated memories.

Indeed, it is a little unclear exactly what Spiegelman witnessed on September 11. In an interview with Claudia Dreifus, Spiegelman states that he and his wife 'had just walked out our door when we saw that first plane crash into the tower about 10 blocks south of us'. In *In the Shadow*, by contrast, Spiegelman first notes that he 'saw it all live – unmediated' (1), but subsequently depicts both crashes as having been witnessed second-hand. The first plane crash is heard by Spiegelman and his wife, who have their backs to the tower, but reflected visually through the reaction of a woman facing them. The crash into the second tower is described, like the first, in a dissociated, heterodiegetic voice: '[h]e ran back home to phone the school, so he only saw the second plane smash into the tower on TV . . . Though he heard the deafening crash right outside his window' (2). In both cases the auditory experience is first-hand, while the visual experience is variously mediated. As Marita Sturken suggests regarding inconsistent narratives such as these, the significance lies not so much in the memory's questionable truth value, but rather 'what its telling reveals about how the past affects the present' (2). Just so, Spiegelman's narrative strategies here convey his unease concerning the persistent and potentially misleading power of mediation in the encounter with the events of September 11. Thus in Plate 6 a Spiegelman figure falling from one of the towers is 'haunted now by the images he *didn't* witness' (original emphasis), that is, those he experienced in mediated fashion. Besides the narrative, Spiegelman's visual strategies also call attention to the Gordian knot of mediated and first-hand experiences; the computer-generated image of the incandescent towers repeated on every plate of *In the Shadow* is deliberately artificial in appearance, and thus, as Martha Kuhlman observes, 'draws attention to the mediated incarnations of the event on television and in photos' (851).

If the mediating role of television in particular, and its complicity in helping to foster support for the Bush administration's response, is a key theme of *In the Shadow*, the role of mediation, particularly in combination with repetition, is even more explicitly broached in Foer's novel. Oskar and his grandmother's experience of 9/11 in particular is described, in a chapter narrated by the latter, in terms of insistent and mediated repetition:

The same pictures over and over.
Planes going into buildings.
Bodies falling.
People waving shirts out of high windows.
Planes going into buildings.
Bodies falling.
Planes going into buildings. (230)

This passage goes on to repeat the same phrases many times more, and as with a number of other instances in *Extremely Loud*, formal repetition not only comments on but reproduces the initial effect. The unbidden traumatic flashbacks suffered by Grandmother and Oskar in *Extremely Loud* are notable for being caused by mediated and repetitive causes. This tallies with Alexander's argument cited above, and the connection Simpson makes between mediation and collective trauma in the specific case of 9/11, bluntly noting that numerous people across America even with little or no direct connection to the events 'reported feelings of acute personal anxiety and radical insecurity, but there was never a point at which this response could be analyzed as prior to or outside of its mediation by television and by political manipulation' (13).

Broaching the notion of collective trauma raises the question of what may be objectionable about the phenomenon in general and, more specifically, about thus conceptualising the reaction of Americans in the wake of 9/11. As suggested above, relying as it does on a rather tenuous set of extrapolated metaphors, the concept itself is unsatisfactory and unproven. In the context of 9/11, though, it is perhaps the political manipulation of a constructed sense of collective trauma that is so troubling. Writing before the events of 11 September 2001, Kirby Farrell noted, with reference to the political potential of the notion of collective trauma, that '[p]eople not only suffer trauma; they use it, and the idea of it, for all sorts of ends, good and ill. The trope can be ideologically manipulated, reinforced, and exploited' (21). Also predating 9/11, Judith Herman similarly observed that '[d]emagogic political leaders well understand the power of [trauma sufferers'] rage, and are only too willing to exploit it by offering to aggrieved people the promise of collective revenge' (242). In the aftermath of 9/11, these seem prescient words indeed. As Žižek asks, '[i]n the traumatic aftermath of September 11, when the old security seemed to be momentarily shattered, what could be more "natural" than taking refuge in the innocence of a firm ideological identification?' (45). This deceptively innocent 'firm ideological identification' is precisely what the Bush administration sought to cement post-9/11, through fostering a feeling of collective trauma. An ideological narrative was rapidly constructed, beginning with a sense of collective victimhood and moving then, as if inevitably, to a desire for revenge. Countless cultural manifestations underscored this idea. To cite just one, Stone's

World Trade Center demonstrates a decontextualising tendency throughout that evolves into an endorsement of the subsequent Middle East excursions by the Bush administration. The film's stereotypically heroic ex-marine, Dave Karnes, becomes involved in the rescue effort, and his reaction to the wreckage – significantly placed near the end of the film – is that 'we're gonna need some good men out there, to avenge this'. There is nothing in the film to suggest that this view is to be challenged.

Again, the process of mediation and the mass media's role in 'shaping how the traumatic event was to be perceived' was a key element in the 'construction of a consensus' (Kaplan 13), and once more, dominant trauma theory may be identified as providing a foundation for this ideological process. As Rachel Greenwald Smith suggests, the construction of collective trauma following 9/11 'was one of many factors in the development of a new national myth, one that drew from therapeutic discourse to suggest that prior to the attacks, the United States was itself a fully constituted whole until it endured an unexpected and unidirectional assault from outside' (156). This again has serious ramifications for trauma theory, since the sense of collective trauma provided such an opportune moment for 'the nation's leaders to pursue the agenda to which they are committed and pass it off as the response to the time's hard necessity' (Brooks 51). In other words, collective trauma was instrumental in the bloody process noted by Simpson: '[i]n less than two years we went from the fall of the Twin Towers and the attack on the Pentagon to the invasion of Iraq, a process marked by propagandist compression and manufactured consent so audacious as to seem unbelievable' (4). The manufacture and manipulation of collective trauma is one of the key drives behind the political anger of Spiegelman's *In the Shadow*. As Jenny Edkins points out, what New Yorkers generally desired post-9/11 was not a 'rush to war and the imposition of even greater state control in the name of security' but above all 'not to repeat the trauma, not to impose on others what they are suffering' ('Absence'). Spiegelman underlines that rather than responding sensitively and creatively to the hurt of New Yorkers, the Bush administration, in collusion with the media, produced a narrow and dehistoricised narrative of 9/11 wherein 'September 11 was presented as the beginning of a sequence of events that was yet to unfold. The past had been obscured' (Ryan 29). This in turn was used to manipulate the public through the resultant spurious sensation of collective trauma. For Spiegelman, Edkins and others, its spurious character is revealed precisely by the desire, through escalation, to enable rather than to prevent repetition.

Ann Kaplan illuminatingly compares this government and media construction of collective national trauma to the individual reactions of New Yorkers, noting the spontaneous and pluralistic response she witnessed from wandering the city's streets in the days following the attacks. Here, she encountered various events and objects to mark the catastrophe: 'on the streets something fluid, personal, and varied was taking place' (15). This significantly points to the dangers of collective trauma as lying predominantly in its monolithic assumption of metanarrative status; in the pluralistic sense encountered by Kaplan it is more complex and almost impossible to manipulate. The point, as most critics of the official media and government response to 9/11 have maintained, is that one must resist attempts to develop a monolithic depiction of collective trauma, as this is uniquely usable. As we shall see, Spiegelman's text, not least through its disruptive, multivocal, and fragmented form, is particularly successful in acknowledging the possibility of collective trauma, but resisting its becoming a metanarrative.

By contrast, Foer's novel appears much more accepting of the existence of collective trauma, grouping together an assortment of traumatised New Yorkers in the aftermath of 9/11, of which the central protagonist Oskar is but one. Arguably though, Foer does not adopt the notion of collective trauma unquestioningly or as if it is unproblematic. Matthew Mullins suggests that the arbitrary collection of New Yorkers with the surname 'Black' assembled by Oskar acts as a cross-cultural community of the traumatised. This group forms a resistance to simplistic and exploitable notions of collective victimhood, and Mullins suggests that the novel promotes a sense of 'traumatic solidarity' that transcends national boundaries, proposing instead 'alternative conceptions of identity that encourage global community across existing identity boundaries' (298). Thus, according to Mullins, it is the dangerously nationalistic sense of victimhood, predicated on a stigmatised other, that Foer challenges in *Extremely Loud*. The arbitrary community of 'Blacks' is important in this respect, since 'suspicions and boundaries can be overcome by joining people, even strangers, together in the wake of a trauma like 9/11' (307). The 'community of the traumatised' remains a problematic concept, however; for a start, given that only a limited set of ethnicities are likely to possess the surname 'Black', this community is probably not as inclusive as Mullins suggests. The apparent inclusivity of *Extremely Loud* is largely an illusion, and the ultimately overriding focus on Oskar's trauma precludes a genuine construction of a community, or an inclusive solidarity towards victims of other tragedies. As Smith notes, the apparently inclusive 'we' in Oskar's fantasy of time reversal at the end of the novel is in fact heavily circumscribed: 'Because time cannot spin backward far enough for the "we" of the final line to expand to include the victims of other tragedies, tragedies that might have complex relationships with the attacks, the appeal to safety draws a clear line between the intolerable deaths of 9/11 victims and the much more complicated geopolitical context of the event' (158). Thus the dominance of Oskar's voice as narrator, his predominant failure to overcome his post-traumatic stress, and – as we shall see – vestiges of racism in his own reaction to events, mitigate against *Extremely Loud* providing a sustained critique of the notion of collective trauma.

The phenomenon of collective trauma is criticised more convincingly in *In the Shadow of No Towers*, both formally and thematically. Right from the frontispiece facsimile reproduction of the headline of *The World*, dated September 11 1901, Spiegelman suggests the dangers of becoming locked in self-perpetuating series of collective trauma. In this sense, Spiegelman suggests that a carefully nurtured and continually renewed sense of collective trauma has produced a low-level mass paranoia that in turn may be periodically used as a state ideological apparatus. The dominance of a post-9/11 narrative of paranoia – constructed through the manipulated sense of collective trauma – is suggested in Spiegelman's introduction to the text, where he describes how 'those of us living in Lower Manhattan found our neighborhood transformed into one of those suburban gated communities as we flashed IDs at the police barriers on 14th Street before being allowed to walk home' ('The Sky Is Falling').

The main body of Spiegelman's text includes a series of attempts to critique unthinking acceptance of the notion of collective trauma. The three-panel strip beginning the first plate, entitled 'The New Normal', succinctly satirises the widespread and hyperbolic assumption, as discussed above, that after 9/11 'everything changed' (see Figure 3.1). In the first panel – shown by the background calendar to be set on September 10 – two parents accompany their small child on a couch, complacently dozing in front of a television. The next panel, a day later, depicts the family's horrified reaction to events, all three humans and the cat now awake, agog, and with hair standing on end. The final panel shows the family returned to similar postures as before, the only differences being that their hair remains on end and the calendar has been replaced by an American flag. These differences are telling in terms of notions of collective trauma. The title of the strip, combined with the anonymity of the family suggests that they are to be taken as representatively American, if not necessarily New Yorkers, and so it is plausible to read their behaviour as Spiegelman's wry comment on how the American public were generally supposed to have reacted to 9/11. The third panel shows a return to normality of sorts, but in this 'New Normal', complacency (the repeated slumped posture of the parents) is uneasily accompanied by continued trauma (the hair remaining on end); again, Spiegelman incorporates the key opposition between continuity and a break with the past. Moreover, in the final panel a sense of time passing, as indicated in the first two frames by the calendar's changed date, has vanished. If time now stands still, in its vacuum is a renewed sense of patriotism, as signified by the appearance of the American flag. The flag is a recurring icon throughout the plates, figuring more than once on this plate alone, and as David Ryan suggests, it was deployed in the days following 9/11 in a way which 'obscured divisions in US society and challenged anyone to question US unity' (21). Spiegelman here sardonically and succinctly demonstrates how the resurgent patriotism, and its concomitant ideologies of victimhood and vengeance, are mobilised in the timeless state of the allegedly traumatised collective of typical post-9/11 Americans.

Just as unquestioning assumptions about collective trauma

Figure 3.1: 'The New Normal'. (Source: Art Spiegelman, *In the Shadow of No Towers*, Plate 1)

are thematically challenged, so Spiegelman's form is similarly employed. Many reviews of *In the Shadow* expressed dissatisfaction with the fragmentary nature of Spiegelman's text. Adam Begley, for example, asserts that *In the Shadow*, especially in comparison to *Maus*, 'fails to tell a story: not a whole one, anyway, and certainly not a coherent one'. This echoes Dori Laub's more general demand for a single, coherent post-9/11 narrative: 'Nearly six months after the event that shook our world and our assumptions about our lives, there is no coherent narrative about September 11' ('September 11' 204). Laub's desire for coherence actually reverts to precisely those assumptions about collective trauma that Spiegelman seeks to critique, that is, a coherent, monolithic narrative that can be politically useful. Whereas Ann Kaplan (and, by implication, Spiegelman) welcomed a plurality of responses to 9/11, Laub apparently sought to unify them: '[t]he multitude of diverse voices, public and private, that we are hearing about September 11 testifies to the absence of a coherent narrative voice for the event itself' (211). Such a fragmented and plural response to any large-scale event must always be the case, however, and this is surely desirable, given the risks of dominant master narratives of collective trauma. The fragmented, often chaotic form of *In the Shadow* – the plethora of styles and the heavy borrowings from classic comic strips – instead strenuously avoids the kind of ideologically numbing narrative coherence desired by Laub, Begley et al.

For Spiegelman, one principle for representing 9/11 and its aftermath is to employ as many plural and competing voices as possible, but without dismissing the likelihood of collective trauma. Indeed, there are clear indications that a common set of emotional responses forms a deeper structure beneath individual behaviour, as when he describes how 'most New Yorkers seem to have picked up the rhythms of daily life . . . but right under the surface, we're all still just a bunch of stunned pigeons' (9). Although the experience may be shared, however, Spiegelman's form persistently resists collapsing into a single coherent narrative of collective trauma that might be manipulated. Spiegelman's fractured narrative form demonstrates that a metanarrative of collective trauma is too dangerous, and too easily manipulated, to be allowed to pass unquestioned.

Indeed, much of *In the Shadow of No Towers* is directly concerned with how the sense of collective trauma following 9/11 was used, how Bush and his associates 'immediately instrumentalized the attack for their own agenda' and 'reduced it all to a war recruitment poster' ('The Sky Is Falling'). As this suggests, Spiegelman's text quickly turns its attention from the immediate terror of 9/11 to deal with the political fallout at greater length. This shift occurs before the text's midpoint, as signalled by the opening narration of Plate 4: '[o]ur hero is trapped reliving the traumas of Sept. 11, 2001 . . . Unbeknownst to him, brigands suffering from war fever have since hijacked those tragic events . . .' (original ellipses). Plate 4 is the last to deal directly with the events of September 11, as the focus shifts more fully to the egregious political response. Spiegelman's writing hereafter adopts a more bitingly satirical tone, mercilessly caricaturing both the Bush administration and the complicit media response. In the strip on Plate 10 Spiegelman, in the guise of the 'Hapless Hooligan' (a pastiche of the classic 'Happy Hooligan' strip), is interviewed for NBC as part of a montage of responses to 9/11 from notable New Yorkers. At the urging of his wife, who suggests that this will present Spiegelman with a rare opportunity to voice marginalised points of view, he reluctantly agrees to take part. Asked what he considers to be the greatest thing about America he responds, 'THAT AS LONG AS YOU'RE NOT AN ARAB YOU'RE ALLOWED TO THINK AMERICA'S NOT ALWAYS SO GREAT!' (10). The next (and final) frame of this sequence depicts Spiegelman being booted unceremoniously out of the studio. His dissenting perspective is clearly anathema to the mainstream media's transformation of a shared sense of grief in an ideological national unity based on blind patriotism.

This episode demonstrates not just the media's compliance with the official government line through a feeble retreat into nationalistic clichés, but also, as indicated by the mention of 'Arabs,' the dangerous embracing of racist stereotypes in the period following the attacks. Susan Faludi notes the appalling price paid because of this distortion of the real meaning of 9/11, and the consequences for people of colour, both within and without the US's borders, as America entered a 'dream state' of mystificatory ideology, that allowed certain political choices to unfold unimpeded. These choices and their consequences would play out in increasingly shameful and cruel forms: in the curtailing of civil liberties, the authorization of torture, the scandal of Abu Ghraib, the creation of secret prisons, the "extraordinary rendition" of detainees to foreign regimes where brutality was guaranteed, and, most of all, our reckless fools' errand into Iraq. (294–5)

This re-emerging racism is also alluded to in *Extremely Loud*. Although Oskar has clearly been brought up according to liberal tendencies that at least pay lip service to equality, following the death of his father he expresses fears clearly based on racial stereotypes. 'There was a lot of stuff that made me panicky,' he admits, 'like suspension bridges, germs, airplanes, fireworks, Arab people on the subway (even though I'm not racist), Arab people in restaurants and coffee shops and other public places, scaffolding, sewers and subway grates, bags without owners, shoes, people with mustaches, smoke, knots, tall buildings, turbans' (36). While these elements are arguably linked in some way to his father's death, they also recall the widespread xenophobic paranoia in New York City following the attacks that was so effectively mobilised by the Bush regime.[2] Depictions of this racist retrenchment post-9/11 in Foer's and Spiegelman's texts underline further problems resulting from the unquestioning acceptance of notions of collective trauma, since they are so amenable to exploitation for political ends. While the dangers of collective trauma are more implicitly criticised in *Extremely Loud*, in *In the Shadow* Spiegelman exercises a multifarious critique of the way in which it led to racism and the disastrous foreign policy of the Bush administration.

TRAUMA IN *In the Shadow of No Towers*

The remainder of this chapter evaluates the experimental narrative strategies in *In the Shadow of No Towers* and *Extremely Loud and Incredibly Close* in terms of both the questionable extent to which postmodernist techniques are any longer shocking, and their relative effectiveness for addressing the events of 9/11 and their political aftermath. Spiegelman is clearly haunted by events experienced on 11 September 2001, and this is related through a series of visual and narrative means. For example, the repeated computer-generated image of the glowing towers, in their imminent collapse, remains, claims Spiegelman, 'burned onto the inside of my eyelids' ('The Sky Is Falling'), and thus appears on every plate. In terms of narrative, there are a number of ways in which Spiegelman's text produces a sophisticated and subtle representation of traumatic symptoms through its treatment of time. Although Foer in his novel makes considerable use of analepsis, prolepsis, and repetition, the temporal point from which the narrative is generated remains relatively stable. In *In the Shadow*, by comparison, Spiegelman occasionally introduces a frozen or continuous present tense into the narrating voice. This is sometimes further complicated by Spiegelman's metafictional practices, which are used in a similar way to those of Danielewski discussed in the previous chapter, introducing a temporal dimension to the moment of the narrating act.

This is encountered, for example, in Plate 2, one of the most structurally fragmented episodes of *In the Shadow*. The top strip of the plate contains one of the few explicit discussions of trauma, as Spiegelman, knowingly appropriating popular trauma discourse, explains how he feels frozen in perpetual recollection of September 11: 'I insist the sky is falling; they roll their eyes and tell me it's only my Post-Traumatic Stress Disorder . . . That's when time stands still at the moment of trauma . . . . . . which strikes me as a totally reasonable response to current events!' (2, original ellipses). Underlining the theme of time seeming to stand still, he continues again in a frozen present tense: 'I see that awesome tower, glowing as it collapses' (see Figure 3.2). As Spiegelman speaks, the frames themselves rotate their border, eventually forming a representation of the flaming Twin Towers, appropriately casting a pall over the rest of the plate. The next frame depicts Spiegelman – significantly in his *Maus* persona – asleep at his drawing board. This image not only reveals that the remainder of this plate is Spiegelman's own unbidden dream or nightmare of 9/11, but also, as Mitchum Huehls observes, evokes how a 'safe temporal space from which

Figure 3.2: Spiegelman's PTSD. (Source: Art Spiegelman, *In the Shadow of No Towers*, Plate 2)

Spiegelman can reconcile the conflict between personal and public time' (55) that was available in *Maus* is no longer tenable in *In the Shadow*, since the sleeping Spiegelman is threatened by cartoon representations of Osama Bin Laden and George Bush. Now that the trauma is more personal to Spiegelman than in *Maus*, even the moment of narrative inscription is threatening. This may be read as a retreat into the nostalgia of classic cartoon strips, as 'history becomes a time to escape to, rather than a trauma to run from' (Huehls 55), but this retreat is constantly problematised by Spiegelman's metafictional practices of foregrounding the present moment of the narrating act, and thus the difficulty of accurately representing the events of the day. Experiments in form here also emphasise the subject's diminished sense of time passing since the attacks; they are narrated as both in the past and still happening in the present moment of inscribed narration. In this and the next two plates narrative time, as he and his wife race to rescue their daughter from her school near the towers, notably decelerates, again suggesting that time has both slowed and remained permanently etched on Spiegelman's narrating present.

Another important experimental ingredient in Spiegelman's representation of trauma is his disruption of a stable sense of subjectivity. Remaining with Plate 2, we notice that the sense of a sudden transformation of the world at the precise moment the plane hits the first tower is underlined by the way in which the style of drawing abruptly changes to a less realist, more cartoon register (see Figure 3.3). In one frame Spiegelman and his wife are depicted in a stylised but broadly realistic form, and they are signalled as relaxed as they stroll through SoHo, smoking. The next frame represents a woman in a far more heightened cartoon style, reacting to the impact. The realist background to the action in the previous frame is replaced here and in a number of subsequent frames with flat colour. The transformed world is further signalled in the following frames, as Spiegelman and his wife are transformed into representations of the Katzenjammer Kids, and instead of their holding cigarettes, the burning component is now a miniature tower on each of their heads. Spiegelman suggests both a loose narrative continuity between the before and after states and a radical discontinuity, underlined by the abrupt shifts in style and

Figure 3.3: The moment of impact. (Source: Art Spiegelman, *In the Shadow of No Towers*, Plate 2)

subjectivity. Again, there is a synthesis of apparent oxymora, with the integration of the exceptional – in the abrupt style change – and the relative – in the simultaneous continuity.

The narration in Plate 2 draws clear links between disruptions to subjectivity and Spiegelman's use of inscribed narration. Here we encounter shifts from an autodiegetic 'I' voice in the narrating present (at which point the narrative is more centred on Spiegelman's personal trauma) and a heterodiegetic 'he/they' voice in the past tense narration of the actual events of 9/11. This has certain implications both for the accusations of solipsism which met the work, providing the beginnings of a shift from the self-centred to a wider viewpoint, and for the broader depiction of trauma. The abrupt and profound shifts in time and narrating persona, which metatextually foreground the moment of the narrative's inscription, extend beyond conventional ways in which writers might adopt new personae in order to be able to represent a traumatic event. The implications in these shifting sections are that, firstly, Spiegelman actually experiences himself as a different person in the weeks and months after the attacks, and secondly, that although the events recognisably affected a mass of people, such are Spiegelman's (self-confessed) neuroses that they have come to seem more centred exclusively on him by the time of inscription.

Further shifts in subjectivity are explicit; in Plate 8, for instance, a transformation back to first person in the previous strip is here acknowledged (albeit, in customarily contradictory fashion, in the third person): 'TIME PASSES. HE CAN THINK ABOUT HIMSELF IN THE FIRST PERSON AGAIN, BUT DEEP INSIDE THE TOWERS STILL BURN'. Spiegelman's tentative recovery is also contingent on form here, and it is significant that *In the Shadow* was initially published as a series of discrete episodes, as this underlines how a temporal element is intrinsic to its narration. As Hillary Chute suggests, the book's initial irregular serial publication 'reflects the traumatic temporality Spiegelman experienced after 9/11, in which a normative, ongoing sense of time stopped or shattered' (230). This underlines how the inscribed narrating in *In the Shadow* conveys a sense of insidious trauma (and muted recovery) in addition to the clearly shattering initial experience. This sense is clear in the final plate, as a conclusion of sorts is broached. Across the final three frames, Spiegelman's narration ends: 'The towers have come to loom far larger than life . . . but they seem to get smaller every day . . . Happy Anniversary' (10, original ellipses).

Spiegelman's experiments with subjectivity continue throughout *In the Shadow*, as he is transformed back into his *Maus* persona, or else adapts identities borrowed from classic comic strips such as 'Bringing Up Father' and the 'Happy Hooligan'. This disrupted subjectivity is most radically conveyed in Plate 9, the text's most formally and thematically experimental strip. This plate draws on a striking variety of styles, everything from a *New Yorker* pastiche to EC Comics' Cards, Spiegelman's own brutalist *Maus* style, plus the by now familiar manic paranoia of *In the Shadow* itself, in the panels depicting Spiegelman uneasily sharing a bed with other New Yorkers. The strip entitled 'Weapons of Mass Displacement' most clearly demonstrates Spiegelman's consciously ludic depiction of subjectivity. In each of the six frames Spiegelman's head, his shoe, the lampshade, his cat, and his cigarette-holding hand are interchangeable. Moreover, in the final frame, as Spiegelman stands from the chair and hurls the cat off his lap, he is transformed once more into his *Maus* persona. The bitingly satirical text of the strip represents one of Spiegelman's furious critiques of the political fallout from 9/11, in particular the trend of displaced guilt over the deceptions involved in using the events as a trigger for war in Iraq (to which the title of the strip slyly alludes). This strip is also particularly interesting for drawing overtly upon the language of trauma, both in its text and its visual strategies. Form is here effectively interdependent with content, with narrative disruption of subjectivity and temporality representing typical traumatic symptoms. Even more significantly, Spiegelman's use of the trope of displacement from psychoanalytic trauma theory demonstrates his conscious use of experimental narrative techniques in order to represent trauma and its aftermath. This strip, with its savage political critique, and Plate 9 as a whole, offer further repudiation of allegations that Spiegelman's work is solipsistic. The displaced subjectivity in this strip, alongside the fragmented nature of the plate as a whole, incorporating numerous styles and diverse characters, renders this page particularly democratic and pluralistic. Indeed, this plate (along with the following and final plate) captures what we might term a 'collective individual' experience, but without collapsing this into a monolithic form of collective trauma. Again, apparent oppositions – here the individual and the collective – are synthesised through a dismantling of the individual. Quite the opposite of solipsistic, Spiegelman's radical disruption of subjectivity, the construction of this collective individual provokes the reader into a more constructive form of empathy.

Some critics have interpreted Spiegelman's unusual strategies in *In the Shadow*, in particular the fragmentation and non-linear chronology, as demonstrating familiar tropes of the representation of traumatic dissociation. Espiritu, for example, claims that the form necessarily 'demonstrates the extent to which traumatic experiences necessitate a breakdown not only of linguistic mastery, but also of "conceptual continuity"' (187). Use of the word 'necessitate' is telling here. Espiritu follows dominant trauma theory in arguing that any attempt to represent post-traumatic symptoms is impossible without employing an experimental form which fragments chronology and subjectivity. While this is indeed a form here employed by Spiegelman, the claim that this was unavoidable inaccurately suggests a naïvety to his construction of the text. Comparison with Spiegelman's earlier work, however, clearly demonstrates his keen awareness of the experimental formal possibilities of the comics form. Many of the strips in his *Breakdowns* collection, for example, deal with mundane, non-traumatic subject matter, but are considerably more experimental (fragmented, non-linear etc.) than *In the Shadow* (see, for instance, 'Don't Get Around Much Anymore' and 'Nervous Rex: The Malpractice Suite'). To a certain extent Spiegelman's work (in *Maus*, *In the Shadow* and elsewhere) does support aspects of dominant trauma theory, as he seeks experimental forms in order to represent traumatic content. But it is reductive to suggest that this is all he represents through such experimental means, or that he is not cognisant of the implications of his chosen forms. Spiegelman's sophisticated understanding of the portrayal of the post-traumatic conditions should not be underestimated. In his employment of experimental and – in particular – metafictional devices and his synthesis of a number of techniques with which he had experimented before, Spiegelman is aware of their effect, and employs them as an appropriate vehicle for representing his trauma. Rather than a compulsion borne of traumatic material, Spiegelman is fully self-conscious of the techniques employed.

Besides the text itself, Spiegelman's paratextual experiments also unsettle our response to 9/11. The book has been described as, '[a]n artifact, a slab, a monument – this is no mere book. Unpaginated, ungainly and heavy, it seems to demand its own space' (Wolff), and 'an object as much as it is something to read and look at' (Orbán 74). Another contradiction arises: the question of monumentalism, and the extent to which *In the Shadow* in its sheer unwieldy size acts as a memorial to 9/11, lies in perpetual counterpoint to its numerous more ephemeral characteristics. These two opposed elements were clearly important to Spiegelman, who in numerous interviews discusses the twin poles of eternal and ephemeral. To Todd Leopold, for example, Spiegelman explained that the form of the book 'has various resonances for me, and those include the nature of the ephemeral and the eternal – what it is to have something that was never meant to last, like a newspaper, and something meant to last forever, like the pyramids or the World Trade Center towers.' What we encounter in *In the Shadow* is an unusual material object, both in terms of its size and its robust thick card pages. The size itself suggests something weighty and monumental, but also evokes the outsize nature of the old Sunday Supplements about which Spiegelman admits to having become so nostalgic. Thus a clear signifier of the ephemeral and the disposable – a series of comic strips – is transformed into something monumental and eternal. Again, this forms an interesting component of Spiegelman's contradictory artistic response to trauma, looking nostalgically to the past, reimagining that past synthesised through a response to current events, and transforming this new synthesis into something lasting. Spiegelman's analogical connections between the book and the Towers – Chute likens its comic frames to windows (237), and also observes how its two distinct parts and monumental size are clearly intended to evoke such a connection (232) – extend the formal aims of *In the Shadow*. The text thus formally recreates the towers, but this is neither to elide their destruction nor to provide the easy palliative of a conventional narrative of redemption through recovery from trauma.

As suggested above with reference to the final frames, recovery from trauma is equivocal in Spiegelman's text. Certainly there are intimations, especially in the final two plates, that Spiegelman and his fellow New Yorkers are moving towards recuperation. The penultimate plate suggests that a measure of equilibrium is achieved through continued activism and protest; the Spiegelman figure concludes, 'SOMETIMES COMPLAINING IS THE

ONLY SOLACE LEFT' (Plate 9). Espiritu notes that Spiegelman falls asleep after he wakes his bedfellows, and asks whether this 'indicate[s] that he has accomplished what he set out to do since 9/11 . . . engaging in some form of "consciousness raising?"' (194). Presumably so, since the writing and publishing of this very text helps to provide a measure of solace, not least since by this time America has begun to recognise the folly of its post-9/11 actions and, as Huehls observes, 'Spiegelman realizes that he was ahead of his time rather than behind it, and his sense of disconnection and alienation begins to fade' (58). But it is only ever partial; Spiegelman's recovery-through-complaint comes at the expense of terrifying the other New Yorkers, the 'stunned pigeons' (Plate 9) with whom he here shares a bed.

The final plate initially appears more ordered than many of the anarchic compositions, structured as it is by a re-creation of the Twin Towers. Such a reassertion of order might be taken as a further sign of recovery, but this too is belied by its fiery backgrounds, and the aeroplane about to hit one of the towers. Recovery is thus again equivocal, as signalled by the content of the strips, illustrating Spiegelman's continued paranoia and alienation from mainstream American life. Intertextuality and dispersed subjectivity are again related to trauma and recovery in this series of frames. Spiegelman appears here as himself, as the 'Hapless Hooligan', and as the familiar *Maus* representation, this latter underlining the connection with previous traumatic episodes in Spiegelman's life. In this final depiction, Spiegelman dwells in a New York populated by numerous classic comics characters, all of whom cower beneath falling cowboy boots. These represent the unwelcome arrival in New York of the Republican Presidential Convention, evoking once more Spiegelman's alienation from US politics, but also recalling the 'Etymological Vaudeville' strip on Plate 1 concerning the phrase 'waiting for the other shoe to drop'. A return to the beginning of the work such as this cannot help but suggest circularity, therefore evoking repetition and acting out, and thus a partial failure to work through the trauma both for the individual and – given that this frame depicts a crowd scene – the collective.

The complex layout of this final plate also suggests circularity, as the frames in the panels (or windows in the towers) do not appear to run in linear order. This deconstruction of temporality (something which Spiegelman experimented with before in his 'A Day at the Circuits' strip [*Breakdowns* n. pag.]) again hints that recovery is tentative and partial. Once more this manifests as the reconciliation of apparent oppositions, as Spiegelman 'recuperates the trauma of 9/11 – re-building the shattered pieces through comics – while he steadfastly refuses to recuperate by offering a progressive narrative with a proper "end" that would denote closure or healing' (Chute 242). It is worth distinguishing further between individual and collective trauma here, as Spiegelman seems to suggest that levels of recovery differ for the two. The final two plates suggest that while New Yorkers' recovery from their collective trauma is limited, as denoted by Spiegelman's earlier sardonic use of the term 'New Normal' and the final scene of the crowd bombarded by cowboy boots, it is at least in advance of Spiegelman's individual state. Whereas the collective, here and in general, seems to experience a 'routinization processes' (Alexander 23), becoming accustomed to the new, post-traumatic situation, recovery is much more difficult for the individual, and so Spiegelman remains 'constantly wrestling with the problem of closure' (Kuhlman 860–1) at the text's putative conclusion.

This portrayal of a limited recovery and also repetition, both of which reflect Spiegelman's experiences of trauma, is underscored by the text's numerous intertextual relationships, often with Spiegelman's previous work. Describing his post-traumatic symptoms, Spiegelman agonises over his inability to distinguish between the 'holes' in his head 'made by Arab terrorists way back in 2001' and those 'which . . . were *always* there' (6). There is much in *In the Shadow* to suggest that 9/11 reawakened past traumas depicted in *Maus*: the death of his mother and his experience as the child of Holocaust survivors. The intertextual references to and incorporation of numerous stylistic tropes from *Maus* emphasise the connections Spiegelman makes between these traumas. In Plate 3 of *In the Shadow*, for example, Spiegelman depicts himself in the *Maus* persona, discussing links between the smoke in Auschwitz and that in Manhattan following the attacks. Spiegelman's cigarette smoke gradually pervades the frames in a strikingly similar way to the flies in the 'Time Flies' section of *Maus*. The flies hovering over the bodies of Holocaust victims, and the lingering smoke of 9/11 draw an equivalence between the two traumatic experiences. Spiegelman talked illuminatingly about the links – but also the distinctions – between the events in his interview with Dreifus:

I don't posit the scale of what was happening to me on 9/11 to what happened to my parents. But of course, there I was standing at the same juncture of personal and world history . . . I didn't turn into Vladek, with his innate sense of practicality in the midst of disaster – though his admonition to "always keep your bags packed" came to mind.

The intertextual references he employs in order to forge tentative links between the two events suggest Spiegelman moves from what Marianne Hirsch has defined as postmemory, a form of trauma 'inherited' from family memory, to experiencing trauma first-hand. Part of what makes *In the Shadow* so compelling is its bleak narration of this gradual process and the only partial recovery that follows.

TRAUMA IN *Extremely Loud and Incredibly Close*

While *Extremely Loud* has been lauded by some critics for its employment of experimental forms in its exploration of trauma, the following argues that much of this apparent formal daring in fact draws on a relatively formulaic set of conventions. If we consider the novel's representation of time, this broad conventionality may become clear. There is much purportedly experimental treatment of time in *Extremely Loud*: sudden temporal jumps in the narration, the insertion of unbidden flashbacks, and extensive use of repetition are all associated with Grandfather's gaps in memory, his loss of a sense of time, and his insistent repeated questions (not least, in various contexts and with varying significance, 'Excuse me, do you know what time it is?' [112 and *passim*]). As the previous chapters suggest, however, the use of postmodernist literary techniques to represent trauma had already become conventional when *Extremely Loud* was published. Similarly, Oskar's symptoms

– including flashbacks, nightmares, and obsessiveness (as in his compulsive inventing or his counting of stairs) – conform to dominant interpretations of trauma. These are combined with repetitive behaviour, as in his determination to contact all the Blacks in New York City, along with destructive tendencies to self-harm, mood swings, and bouts of depression (which Foer has Oskar coyly refer to as 'heavy boots'). As we shall see, these symptoms fall extremely readily into the kind of popularised trauma discourse that seems to have influenced Foer's writing of the novel.

Similarly conventional – and obviously linked to its treatment of time – is the novel's heavy employment of superficially experimental repetition. Perhaps the clearest example of this is in the repeated narrations of Oskar's father's final telephone calls from the burning tower of the World Trade Center, wherein every repetition of the story adds a little more information. Oskar's description of his father's phone messages is repeated numerous times in the text, and is also itself repetitive in nature, comprising five separate and increasingly desperate messages. Oskar skirts the narration of his return home and encounter with his father's answerphone messages, followed by his witnessing the final call, numerous times before the full story is finally disclosed during Oskar's meeting with William Black near the novel's conclusion. This form of repeating narrative, where something that occurred once in the fictional realm is narrated a number of times, has become prevalent in the narration of traumatic episodes, since it can effectively suggest that a character is haunted by recollections of the event. Typically, the character involuntarily revisits and compulsively renarrates events that brought on the traumatised symptoms, as is the case here, with repetition suggesting not only haunting but also Oskar's understandable difficulty in narrating the incident. Oskar's procrastination, the forestalling of the full story of his hearing the messages (and the revelation of their content) through repetition of only a partial version, is thus effective if unoriginal. As the discussions of Heller, Morrison, and O'Brien in Chapter 1 suggested, this mode of repeating narration is broadly conventional rather than experimental by the time of its use by Foer.

Although again ostensibly experimental, the depiction of Oskar's grandfather's traumatic symptoms is similarly formulaic.

Grandfather is portrayed throughout as silently traumatised, having gradually lost the ability to speak following the firebombing of Dresden. This silence underlines the apparently non-communicable nature of his trauma, as intimated elsewhere when he is unable to describe his story to Oskar (238). His behaviour is also characteristically obsessive, as he tries to document everything from his past through photographs (175), and, like Oskar's, marked by repeated but thwarted attempts to narrate his trauma, as in his twin failed phone calls to his wife after 9/11 (273). All of these – the silences, the obsessive photo-taking, and the repetition of experience and its narration – comprise another fully conventional depiction of traumatic symptoms, indicating that *Extremely Loud* falls comfortably into the category of trauma genre, and suggesting on the part of its author an understanding of trauma gleaned through theoretical publications. A key problem, as we shall see below, is that since these experiences of trauma and its symptomatic manifestations conform rigidly to dominant approved representational norms, they may be enthusiastically embraced by critics as proof of their theories. Such conformity therefore has the unfortunate effect of further strengthening this form of representation as normative.

Foer's paratextual experimentation is initially one of the most striking attributes of the book, in particular that element which has provoked most comment, the extensive use of photographs. The lengthiest series (53–67) purports to represent photographs that Oskar has pasted into his journal, 'Stuff That Happened to Me'. The images themselves are strikingly predicated upon repetition, not only recapitulating aspects of the preceding text, but also frequently comprising doubled, mirrored and/or repeated images (a multitude of uncut keys, a blurred image of Stephen Hawking doubled with an in-focus one seen through a viewfinder, a symmetrical image of an unfolded paper plane, two tortoises mating, etc.). Elsewhere, photographs are similarly characterised by repetition, as in the numerous images of doorknobs, or the controversial flipbook of the falling/reascending man which concludes the book. Some critics have been drawn to make bold claims about the relationship between Foer's use of visual images and his representation of traumatic subject matter. Versluys, for example, argues that 'the mustering of visual, paralinguistic means of communication (photographs, blank pages, illegibly dark pages, pages in cipher) introduce[s] the unsettling nature of the events into the very texture of the prose' (81), and that Foer's visual paratexts mean that '[i]n its very structure, the novel stages a radical decoding of reality followed by a significant recoding' (81). It is debatable, though, whether this material really unsettles the reader to the extent Versluys suggests. Instead, we encounter a banally literal playing out of particularly influential theories of trauma surrounding visual memory. To this extent, it is difficult not to agree with critics who found in *Extremely Loud* a series of gimmicks, as suggested by John Updike's declaration that 'the book's hyperactive visual surface covers up a certain hollow monotony in its verbal drama.' This is especially apparent once we compare the use of conventional metafictional devices here with the more radically unsettling forms found in Spiegelman's text.

More importantly, if we understand the photographs as representing Oskar's scrapbook-journal 'Stuff That Happened to Me', this appears to position the novel – at least the portion narrated by Oskar – as inscribed narration. Certainly the intention appears to be to suggest to the reader that we are encountering at least a simulacrum of 'Stuff', similar to the effect constructed in *House of Leaves*. To this extent we may regard Oskar, like Johnny Truant, as an inscribed narrator; as with Johnny, Oskar's process of inscribing becomes part of the novel's attempts to reproduce Oskar's post-traumatic symptoms. There are, however, obstructions to reading the photographic sections (and, by implication, all of Oskar's narration) as a reproduction of 'Stuff'. Clearly we are supposed to understand the photographs as being those which appear in his scrapbook, but Oskar also mentions pasting particular photos into his scrapbook: pictures of 'a shark attacking a girl, someone walking on a tightrope between the Twin Towers, that actress getting a blowjob from her normal boyfriend, a soldier getting his head cut off in Iraq' (42), 'people who had lost their arms and legs' (240), and 'dead kids' (243). Mercifully, the reader does not see these particular pictures, but this does mean that the version of 'Stuff' that we encounter is an expurgated one. This distinction is important: if the reproduction of 'Stuff' the reader encounters is sanitised then this is an aestheticised, faux inscribed narration. Rather than traumatic metafiction's attempt to address the difficulties of representing trauma, this casts *Extremely Loud* again as a work of trauma genre literature. We return to this point below, both in terms of trauma genre criticism and accusations that this novel aestheticises trauma.

Reinforcing this position, a number of other instances in *Extremely Loud* are arguably amongst the most inappropriately sentimental representations of trauma in contemporary literature. Oskar's series of inventions, for example, involves, 'a special drain that would be underneath every pillow in New York . . . Whenever people cried themselves to sleep, the tears would all go to the same place, and in the morning the weatherman could report if the water level of the Reservoir of Tears had gone up or down, and you could know if New York was in heavy boots' (38). This cloying approach to trauma is echoed in Oskar's description of how he 'woke up once in the middle of the night, and Buckminster's paws were on my eyelids. He must have been feeling my nightmares' (74). These episodes are at least helpful in terms of demonstrating potential effects of the existence of a trauma genre. Coyness or triteness found in these examples represents a serious lapse in what purports to be a sincere exploration of post-traumatic symptoms. Further examples demonstrate an unfortunate willingness to borrow and embody elements of trauma theory, as with Oskar's description of his walk through New York's boroughs: 'I shook my tambourine the whole time, because it helped me remember that even though I was going through different neighborhoods, I was still me' (88). This is not only a cliché, but also demonstrates an implausible awareness on Oskar's part of traumatic dissociation. As Laura Miller suggests, 'Oskar is prone to reflections beyond the emotional sophistication of any kid.' Episodes such as these, through a programmatic exercise of approved elements of theory, undermine Oskar as a convincing character and *Extremely Loud* as a serious exploration of trauma.

Nevertheless, a number of critics have eagerly defended Foer's depiction of trauma symptoms and the array of postmodernist techniques that he uses in their representation. Much of this critical commentary searches specifically for trauma symptoms and aesthetic practices approved by dominant theory, and thus represents what I term trauma genre criticism. In this respect, Philippe Codde's response to the novel is typical, arguing that it is the failure of written language and narrative that is 'precisely what has prompted the controversial form of *Extremely Loud & Incredibly Close*, and why both of Foer's novels are such interesting and convincing representations of trauma' (249). Such an endorsement is problematic, however, when we consider that although *Extremely Loud* may be a 'convincing representation' according to certain aesthetic criteria, this fulfilment and its laudatory reception by critics inevitably works to limit how trauma can be represented. Foer's novel, with its allegedly alienating and experimental techniques, is perfectly moulded to fit certain critics' idea of what a trauma novel should be. In other words, a body of dominant trauma theory exists and is accorded considerable currency in both popular and academic discourse. When fictions such as Foer's are written in compliance with this dominant model it is hardly surprising either that they endorse its criteria of representation, or that they are well received by critics who wish to see their own theories validated. As suggested in the Introduction, a vicious circle develops whereby dominant theoretical models inspire works of fiction which are then taken to endorse and therefore somehow prove the theory's validity.

Clearly, this is a large claim, but there is considerable evidence that Foer's text was influenced by trauma theory, much of which, ironically, emerges from critics most concerned to validate their theories of trauma through Foer's work.[3] For example, in the character of Grandfather, Foer apparently adopts the notion of constriction from Judith Herman, whereby sufferers aggravate trauma symptoms by trying to ward them off. This is noted by Versluys, who observes that Grandfather 'become[s] the impersonation of constriction' (87). Versluys actually approves of a fictional character literalising a key trauma theory concept, and praises the understanding of trauma theory thus revealed: '[f]ar from being an artistic lack or fault, the flatness of the character of Grandpa proves Foer's acquaintance with and utmost respect for the essence of trauma: its inescapability' (87). This reveals that Foer is demonstrating 'utmost respect' for a narrow, albeit dominant, theoretical conception of trauma, however, in order to produce an embodying character, and thus working within a genre of trauma literature that is merely a simulacrum of the serious literary investigations of trauma discussed in Chapter 1. A clear contrast between trauma genre literature and traumatic metafiction may also be drawn here: Chapter 2 described Danielewski's parodic graphic provision of the symbol of a 'key' to unlocking trauma, whereas in *Extremely Loud* Oskar's search for the owner of the key left by his father is ingenuously symbolic.

Perhaps the clearest – although by no means the only – instance of the vicious circle of approving criticism in relation to Foer's novel is provided in an essay by Francisco Collado-Rodriguez. Noting the roots of its magic realism in writing classes Foer took under Jeffrey Eugenides, and its heavy employment of repetition, Collado-Rodriguez writes, '*[f]rom his classes on fiction*, Foer has possibly learnt about the metaphorical importance of the cycles of infinite repetitions that saturate the pages of writers like T. S. Eliot, William Faulkner, Jorge Luis Borges, or Gabriel García Márquez' (52, emphasis added). Collado-Rodriguez is accurate regarding Foer's influences, but does not appear to perceive the willingness to adopt ideas and forms as problematic. The same may be said with regard to Foer's approach to theory which, as Collado-Rodriguez notes, apparently embraces an aesthetic programme prescribed by influential critics such as Cathy Caruth and Anne Whitehead. Unfortunately, instead of challenging this transformation of theory into literary form, a number of critics are keen to evaluate fictional works according to those same theoretical criteria. Collado-Rodriguez, for example, overtly sets out to test the fiction by its compliance with theoretical models: 'following Whitehead's views on trauma fiction, we should evaluate the existence of strategies related to experimentation . . . Let us now consider if these strategies are traceable in *Extremely Loud & Incredibly Close*' (57). Unsurprisingly, these patterns are indeed found, and Collado-Rodriguez consequently applauds the novel: '[f]ollowing the already typical patterns of trauma fiction, Foer has wisely combined testimonial elements with different subject perspectives to create a dialogical structure of witnessing that forces readers into an ethical evaluative position (compare Vickroy

2002: 27)' (59).[4] The word 'wisely' is immensely telling; Foer is, in other words, to be praised for following patterns established by existing fictional and theoretical work on trauma, since it reinforces the strength of the critic's own perspective. This echoes Sien Uytterschout's reading of the novel, wherein she praises how it 'conforms perfectly [to] the task of literature in the aftermath of a catastrophic limit event', as it 'seriously founders any reader's expectation of a smooth, straightforward narrative' (68). Finally, Collado-Rodriguez suggests that the 'experimental devices' (56) in Foer's novel encourage an emotional-ethical response in the reader, that the elisions and gaps 'end up being a strategy of participation, of an emotional communication' (57). But it is worth pondering whether such calculated and coercive employment of the prescribed metafictional devices of the trauma genre results in any form of communication in which the reader can truly be said to participate.

Discussing the 'aesthetic of 9/11', Claire Kahane proposes that the event itself possessed a traumatic sublimity, 'a certain beauty in the formal image of devastation' (114). Foer's response to 9/11 stands in interesting relation to this question of aestheticisation, as the discussion of Oskar's scrapbook above suggested. *Extremely Loud* is, as we have seen, heavily laden with postmodernist formal devices, not least in both narratives by Oskar's grandparents. The layout of Grandmother's narrative, especially with its unusually lengthy gaps between sentences, resembles a modernist prose poem (see, for example, 174). This being the case, it may be argued that trauma genre works such as *Extremely Loud* draw extensively not only upon trauma theory but also upon venerable literary aesthetics. Again, however, certain critics are enthusiastic about Foer's employment of such an aesthetic. Versluys, for example, suggests that Grandmother's blank pages are effective evocations of trauma, that they 'stand for the hiatuses in her life' (98), while Grandfather's blackened pages 'illustrate the sterility of expression turned inward, the limits of language and the ineffability of trauma' (98). Similarly, Codde reads the grandparents' blank/black pages as examples of incommunicable trauma, since 'attempts to recreate linguistically one's traumatic histories are doomed to end in the emptiness of the blank page or in total blackness' (245). In terms of aestheticisation one might also mention Oskar's turning his father's final phone messages firstly into Morse code and then into a necklace for his mother. Holloway finds this 'a perfect sublimation' (117), rather than coy or grotesque, but it is worth asking whether such devices are really anything more than an affectation, an aestheticisation that expresses a writer's conception of trauma drawn from overwhelming exposure to popular trauma theory, rather than a sincere urge to explore the characters' experience of it. Interestingly, Saal uses the same term in criticising Grandfather's unlikely description of the Dresden bombing: 'his heavy emphasis on apocalyptic imagery and vivid colors aestheticizes the event in the manner of a baroque allegorical painting' (466). As Elizabeth Anker observes, a key danger here is that aestheticisation 'collapse[s] the trauma of 9/11 into the psychic economy of the spectacle, with the ultimate effect of subduing 9/11's fraught sociopolitical meanings' (464). Again though, this kind of programmatic aesthetic representation, with its tendency to transform historical event into sublime spectacle, is too often celebrated by adherents to dominant trauma theory, as the various approving commentaries by Versluys, Uytterschout, Codde, Collado-Rodriguez, and Atchison clearly demonstrate. Such a transformation is undesirable primarily because it is, as with the decontextualising tendency discussed above, heavily depoliticising; as Anker notes, it tends to extinguish 'the ambiguities that riddle 9/11 as a sociocultural and political reality, ironically purifying it of indeterminacy through hyperbole' (473).

Perhaps the most notorious example of Foer aestheticising trauma is the flipbook of the man reascending the Tower that concludes the novel. Chapter 5 examines a number of post-9/11 texts which employ the mode of counterfactual history in order to deal with traumatic themes, but we find the same phenomenon here in Foer's novel. Oskar is prone to fantasy episodes, which are generally narrated to the reader as if they really happened, before he reveals the reality. The episodes generally concern Oskar fantasising about temporarily eschewing polite behaviour and fully indulging his post-traumatic feelings of rage (for example, trashing his psychiatrist's office [203] or disrupting his school production of *Hamlet* [147]). As mentioned in Chapter 1, Judith Herman writes that as well as recreating the traumatic event, sufferers not infrequently reenact a fantasy version with a different, more positive outcome (39). Oskar's fantasies of articulating out loud how he feels enact this very sentiment.

Of course, the most prominent (and ultimately notorious) examples of this reversal wish occur at the end of the novel. As with so much in this and other trauma texts, this ending is predicated on repetition, and there are three instances of wished alternate reality. Firstly, and recalling Vonnegut in *Slaughterhouse-Five* so overtly that it must be conscious, Foer has Grandmother mentally revisit Dresden: 'In my dream, all of the collapsed ceilings re-formed above us. The fire went back into the bombs, which rose up into the bellies of planes whose propellers turned backward, like the second hands of the clocks across Dresden, only faster' (306–7). Still reversing time, her dream continues a few pages later: 'Lovers pulled up each other's underwear, buttoned each other's shirts, and dressed and dressed and dressed' (311). The significance here lies in the implications of this reversal: if there is no sex, there is no procreation, therefore no birth, and therefore no death. This becomes clearer a few pages later when we encounter Oskar pondering: 'I wondered how many things had died since the first thing was born. A trillion? A googolplex?' (319).

Secondly, we encounter Oskar's own fantasy reversal wherein he imagines his father moving backwards from the devastated scene of 9/11, all the way to home and safety. Finally – and most controversially – Oskar reverses photographic pages from 'Stuff That Happened to Me', which produces the graphic escapist fantasy of the flipbook of the male figure reascending the Towers that concludes the novel. Foer was castigated by a number of reviewers for this 'flip' conclusion in particular, but some defenders have subsequently emerged. Versluys suggests that Oskar's fantasy helps towards his recovery, as he 'adopts his grandmother's dream logic, by which the order of events is reversed and history goes back upon itself so that the "worst day" never happens . . . Thus trauma is resolved by the creation of an alternative world' (118–19). The notion that trauma is somehow 'resolved' through these strategies is dubious, however. In her essay 'Writing Wrong', Sandra Gilbert writes movingly about her desire to rewrite events following the death of her husband during a hospital procedure. Ultimately she finds this dissatisfying, since attempting to rewrite trauma by reversing time is always 'a hopeless effort at a performative act that can never, in fact, be truly performed. You can't, in other words, right wrong by writing wrong' (261). In a more convincing reading than Versluys's, Codde argues that far from being glib, this final section deliberately represents a failed redemptive fantasy: 'the entire closing section of the novel is written in the past conditional mood, which clearly indicates the illusory nature of the entire endeavour' (251). Codde's qualifying observation is useful, but it remains difficult not to feel uneasy about the way in which this final sequence gestures towards escapism as a response to trauma. As this suggests, the rejection of escapism found in Vonnegut's work in Chapter 1 is not necessarily shared with writers and artists post-9/11. In part, this is a subset of the retreat into comforting fantasies in post-9/11 writing that Richard Gray condemns in *After the Fall*. *Extremely Loud and Incredibly Close* largely indulges the escapist fantasies of its young protagonist, and concludes with precisely the type of escapist backwards-chronology narrative that is rejected as a facile response to trauma in *Slaughterhouse-Five*.[5]

This chapter has argued that Spiegelman's text interrogates the trauma of 9/11 in a much more sophisticated and pluralistic way than Foer's ostensibly experimental novel. Spiegelman's genuinely polyvocal and fragmented text mounts a political rebuff to attempts to construct a metanarrative of 9/11 that may be manipulated. The series of synthesised oppositions in *In the Shadow* represents a refusal of simple, monolithic readings of 9/11 which elide the complex mediation process involved in the construction of collective trauma. *Extremely Loud*, by contrast, demonstrates the dangers of the formulaic adoption of elements of theory in order to lend trauma texts verisimilitude, both in terms of the self-sustaining circle of trauma genre criticism this enables, and the tendency of this criticism to obscure agency behind notions of passive victimhood, which may then be mobilised for retributive action. Sigrid Weigel traces this back to Caruth's much cited interpretation in *Unclaimed Experience* of Freud's reading of Tasso which, Weigel argues, repositions the perpetrator as a victim (91).[6] Importantly, this again implicates trauma theory in the post-9/11 mediation process, since it suggests that the true motive of collective trauma is to refigure the self as a victim rather than a perpetrator. The perpetrator is therefore precisely the repressed in Caruthian theory which here returns, thereby raising the troubling question of whether the strenuous ethical denial of interest in the perpetrator in cultural trauma studies represents an attempt to deny Americans' possible status as perpetrators. The next chapter considers this difficult question in terms of the traumatic experience of US soldiers in Iraq.

NOTES

1. *In the Shadow of No Towers* is an unconventional work not only in terms of form, but also in content. It comprises the introductory essay, 'The Sky Is Falling'; ten original full-colour double spread plates, all bearing the heading 'In the Shadow of No Towers'; a further essay, 'The Comic Supplement', which discusses Spiegelman's post-9/11 renewed admiration for classic New York comic strips and artists; and seven double spread reproductions of classic strips.

2. Other works emerging around the same time reinforce this point. Mohsin Hamid's *The Reluctant Fundamentalist* describes how 'the FBI was raiding mosques, shops, and even people's houses; Muslim men were disappearing, perhaps into shadowy detention centers for questioning or worse' (107). Mira Nair's section of the portmanteau film *11'09"01*, based on a true story, depicts the arrest of many people of colour, while the featured (Indian) family's father despairs that 'there's no safe place for Muslims anymore'.

3. See, for example, essays by Atchison and Uytterschout ('Tin Drum').

4. The citation of Vickroy is deliberately retained in this quotation in order to underline the cross-fertilisation between theoretical criticism and literary practice.

5. Compare escapist Iraq War era fare such as Quentin Tarantino's *Inglourious Basterds*, wherein American intervention overseas has notably greater success than in reality, compared to either

the 1940s in which it is set, or the 2000s when it was made. Fantasies of backwards-chronology as a solution to trauma also appear in works including Frédéric Beigbeder's *Windows on the World*, wherein David daydreams that his father 'could spin the earth in the opposite direction and make time go backward two hours, that way none of this would have happened' (Beigbeder 213), while Richard Gray mentions the play *The Guys* by Anne Nelson, wherein one character, Jean, 'dreams of rewinding history: "Let's just play the tape backwards," she suggests' in order that the planes fly backwards to Boston and everyone is safe (153).

6. Caruth here glosses Freud's reading of Torquato Tasso's *Jerusalem Liberated* from *Beyond the Pleasure Principle*. In the tale Tancred accidentally kills his lover, Clorinda, and then in his anguish also kills a reincarnated version of her. For Caruth, the tale is thus one which underlines the 'belated experience' of trauma, 'its endless impact on a life' (*Unclaimed Experience* 7), but she has been much criticised for understanding Tancred in this scenario as a trauma victim rather than a perpetrator.

CHAPTER 4

Gulf War Memoirs and Perpetrator Trauma

John Pilger notes that the US and UK used over 300 tons of depleted uranium in the second Iraq War, leaving numerous devastating effects. This scenario would appear to draw a clear demarcation between perpetrators and victims. In a process I began to outline in the previous chapter, however, much of the American literature concerning the Gulf Wars attempts to overturn perpetrator status. Thus the diverse traumas of witnessing death and experiencing physical or psychological injury for overseas victims of American foreign policy become rewritten as trauma for the perpetrators. This chapter examines a number of rhetorical tropes employed by American writers to enact this reversal, to deny agency, and to project aggression onto the other. This is not to deny that the writers discussed below are sufferers of trauma, but to demonstrate that they also exist in that 'grey area' where they are also, on an individual and collective basis, perpetrators. As we shall see, the projection of sufferer or victim status onto members of the American armed forces entails a kind of doublethink, requiring the minimising of responsibility for one's actions, and therefore associated guilt. But this is in tension with a military training and profoundly masculine discourse of war narrative that demands agency. This chapter also explores that tension, and notes its contrasting absence in female narratives of the wars, which much more convincingly position the protagonist as a victim.

This chapter analyses two accounts of the Gulf War following

Iraq's invasion of Kuwait in 1990, Anthony Swofford's *Jarhead* and Joel Turnipseed's *Baghdad Express* (both published in 2003). We then turn to an examination of a number of accounts of the Iraq War which began in 2003: Evan Wright's *Generation Kill* (2004), Nathaniel Fick's *One Bullet Away* (2005), Kayla Williams's *Love My Rifle More than You* (2006) and a selection of short works from the collection *Powder: Writing by Women in the Ranks* (2008). Swofford and Turnipseed were increasingly reluctant marines during Operation Desert Storm, Swofford a sniper and Turnipseed a driver of tractor-trailers; Wright was an embedded journalist for *Rolling Stone* travelling with a recon marine platoon commanded by Lieutenant Nathaniel Fick, author of *One Bullet Away*, in the 2003 war with Iraq, in which Williams was an army specialist translator.

One element about which most theorists writing on trauma and war agree is the essential link between the Vietnam War and emergent and popularised notions of trauma in America. This link is played out again through the haunting shadow cast by Vietnam over trauma narratives of the two Gulf Wars and, indeed, over the actual conduct of the later conflicts. Uneasy residual feelings are alluded to in Swofford's memoir, through his mistrust of the euphemistic public language still employed in the wake of Vietnam: 'I'm a soldier, in a "conflict." A "conflict" is much easier for the American public to swallow than a war. *War* still has that messy Vietnam feeling' (175). Kalí Tal, one of the few theorists to consider perpetrator trauma in any depth, observes that whereas in the 1960s and 1970s 'comparisons were regularly made between American soldiers committing atrocities in Vietnam, and *German* soldiers committing atrocities during the Nazi regime' (11, original emphasis), by the time she is writing (1996) this sounds shocking. Tal notes that 'U.S. soldiers were hailed triumphantly by the American public when they returned from war in the Persian Gulf in 1991, and the Vietnam veteran as icon is firmly established in the American heroic tradition' (12). As Tal comments, former comparisons between American soldiers and Nazis by this time seem 'jarring and incredible' (12), although this may have changed again in the time since she wrote, following the Iraq War and revelations such as Abu Ghraib.[1] While Kirby Farrell suggests that the culture had shifted before the first Gulf War, having 'turned Vietnam veterans from agents of genocide into victims of trauma, and thereby rehabilitated the military for the Gulf War in 1991' (16), David Ryan notes a more specific cause and effect, arguing that the overdetermined causes lying behind both Gulf Wars included a war on 'that corner of the US mind that felt emasculated after Vietnam' (103). The gendered language used here is, as we shall see, crucial to the experiences of soldiers, male and female, in both Gulf Wars, but more significant here is the function of these wars as a means to work through the collective public trauma of Vietnam. Certainly, themes of redemption and rehabilitation are prominent in these texts. Near the end of *Jarhead*, for example, a Vietnam veteran boards the bus driving the victorious returning soldiers through cheering crowds in California, and thanks the marines for 'making them see we are not bad animals' (251). Unsurprisingly, since the book was adapted for the screen by Vietnam veteran, William Broyles Jr, this scene is retained in the film. This scene is mirrored in Turnipseed's *Baghdad Express* (198) and Williams's *Love My Rifle More than You* (276), these examples demonstrating a compelling need to work through the collective public remnants of the trauma of Vietnam. Like that war, however, the two incursions in the Gulf construct amongst the American soldiers a complex matrix of trauma deriving in varying measure, as this chapter explores, both from their status as victims and perpetrators.

The texts considered below are, indisputably, trauma narratives, even if they are told predominantly from the perspective of what we would understand as the perpetrator. A widely quoted figure, cited by Lambèr Royakkers and Rinie van Est, states that 'almost twenty percent of the soldiers returning from Iraq or Afghanistan have post-traumatic stress disorder or suffer from depression . . . causing a wave of suicide' (289). Each of the texts discussed in this chapter contains ample evidence of first-hand experience that produces various traumatised responses. At some point in each narrative, for example, the author endures the absolutely overwhelming experience of coming under attack, which tends to produce attendant experiences of dissociation, time dilation and sensory shutdown.

Swofford's account is notably driven by elements of trauma, before, during and after the Gulf War. Significantly, the subtitle of the American edition, *A Marine's Chronicle of the Gulf War and Other Battles*, looks beyond the war itself for evidence of Swofford's traumas. But the most affecting traumatic experiences are described as occurring during Swofford's time in Kuwait. These include encounters with countless burnt or decomposing corpses, nearly committing murder and suicide in two separate incidents of combat stress, almost being killed by a booby trap in the post-war clean-up, and the sheer terror of several times coming under enemy and friendly fire. Turnipseed's most clearly traumatising experiences are similarly rooted in coming under fire. Although his description of this experience entails a delay in cognition, it is of much shorter duration than conventional definitions of PTSD would suggest. Following a mortar attack so sudden that, '[n]o cognition was involved', Turnipseed explains that, '[i]t wasn't until we saw one another, sitting in the bunker wearing fogged-up gas masks, that we were able to piece together the events: Alarm. Explosion. Shelter. Gas Masks. Weird, incomprehensible stares' (146). The suggestion here is that the communal attempt to reconstruct traumatic events shortly after their occurrence is a successful means to address potential trauma, since after a short period of silence the soldiers 'collectively shrugged' and returned to their tent (146).

Fick similarly discusses the way in which, immediately after especially traumatic incidents, the soldiers relive events communally in an attempt to recuperate them into memory. After Fick's platoon almost miraculously survives a fierce gun battle while driving through the town of Al Gharraf, the recounting represents a conventional way of coping: '[e]very fight is refought afterward . . . The telling and retelling are important. Platoons have institutional memory' (219). Sensations and memories prove to be highly unreliable under such strain, however: '[f]requently, I found that my memory of a firefight was just that – mine. Afterward, five Marines told five different stories' (219). Fick is also prone to more conventional experiences of trauma, such as coming under fire and experiencing extreme sensory displacement, his disorientated response to these incidents suggesting reasons for the incompatible and competing memories of violent events amongst his platoon. Wright, the journalist embedded with Fick's platoon, experiences similarly dislocated perception during the journey through Al Gharraf, including 'time dilation, a sense of time slowing down or speeding up; vividness, a starkly heightened awareness of detail; random thoughts, the mind fixating on unimportant sequences; memory loss; and, of course, your basic feelings of sheer terror' (182). Both Fick's and Wright's experiences here are disturbing but roundly conventional in terms of trauma. As Judith Herman describes, the dissociation in such devastating events frequently produces sensory confusion: '[p]erceptions may be numbed or distorted, with partial anesthesia or the loss of particular sensations. Time may be altered, often with a sense of slow motion, and the experience may lose its quality of ordinary reality' (43).

As with the other writers discussed in this chapter, Kayla Williams's experiences in Iraq consist of a kind of attritional and incremental trauma interspersed with more sudden and overwhelming episodes. The latter include her attempts to aid some of the most severely injured Iraqis after unexploded ordnance detonates, and as with Fick's account, a difficult return to normality once back in America after the War. Williams exhibits symptoms of constriction when swerving 'to avoid trash in the road. In Iraq it could be an IED [improvised explosive device],' and flashbacks and nightmares: 'I had real trouble sleeping. I rarely had trouble before combat. Now I woke up with my sheets soaking wet' (281). These are unquestionably trauma narratives, citing a range of archetypal post-traumatic behaviour and, moreover, in many ways so similar that they reconfirm generic norms in war writing.

PERPETRATOR TRAUMA

Before looking in more detail at the particular texts, it is necessary to develop further the idea of perpetrator trauma broached in the Introduction. As suggested there, the traumatic symptoms suffered by those who are not (wholly) in a position conventionally recognised as that of the victim represent a phenomenon that theorists of trauma have been reluctant to acknowledge and therefore a little slow to examine. In one respect this reluctance is surprising, given that the defining of PTSD was dependent on 'a political struggle waged by psychiatric workers and activists on behalf of the large number of Vietnam War veterans who were then suffering the undiagnosed psychological effects of war-related trauma' (Young 5). Ironically, then, while PTSD depended as a concept upon the lobbying of perpetrator trauma sufferers, their particular condition has been marginalised in the years since the acceptance of PTSD as the principal trauma paradigm.

Dominick LaCapra is amongst the few theorists to address the issue of perpetrator trauma, but his writing is characterised by a distaste for examining the phenomenon beyond a superficial level. Approaching the issue from the perspective of his distinctions between subsets of trauma he terms absence and loss (discussed at greater length in the next chapter), LaCapra asserts that when these two types are conflated, 'one encounters the dubious ideas that everyone (including perpetrators and collaborators) is a victim, that all history is trauma' (64). LaCapra resists such a conflation, since although everyone experiences the structural trauma of absence, by contrast with 'historical trauma and its representation, the distinction between victims, perpetrators, and bystanders is crucial' (79). Traumatic loss, the result of particular and local circumstances and events, produces a division between perpetrators and victims for LaCapra: 'not everyone traumatized by events is a victim. There is the possibility of perpetrator trauma which must itself be acknowledged and in some sense worked through if perpetrators are to distance themselves from an earlier implication in deadly ideologies and practices' (79). On one level this is a genuinely clarifying distinction, but the moral dimension upon which LaCapra insists produces its own difficulties. LaCapra's overarching attempt to address the difficulty of representing trauma is through what he terms empathic unsettlement, forms which enable the reader or viewer to achieve an uneasy understanding of the traumatic experience being described. But he remains 'dubious' about seeking empathy with perpetrators because this may foster 'a confused sense of identification with or involvement in certain figures and their beliefs or actions in a manner that may well subvert judgment and critical response' (202–3). This is an understandable objection, but it assumes an inability on the part of the reader not to adopt a fixed sense of identification that inevitably clouds moral judgement. Most overtly in this respect, LaCapra insists that we should seek 'empathy with the victim and repulsion toward the perpetrator' (133). But is this necessarily the case? As critics of trauma narratives, both factual and fictional, one might question whether we should seek moral empathy or repulsion rather than analysis and understanding of both the victim and the perpetrator.

Moreover, it is necessary to observe that these categories are often insufficiently stable in narratives to make clear distinctions between perpetrators and victims. The texts examined in this chapter uniformly place their narrator-protagonists in a liminal position of restricted agency. Thus whatever deplorable actions in which they are directly or indirectly involved, these narrators are nevertheless also simultaneously victims of traumatising circumstances over which they have no control. As Tal observes, albeit making the opposite point, '[t]he soldier in combat is both victim and victimizer' (10). At a more fundamental level, Michael Rothberg questions categories in trauma studies which have conventionally marginalised so-called perpetrator trauma texts, arguing that the moral distaste for analysing such texts 'derive[s] in part from a category error' of eliding 'the category of "victim" with that of the traumatized subject' (*Multidirectional Memory* 90). As Rothberg further suggests, while we can

speak conventionally of . . . a "victim of trauma," such a formulation of victimization has a different ontological status from the distinction between perpetrators and victims with which it is often confused. Thus, on the one hand, we can conceive of a victim who has not been traumatized . . . On the other hand, being traumatized does not necessarily imply victim status. As LaCapra has frequently pointed out, perpetrators of extreme violence can suffer from trauma – but this makes them no less guilty of their crimes and does not entail claims to victimization or even demands on our sympathy. (*Multidirectional Memory* 90)

Perpetrators can also suffer trauma, but studying representations of such trauma neither absolves the perpetrator of guilt, nor invalidates the academic work of analysis through making it somehow complicit with their acts. As Rothberg further points out, 'the concept of trauma emerges from a diagnostic realm that lies beyond guilt and innocence or good and evil' (*Multidirectional Memory* 90). The moral elements involved in judgements regarding perpetration and victimhood actually obstruct clear analysis of trauma or, as Rothberg maintains, '[p]recisely because it has the potential to cloud ethical and political judgments, trauma should not be a category that confirms moral value' (*Multidirectional Memory* 90).

Bearing in mind a more complex and shaded model of trauma, and distrusting straightforward Manichean distinctions between perpetrators and victims, there is clearly considerable value in investigating so-called perpetrator trauma.[2] We may well – and often appropriately – retain a moral distaste for the phenomenon, but it demonstrably exists, writers and artists have written about it and represented it, and it is therefore a dereliction of analytical duty for academics to refuse to examine it. This is especially true since the texts discussed below sometimes make dubious claims to victimhood, or employ rhetorical tropes to overturn the political realities underlying destructive American incursions into Afghanistan and Iraq. Ignoring perpetrator trauma might thus make critics complicit with a discourse which inverts victim status and projects it onto America, by allowing it to pass unchallenged. Moreover, perpetrator trauma clearly possesses distinct characteristics that differentiate its manifestation and, therefore, its representation from the kinds of trauma more commonly identified exclusively with victims. For example, perpetrator trauma questions the assertion, which forms a core definition of PTSD and Caruth's model, that trauma is always the result of a single, shattering and overwhelming event. As the introduction argued, this model of trauma has already come under criticism, in particular from a number of postcolonial critics who have exposed its western bias and its exclusion of, for example, what Laura Brown describes as 'insidious' trauma – that is, 'the traumatogenic effects of oppression that are not necessarily overtly violent or threatening to bodily well-being at the given moment but that do violence to the soul and spirit' (107). To recall, insidious trauma includes 'repeated forms of traumatizing violence, such as sexism, racism, and colonialism' (Rothberg, *Multidirectional Memory* 89), and is therefore appropriate for the study of the daily violence experienced by the writers considered in this chapter.

Although here emerging more from the direction of the oppressor than the oppressed, a gradual rather than sudden causation of trauma – what Elisabeth Piedmont-Marton terms 'a kind of boredom-induced trauma' (263) in Turnipseed's memoir – pervades the narratives examined in this chapter. While this gradual process is examined in a little more detail with direct reference to the texts later in the chapter, it is possible here to suggest some provisional answers as to why perpetrator trauma may be particularly marked by a gradual rather than instant or sudden process. An insidious accretion of guilt coupled with disillusionment about the cause being fought for evidently prompts perpetrator trauma in some of the texts considered here. Perpetrator trauma in this sense is often the result of guilt or shame over a series of acts of increasing intensity or depravity.

This departure from more recognised experiences of trauma is reflected through the employment of unconventional literary techniques. Swofford's frequent use of a continuous present, for example, helps to underline certain dislocating effects of perpetrator trauma in a number of ways. When he talks of a 'collective fear and terror' of coming under fire, which causes time dilation and a vision of 'all of our broken faces, caught in this eternal moment' (197), the continuous present obscures distinctions between the moment recalled and the moment of writing. If, as Swofford suggests, 'the now of these moments is a blur' (197), then the precise nature of the 'now', whether it refers to the event or its traumatic memory, is appropriately unclear. Clearly this blurring of the two deliberately evokes a lingering traumatic haunting which built slowly over time.

A linked way in which the overwhelming presence of trauma manifests itself for Swofford both during and after the Gulf War is in a frequent and extreme sense of temporal disorientation. Analepses which simulate episodes of traumatic flashback are familiar formal devices in trauma narratives. The key point with regard to Swofford's extensive use of analepsis in *Jarhead*, though, is that unlike a number of more conventional trauma victim narratives (but similar to some of those discussed in Chapter 1), there is no suggestion that what has traumatised Swofford – including actions for which he is responsible and feels a measure of guilt – is either unavailable to conscious memory or manifested only through unbidden flashbacks. The disrupted chronology of his text represents the unusual connections made by his traumatised memory rather than *Nachträglichkeit*. Swofford's conscious mind is in fact plagued by a persistent memory of events; indeed, it is this persistence rather than any absence which is the problematic symptom that marks his and others' experience of perpetrator trauma. The persistence of conscious traumatic memory is considered to be such a major part of Williams's post-war life, for instance, that she baldly asserts in her introduction, 'I don't forget. I can't forget any of it' (17). Unconventional use of anachrony in *Jarhead* and, to a lesser extent, the other texts, effectively communicates the distinct element of perpetrator trauma where the memory is consciously tormenting rather than suppressed into the unconscious. That it is predominantly perpetrator trauma is underlined by the fact that guilt is so often behind the memories. This pattern of guilt-related perpetrator trauma is borne out by researchers into trauma and suicides among serving and veteran members of the US armed forces. Ed Pilkington discusses the work of William Nash, a Navy psychiatrist who directed the marines' combat stress control programme, and whose team developed the concept of 'moral injury' to cover guilt caused by diverse events in battle. The most common of these are witnessing the death of a comrade, experiencing or witnessing 'friendly fire', and 'the guilt that follows the knowledge that a military action has led to the deaths of civilians, particularly women and children', all of which may cause 'damage to your deeply held beliefs about right and wrong' (qtd in Pilkington). Nash's team found that these forms of guilt are actually more common as triggers of trauma than the terror described in some of the incidents above.

As the above suggests, the issue of *Nachträglichkeit*, or latency period, is different for the perpetrator than for the unambiguous victim of trauma. In perpetrator narratives, memory appears to be more often characterised by conflicting urges towards both silence and confession. Moreover, when they do exist, latency periods in perpetrator narratives may occur because of the lack of an appropriately receptive audience. The perpetrator may wish to tell of their traumatic experience, but there is clearly – as the paucity of theoretical discussion of perpetrator trauma mentioned above suggests – a moral resistance to perpetrator narratives. This may be particularly true of war narratives. Ben Shephard suggests that the individual soldier's measure of guilt may be in large part dependent upon consensus back home about the war. Thus German soldiers who committed atrocities often felt little guilt, because they felt their actions were supported at home, '[b]ut after Vietnam, many American soldiers on returning home began to develop intense feelings of guilt about what they had done . . . because their society did not endorse what they had done' (Shephard 371–2). This is a useful idea, since it may enable us to draw certain distinctions between narratives of the Gulf War and the Iraq War. The first war, with the wider international coalition and the clearer aim of expelling Iraqi forces from Kuwait, was markedly more popular than the second, which was widely seen in the West as unclear in aim, and having been based on spurious and ulterior motives. Certainly, the narratives considered in this chapter from the Iraq War figure protagonists who are markedly more alienated from their peers at home and more traumatised than Swofford or Turnipseed. The guilt of the perpetrator informing the narrative of trauma is much more keenly felt among combatants involved in the Iraq War. Having made this distinction, it is important to recognise that there is always a degree of alienating division between the soldier-narrator and the reader of these testimonies. As Broyles puts it, 'I suffered, I was there. You were not. Only those facts matter. Everything else is beyond words to tell,' and so doubts over the existence of a receptive audience therefore always arise.

A final significant formal device employed by Swofford to evoke perpetrator trauma is his use of second-person address. As with some of the other techniques he uses, it might be argued that the 'you' address is introduced as a means of dispersing or portioning off blame for events over which Swofford feels guilt, by seeking a division between the writer now and the soldier then. The section on *Jarhead* below discusses in more detail twin tendencies in Swofford's narrative both to seek to invert perpetrator-victim status, and to attempt to forge empathic links with the Iraqi soldiers. The use of second-person address is another formal means which reinforces these twin strategies. Near the end of book, back in America, Swofford again contemplates his time in the Gulf:

> Sometimes you wish you'd killed an Iraqi soldier . . . During the darkest nights you'd even offer your life to go back in time, back to the Desert for the chance to kill. You consider yourself less of a marine and even less of a man for not having killed while at combat. There is a wreck in your head, part of the aftermath, and you must dismantle the wreck. (247)

Significantly, the passage concludes with a measure of defeat: '[b]ut after many years you discover that you cannot dismantle the wreck, so you move it around and bury it' (247). Burying and repressing are conventional, if self-destructive, responses to trauma, but even these prove difficult for the perpetrator-sufferer to achieve.

ANTHONY SWOFFORD'S *Jarhead* AND JOEL TURNIPSEED'S *Baghdad Express*

A sizeable part of the trauma that both Swofford and Turnipseed represent themselves in their memoirs as having endured appears to derive from their peculiar feeling of having been somehow cheated of an experience of war. This experience, which both authors – regardless of their overt scepticism about the war's cause – seem to expect as a rite of passage, is denied them by the unusual circumstances of the conflict in Kuwait. In other words, the war was concluded so rapidly that both writer-marines feel that they were barely involved. Kathy Phillips suggests that there is a basis for this feeling in the typically gendered attitude to military experience. Phillips is discussing Vietnam, but the following applies more generally, and certainly to the texts considered here. An ideological misconception of gender employed in patriarchal society in order to encourage men to fight, Phillips argues, 'elevates fighting

– in the abstract, for no cause or even for a known bad cause – into the one irreplaceable "proof" that a man is not that lowly creature, "sissy" or "pussy"' (142). Thus the desire to prove one's masculinity overrides an awareness of the emptiness of the cause, even in literate and educated men such as Swofford and Turnipseed.

Like Swofford, Turnipseed expresses a twin attraction and repulsion towards witnessing and participating in war. This is evident before he has seen any real action: 'even though I felt deep within me that this was a stupid war, an avoidable war, I wanted very badly to see the worst of war' (62). This seems to confirm that despite his declared scepticism not only about causes but also regarding conventional notions of military masculinity, the gendered notion of proving manhood retains, in his mind, some power. This feeling is, moreover, revisited and reinforced post-war when, although he has more or less 'escaped without harm', Turnipseed attests that, '[r]ather than feeling lucky, I felt cheated – as if my war had been undermined or stolen from me' (185).

Swofford's sense of anti-climax, as his rigorous sniper training is rendered useless when the war progresses to a conclusion many miles ahead of his position, is similarly couched in gendered terms suggesting impotence. A particularly disturbing example of this occurs when Swofford witnesses acts of revenge during the mop-up operation. These acts of rage at having been cheated of war and thus a chance to prove one's masculinity are displaced and inflicted upon Iraqi corpses: '[t]he platoon continues collecting relics for the same reason Crocket puts the damage to the corpses – in order to own a part of the Desert' (242). Swofford's fellow marine, Crocket, is the most disturbed by this process of emasculation, and he embarks on a repetitive campaign of the compulsive mutilation of a particular corpse: 'again and again, day after day . . . he punctures the skull and with his fixed bayonet he hacks into the torso. And he takes pictures' (239). Despite orders to stay away from the corpse, he either won't or cannot: 'Crocket is being driven mad by that corpse. I understand what drives Crocket to desecrate the dead soldier – fear, anger, a sense of entitlement, cowardice, stupidity, ignorance' (239). To these overdetermined reasons is added the familiar cause of the long, boring wait, 'and finally the letdown, the easy victory that just scraped the surface of a war' (239). Crocket is thus, ultimately, 'fighting against our lack of satisfaction' (239). Again, this rage may be traced to the ideological misrepresentation of the war, even to the American troops. As Douglas Kellner maintains, 'the war against Iraq was really a carefully orchestrated high-tech massacre' (234, n.34), and was arguably not a war at all, but a 'cyberspectacle in which the pitifully overmatched Iraqi troops were overwhelmed by the most massive and awesome military force ever assembled' (217). It is therefore hardly surprising that this simulation of a war allowed little chance for the servicemen to validate their masculinity.

Certainly, it is tempting to read these actions, as Phillips does, strictly in gendered terms, and provoked by the withdrawal of the opportunity to prove masculinity. A short piece by Terry Hurley, a female soldier who served in the same war, suggests however that the feeling of being cheated runs deeper than the exclusively masculine. Hurley describes how she and other soldiers were involved in surreptitiously circulating a collection of photographs of Iraqi corpses following the war, the 'Dead Iraqi Album' after which her memoir is named. Hurley asks why this degrading action seemed 'necessary', and the answers are similar to those given in Swofford's attempt to account for the actions of Crocket: 'I guess we all wanted to see the carnage. We wanted to participate on a more personal level in the defeat of the enemy force. Too long in the desert, we wanted proof we were really there for the liberation of Kuwait's people and not for another paperwork-ridden training exercise' (56). The requirement to prove one's mettle runs so deep in US military training and ethos that it apparently transcends divisions of gender. Certainly there is no evidence from Hurley's piece that the circulation of the photographs or her frustrated desire for the experience of having been in a recognised war results from any pseudo-masculinity, as Phillips's reading might suggest. Whether or not this is the case, it is important to acknowledge that the character of the Gulf War, with many weeks of waiting in a more or less barren space followed by a swift conflict that left many soldiers behind, hundreds of miles from the advancing frontline, caused some peculiar and complex effects of perpetrator trauma upon the combatants.

The components of boredom and frustration in these sol-

diers' experiences are importantly related to the insidious character of perpetrator trauma. The kind of trauma experienced by
Turnipseed, for example, is gradual, consisting of 'soul-rending
boredom, fear, the ache of lost love, murder, death' (41). This
is actually not unique to the Gulf War, as is confirmed by
Turnipseed's staff sergeant, who experienced similar monotony in
Vietnam. Drawing on his experience of the earlier war, he warns
the marines under his command that 'it's going to get so boring
you won't feel like doing anything. Not reading, not sleeping, not
shitting, jerking off, nothing . . . . Boredom creeps up on you like
a sickness' (41–2). Certainly Turnipseed's experiences seem to fall
into this general pattern predicted by his staff sergeant, and thus
repeat patterns familiar from the earlier war. The ubiquity of the
crushing boredom experienced by so many of the writers during
the Gulf War, however, suggests that it was an even stronger
feature of trauma in this conflict. This certainly characterises
Swofford's experience in *Jarhead* (and this is equally captured by
a series of montages and Jake Gyllenhaal's increasingly unhinged
performance in the film adaptation), but is also seen in narratives of the second war. Kayla Williams, for example, finds that
'[d]eployment in Iraq was like this yearlong invitation to think
. . . You started to go crazy with the thinking and the waiting and
the sitting around' (25). This alienation conveyed by boredom
and frustration is a defining characteristic of the US soldiers'
experience of the Gulf, and also a clear challenge to the dominant
event-based model of trauma. The insidious nature of perpetrator
trauma, as we shall see throughout this chapter, is a defining difference from the dominant model.

At this point, certain tropes for the depiction of trauma in
these texts need further examination, in order to establish more
precisely the degree to which the protagonist-trauma sufferers are
responsible for their actions. A common facet of the texts discussed
in this chapter, albeit employed to varying degrees, is that they
seek to diminish the extent to which the writer is a perpetrator
and refigure them as victims of circumstance, lacking in agency.
Jarhead, especially, contains a number of strategies for problematising Swofford's culpability and therefore the text's status as a
perpetrator trauma narrative. These strategies are worth further

investigation, since they synecdochally reflect broader attempts to refigure aggressive American foreign policy as defensive and acting in the world's best interests. A significant scene in this respect occurs when Swofford strays momentarily from his unit in order to relieve himself and encounters a circle of dead, burned bodies of Iraqi soldiers. Witnessing the purported enemy in this diminished state causes a physical reaction: 'I smell and taste their death, like a moist rotten sponge shoved into my mouth. I vomit into my mouth. I swish the vomit around before expelling it, as though it will cover the stink and taste of the dead men' (224). While this may clearly represent a traumatic experience and reaction, the question remains as to Swofford's personal responsibility and therefore his status as a perpetrator. As a marine sniper, Swofford is part of a large organisation which regularly perpetrates acts of violence, often against people of colour and in the cause of an aggressive foreign policy dedicated to economic expansion and control of markets. There is, therefore, an observable guilt by association, since Swofford, Turnipseed et al. are part of the military machine or organisation that has perpetrated violence. (As we shall see later in the chapter, considering the soldiers as a mechanised component in a larger organism has profound implications for interpreting their experience as traumatic.) In the episode where Swofford and his team look upon the scorched earth of the battlefield strewn with Iraqi corpses, he describes how they 'look at one another with blank, amazed faces. Is this what we've done?' (222). The use of first-person plural is instructive; since he was not a part of this battle, Swofford does not use 'I', which would imply an assumption of direct guilt, but neither does he use 'they', which would entirely repudiate it. The pronoun used instead underlines a guilt-by-association, and acknowledges Swofford's being part of the military machine. He is also more or less willingly a part of it, having voluntarily enrolled for the marines, even though early in his training he comes to regret his decision and unsuccessfully seeks a discharge. In short, Swofford (along with Turnipseed and Williams, if not the other writers discussed in this chapter) is in a liminal position, part of the violence-perpetrating organisation, but also victimised and exploited by it, as the opening boot camp scenes serve to emphasise. Indeed, the conventional-generic character of the boot camp episode, strongly reminiscent of Kubrick's *Full Metal Jacket*, serves to underline that the general status of soldiers as comprising an uneasy admixture of victim and perpetrator has become a staple of war narrative. This profoundly fluid liminal status is, as even a brief survey confirms, common to much American war literature. In O'Brien's *If I Die in a Combat Zone*, for example, readers encounter the startlingly rapid oscillation in the US soldiers from victims, as they come under a terrifying mortar attack and lose men to boobytraps, to perpetrators, as they take revenge on civilians (119–20). Significantly, episodes such as these reveal a common way of attempting to cope with perpetrator trauma, which is to suppress the knowledge of oneself as a perpetrator and instead appropriate victim status. As we shall see, this is a strategy also later adopted by Swofford. But it is also a strategy employed on a broader political level, both generally and in the specific instances of the Gulf Wars. Keith Brown and Katherine Lutz, for example, note how an ideological inversion of perpetrator and victim status – of the type suggested towards the end of the previous chapter, where America envisions itself as the latter in the face of facts which suggest the contrary – is a regular practice, resulting in a 'standard-issue U.S. war story, in which civilization faces savagism and every war is defensive and inevitable, rather than chosen, one that involves payback for a sneak attack by a duplicitious [sic], racialized Other' (326). In an essay examining the implications of the use of torture on the Guantanamo Bay detainees, Nina Philadelphoff-Puren similarly identifies American policy-makers, and by extension soldiers, as performing this shift from perpetrator status to conceiving oneself as a victim. However, torture testimony from the inmates at Guantanamo is identified by Philadelphoff-Puren as revealing the falsity of America's assumed victimhood (169). As we saw in the previous chapter, the attacks of 9/11 were swiftly mobilised as a tool of aggressive revenge, rapidly diminishing sympathy for America's victim status. One argument for interpreting the soldier-authors discussed in this chapter as perpetrators is that their individual experience can be mapped onto the broader actions of the country as a whole, in particular the political leaders who reimagined 9/11 as an initiating act of war.

The same rhetorical shift of American troops from perpetrators to victims is evident in *Jarhead*, where it represents a further strategy for attempting to recover from the trauma of guilt. At its most basic, this tendency is characterised by figuring oneself as a victim of circumstances rather than a perpetrator, part of an invading force. This conflation of perpetrator and victim, or transformation of one into the other, occurs in numerous ways throughout *Jarhead*. One chapter begins, for example, '[t]he man fires a rifle for many years, and he goes to war, and afterward he turns the rifle in at the armory and he believes he's finished with the rifle. But no matter what else he might do with his hands – love a woman, build a house, change his son's diaper – his hands remember the rifle and the power the rifle proffered' (123). A number of important formal and thematic ideas emerge here. Swofford relates this using a third-person voice, universalising the episode to depict soldiers or men in general, and thus distancing himself from the uncomfortable inescapability of his individual violent past. The passage also suggests that the firing of the rifle, an act of violence, somehow makes a victim of the man, as if he is subsequently, as in the conventional conception of a trauma victim, haunted by events. Inversion of perpetrator and victim occur when the 'power the rifle proffered' is ultimately turned against the one who had wielded it.

An even more pervasive and striking rhetorical trope in *Jarhead* overturns the notion of invasion, suggesting that rather than being aggressors, the thousands of individual soldiers comprising the US forces are actually the victims of invasion. Throughout, Swofford employs sand, and its invasive qualities, as an appropriate metaphor for this process. The reader is thus frequently confronted with the suggestion that it is not so much that America is invading the Middle East, but that the Arabian and Kuwaiti desert is instead invading the US soldiers' very bodies. Near the start of *Jarhead* this takes the form of a Proustian rush, as Swofford opens his rucksack after many years and extracts a map, out of whose folds sand emerges (2). This potent symbol of buried trauma – buried in the sand and re-emerging – begins a series of memories comprising 'dreams and the naïve wishes, the pathetic pleas and the trouser-pissing horror' (2). A little later, Swofford starts recounting his time in Saudi Arabia before the war begins:

After only six weeks of deployment, the desert is in us, one particle at a time – our boots and belts and trousers and gas masks and weapons are covered and filled with sand. Sand has invaded my body: ears and eyes and nose and mouth, ass crack and piss hole. The desert is everywhere. The mirage is everywhere. Awake, asleep, high heat of the afternoon or the few soft, sunless hours of early morning, I am still in the desert. (15)

Here, for the first time, the invasive qualities of sand are clearly described and the inversion of perpetrator status – that is from invader/perpetrator to invaded/victim – is begun in earnest. The invasive quality is, like the insidious perpetrator trauma itself, gradual, and pervades not only the soldiers' every bodily orifice, but also their equipment (including both defensive, the gas masks, and offensive, their weapons). It is also ubiquitous in terms of both space ('everywhere') and consciousness ('awake, asleep'). And again, through Swofford's use of the continuous present – 'I am still in the desert' – the narration merges the events described with the moment of inscription. This use of tense conflates the period described with the moment of writing, once more suggesting the haunting traumatic presence of this invasive force of the desert.

As the fighting finally begins and conditions become more stressful, so for Swofford the desert takes on a more aggressive tenor. On one long hump, Swofford describes how his 'crotch is sweaty and rancid and bleeding. I can feel sand working into the wound' (223). Noticeably, it is now Swofford's genital area that is affected by the sand, as if the invading sand registers a wound upon the masculinity that Swofford's membership of the marines was supposed to confirm. Again, the language is couched in such a way as to invert the reality of the situation, suggesting that Swofford is carrying out a defensive action in response to aggression, rather than being himself actually part of an invading force.

Not only is the inversion process from perpetrator to victim common to a number of war narratives, but even the use of the sand metaphor is not confined to Swofford's memoir. Turnipseed, for example, significantly refers to entering the desert world of the Gulf as a descent 'into a world of swirling sands and uncertainties'

(44). After the war a returning marine who was more involved in the conflict than Turnipseed is described as 'not so much covered as suffused with dust and sand' (172). Appropriately, given its symbolic status as a quagmire in which the US became increasingly trapped, the sand metaphor continues on into narratives of the Iraq War. Williams, like Swofford, is threatened both by its ubiquity and its somatically invasive qualities, describing a 'world of sand and grit, thick enough some days to stick between the teeth and cloud the air to hazy white' (69), before encountering a ferocious sandstorm, during which 'it was in your eyes, your hair, your mouth . . . When we woke, the dust had coated every orifice that was at all moist – eyes crusted shut, lips and nostrils caked in grit, and tongue and throat coated with a film of dirt. It was horrible' (88). Interestingly, Wright tends to refer in *Generation Kill* to dust rather than sand: 'Everyone is covered in dust' (31), he explains, or he describes how the air 'is heavy with dust particles' (200). The symbolic associations of dust with death (as opposed to the association of sand with time and therefore with boredom) may thus be significant in terms of understanding distinctions between American interpretations of the two wars.

Besides inversion, the other key rhetorical trope whereby Swofford tries to subvert perpetrator trauma in *Jarhead* is through the construction of empathy with the Iraqi soldiers. Swofford's attempted empathy stands in direct opposition to his marine training; as Gary Olsen notes, a key element of military conditioning is overtly anti-empathic: '[i]f empathy is putting oneself in another's shoes, the indissoluble combination of core masculinity with brainwashing, degradation, and stripping away any sense of self aims to foreclose this response.' This is where the doublethink entailed in inverting one's perpetrator status is most apparent, since empathy and passivity are diametrically opposed to the masculine aggression demanded of soldiers. There are, nevertheless, numerous occasions where Swofford tries to blur the distinction between himself and the Iraqi soldiers and thus, at a broader level, between the US and its enemies. The most vivid of these occurs when Swofford is punished by being given the task of manually processing the waste from the company's toilet facilities: '[t]he smell is atrocious, vomitous, bilious. I stir the burning shit and wonder if somewhere in

Kuwait or Iraq my peer enemy might at this moment be stirring the burning shit of his regiment . . . And I'm sure the poor man, my brother in arms at the moment, is also feeling sick to his stomach, about to vomit' (102). On the one hand, Swofford's recourse to the cliché of 'brother in arms' perhaps attests to the spuriousness of this identification with the other. Nevertheless, the episode is echoed elsewhere in the narrative, where empathy works according to the internally structured homosocial bonds of the military. This means that a US serviceman such as Swofford can claim to identify more with the purported enemy than with American non-combatants. In other words, although there is an anti-empathic imperative in military training, other elements of that same training in fact work, albeit inadvertently, in the opposite direction.

This empathic tendency in *Baghdad Express* is given an additional racial dimension. For an extended period, the Caucasian Turnipseed is in a unit with mainly African-American soldiers, and he notes their greater ability, clearly in part because of race, to identify with the oppressed. When the brief war has been more or less won, Turnipseed's unit hears stories about 'the "Highway of Death"' where Iraqis 'frantically trying to escape' from Kuwait City to Basra are bombed, leaving 'miles of burnt-out tanks, trucks, buses and bodies' (168). Turnipseed describes the collective sense of outraged guilt that pervades the unit after hearing this news: '[t]his was a brand new flavor of fucked-up, served cold. Having seen the Iraqi POWs in their cattle cars . . . it was hard for us to consider them our enemies. It was hard, thinking of their slaughtered brothers, not to remember other injustices – whether they occurred at Fort Pillow or Tuskeegee or My Lai' (168). This episode is thus linked, through a common occurrence of violence against people of colour, to previous shameful episodes in American history, a connection which becomes clearer when Turnipseed's African-American friend Ebbers describes it as '[b]rothers running away and we go and shoot them in the back' (168). When one of the white members of the platoon objects that Ebbers had not previously empathised when they were under attack from Iraqi missiles, he receives this response: '"You hear any alarms, Luke?" shouted Ebbers. "Shit, just like a white man to say something like that"' (168). As the next section discusses, the tendency of, especially, ethnic minority members of the US forces to forge empathic links with the minority other as a means to mitigate the effects of perpetrator trauma is evident also in narratives of the Iraq War.

EVAN WRIGHT'S *Generation Kill* AND NATHANIEL FICK'S *One Bullet Away*

One of the most memorable characters appearing in Wright's and Fick's narratives of Bravo Company's experiences during the Iraq War is Antonio Espera, a 'part Native American, part Mexican and a quarter German' (Wright 114) marine sergeant. Partly as a result of his ethnic minority status, Espera is sceptical regarding US foreign policy, in particular its treatment of the racial other. Espera's alienation from cherished American ideologies is increasingly voiced in terms that disparage the US mission, express a 'low-grade case of invaders' guilt' (Wright 115), and seek empathy with the Iraqis as ethnic others in part through a critique of attitudes towards race in America. Similar to the African-American marines in *Baghdad Express*, Espera is more able to empathise with the Iraqis than many of the white troops in the platoon. Indeed, the possible beginnings of his own perpetrator trauma – again experienced incrementally – are couched in language that suggests a growth in empathy. Before the company entered Iraq, Espera claims to have 'fucking hated Arabs', but as he encounters the Iraqis, he identifies with these people of colour and victims of American imperialism: 'I just feel so sorry for them . . . I don't want to kill nobody's children' (Wright 150).

Similar to the narratives of the Gulf War, *Generation Kill* and *One Bullet Away* present a further challenge to the instantaneous model of trauma, albeit for different reasons. Whereas in Swofford's and Turnipseed's texts perpetrator trauma was predominantly the result of overwhelming boredom, in the Gulf War Two texts the insidious trauma may be linked to the gradually worsening situation and, in particular, the steady attrition of the US forces' Rules of Engagement (ROE). Surveying a range of Iraq War literature, Brown and Lutz find symbolic significance in the ROE: '[t]he changes in wording and tacit acceptance of flexible interpretation of these rules are identified in these first-hand accounts and serve as a metaphor for the entire enterprise in Iraq' (326). The importance of the ROE lies not only in metaphor, however, since their gradual erosion and 'flexible interpretation' can be seen as a contributory factor to the occurrence of perpetrator trauma. Fick, especially, gradually recognises that the attrition of the ROE, and the commission of certain atrocities which is partly the result, represent an assault on his former assumption of moral rectitude. This is revealed by the contrast between his belief on entering the war that the ROE would allow him to 'control the justice of [this war's] conduct within [his] tiny sphere of influence' (182), and his subsequent disillusionment and disgust when his platoon shoots two shepherd boys (239). Fick and his platoon are further alienated when his commanders initially refuse to treat the boys: 'I wanted to tell the major that we were Americans, that Americans don't shoot kids and let them die, that the men in my platoon had to be able to look themselves in the mirror for the rest of their lives' (240). On one level, it is striking how Fick's concern emerges not primarily as guilt, but regarding his men's psychological well-being through its avoidance. This flows directly from Fick's initial aim for his personal war, having set himself the two-fold task of 'winning and getting my men home alive. Alive, though, set the bar too low. I had to get them home physically and psychologically intact,' and having 'retained their humanity' (241). Fick becomes morally caught between outrage at what he sees as the decaying values of the US cause and resolute concern for the operational capacity and wellbeing of his men, who 'were being abandoned to suffer the consequences of other people's poor decisions' (240). Fick's disillusionment and moral confusion emerges most fully when, exhausted from many days under extreme stress, and in particular following a near-disastrous experience of being ambushed, he finally finds some quiet time alone in the dark: 'I felt sick for the shepherd boys . . . and for all the innocent people who surely lived in Nasiriyah, Ar Rifa, and all the other towns this war would consume' (243). By this point Fick is himself consumed by guilt, close to Nash's state of 'moral injury' discussed earlier, which, to recall, may be brought on by shame over culpability in the deaths of civilians.

Besides the morally troubling position into which the ROE put the marines, another source of trauma lies in the alienating and sometimes incompetent behaviour of their commanding officers. Wright, for example, describes the attempt of Fick's immediate commanding officer to call in a 'danger close' artillery strike (205–6), that is, a strike within 600 metres of his own troops (cf. Fick 229). An even more stark example of this incompetence is the disastrous insistence by Fick's CO that an order given in error higher up the chain of command to clear mines at night is carried out. This results in the loss of a leg by one man and an eye by another (Wright 427–33), but no sense of wrongdoing in the mind of the CO. Regarding his CO, Fick concludes that '[h]is poor decision making since before the start of the war had sapped every bit of natural trust that Marines are taught to have in their chain of command' (Fick 305). As an outsider with a wider perspective, Wright notes how the perceived incompetence of their superiors, combined with being kept uninformed about operational objectives, finally alienates Fick's platoon. After the terrifying drive under heavy fire through Al Gharraf, for example, Wright observes how '[t]he lack of information provided to the Marines about their role in the grand scheme of things is beginning to erode morale' (193).

Even Fick, initially a highly loyal officer and firm believer in the justified nature of their cause, is ultimately outraged by the failures of the operation. When he and his company find themselves coming under friendly fire from a logistics convoy '[r]age followed cynicism as I thought indignantly of how we had spent the entire day sitting in this dangerous spot, making it safe for their passage' (232). Coming under friendly fire – to recall, another trigger for what William Nash describes as 'moral injury' – combines two key responses to perpetrator trauma seen in these memoirs: the inversion of perpetrator/victim status, and the attempt to construct empathic links with the enemy. Fick and his company are part of the same (perpetrating) organisation that in this instance mistakenly victimises them; this is especially noticeable in Wright's account of the same incident which follows only a few pages on from Fick's company having themselves fired erroneously on civilians (199–200). Combatants placed in potentially hazardous positions, where they are subject to the whims and incompetence of their commanding officers, may well come to believe that they are more victim than perpetrator in particular situations. This is a plausible reaction to coming under friendly fire, which clearly enables empathy for an enemy even more regularly facing the lethal power of the US military machine.

We may borrow from Fredric Jameson's notions of alienation, reification, and the political unconscious in order to demonstrate another way in which perpetrator trauma seems to be experienced by soldiers in these circumstances. The models of masculinity enforced in the military environment, in particular its mechanising of the individual, are revealing in this respect. As an embedded reporter, Wright can distance himself from the hyper-masculinity on display from the marines, so his memoir occasionally comprises a sardonic ethnographic study of the masculine homosocial subculture he encounters. He notes, for example, that the Recon Marines are male only, and thus 'one of the last all-male adventures left in America', and the pride exhibited in a hyperbolic masculinity: 'few virtues are celebrated more than being hard – having stronger muscles, being a better fighter, being more able to withstand pain and privation' (38).

Numerous writers have observed how the military manipulates particular forms of masculinity in order to produce aggression, noting how military power structures seek to 'colonize the soldier's gendered identity and to develop a militarized body that must be permanently hard and function with mechanical efficiency' (Jarvis 137). This functionality comes at an extreme cost, however, since male soldiers are forced to stifle any attribute perceived as feminine. 'The hyperbolic masculinity imposed by military discipline,' Brian Jarvis suggests, 'ensures that trauma is inseparable from the corporeal cartographies of gender identity' (137). Thus, the very processes that manipulate the individual soldier into the military unit traumatically appropriate and distort his gendered identity. This conception of the individual body as mechanised, a small component in a larger machine, clearly evokes Jameson's notions of reification. Phillips, for example, describes how military powers manipulate masculinity by portraying universal feelings of fear as somehow womanly, and therefore to be shunned. This repression, Phillips argues, ultimately produces a 'breakdown' whereby soldiers are either unable to continue in combat or can fight 'only when numbed.￼ The more frequently soldiers switch on this enabling numbness, however, the more likely it is that they cannot switch it off, so that they return to civilian life emotional cripples' (178). The ideological manipulation of the individual's masculinity in order to transform them into fighters, according to Phillips, inevitably produces trauma.

Both *Generation Kill* and *One Bullet Away*, through their depiction of a key member of Fick's platoon, Sergeant Rudy Reyes, provide an interesting challenge to universal models of military masculinity. Wright describes Reyes on the one hand as possessing 'the insanely muscular body of a fantasy Hollywood action hero', but on the other as 'one of the gayest', of the marines, and although not sexually gay and actually married, 'he is at least a highly evolved tough guy in touch with a well-developed feminine side' (63). Despite his military-approved dedication to bodybuilding and martial arts, Reyes simultaneously accommodates a less essentialised masculinity. Surprisingly, Reyes earnestly describes himself to Wright as having, 'very low self-esteem. I need to empower myself daily through physical training and spirituality. I identify with redemption stories like *The Color Purple*. I love the journey of a woman from weak and less-than to someone who is fully realized' (64). Reyes provides an arresting exception to blanket assumptions about military masculinity, but is also relevant in terms of trauma. Reyes was the only member of the platoon to reprise his role, playing himself in the HBO television mini-series adaptation of *Generation Kill*. It is unlikely that someone truly traumatised by a series of events would be willing to revisit them in such a structured, public and literal way. Despite experiencing the same harrowing events as the rest of Fick's platoon, Reyes, perhaps because of his refusal of the inhibitory mechanised masculinity generally required by the military, is markedly less traumatised.

Another source of alienation among the troops relates to the cause(s) for which the wars are fought. Combatants' homosocial bonds are characteristically interpreted as superseding any concern with causes, both in war in general, and the Iraq wars in particular, Phillips noting that '[i]n both Iraq wars, servicemen boast of knowing the motives are bad ones, as if awareness absolved the knower from acting on his revelation' (192). Certainly, the suspicion that the real aim is to secure oil rights is addressed even in *Baghdad Express* and *Jarhead* (in the latter, Swofford notes how shortly before deployment the marines 'joke about having transferred from the Marine Corps to the Oil Corps' [11]), as well as in the memoirs concerning the second war. Wider causes are thus also marginalised in *Generation Kill*, where 'the marines skip away from community goals to more important personal ones' (Phillips 192). Wright soon notices, for example, that 'external facts about the looming war don't really seem that important to these guys. The dominant feature of their lives is simply the fact that they are all together, which they enjoy tremendously' (44). The combatants' attitudes towards causes may be more complex, however, and certainly less homogenous than this suggests. Sometimes, for example, it appears that the alienation entailed in the soldiers' dual awareness of the spuriousness of their cause and the suppression of that knowledge produces precisely the kind of political unconscious that Jameson describes. Significantly, in accounts of the second war this suppression is often manifested in instances of traumatised acting out. In *One Bullet Away*, for example, Fick describes the cynical assessment of causes voiced by his driver, Corporal Josh Person: 'I guess I'm fighting for cheap gas and a world without ragheads blowing up our fucking buildings' (251). While Person is clearly conscious of the underlying basis of the war, this can be read as a Jamesonian political unconscious in that it is the war's irreconcilable ethics that produce his habitual acting out in the form of angry tirades, constant talking and singing, and, like the other soldiers, occasional extreme violence.

Antonio Espera, who, as we have already seen with regard to issues of race, is clearly one of the more reflective members of Fick's platoon, voices a more complex assessment of causes. Espera gives semi-ironic expression of a wish to export capitalist values worldwide forcibly, and these speeches make it clear that he is aware that the form of freedom that the US forces offer is a spurious and debased one. Notwithstanding his earlier critique of the white man's colonialist exploitation (with its echoes of Richard Slotkin's *Regeneration Through Violence*), Espera recognises and expresses ambivalent feelings regarding his role in the process, a job he seems to relish with equal parts pride, cynicism, and self-loathing. He says, "The U.S. should just go into all these countries, here and in Africa, and set up an American government and infrastructure – with McDonald's, Starbucks, MTV – then just hand it over. If we had to kill a hundred thousand to save twenty million, it's worth it . . . Hell, the U.S. did it at home for two hundred years – killed Indians, used slaves, exploited immigrant labor to build a system that's good for everybody today. What does the white man call it? 'Manifest Destiny'". (Wright 296)

Other statements made by Espera during the course of both Wright's and Fick's accounts suggest that this is not a sincerely held point of view – especially the idea that the US presides over 'a system that's good for everybody' – but more his deconstruction of the real motives behind American foreign policy. In this respect, Espera's position echoes the viewpoint espoused in Mark Simpson's essay 'Attackability', which argues that in order to open up markets and to keep the poorer part of the world feeling vulnerable and therefore compliant, war is an essential part of American imperialist capitalism, not an unfortunate and occasional by-product. Espera's wearily sarcastic advocacy of US imperialism reveals alienation from the war's causes, and suggests reasons why causes are generally of necessity suppressed into the soldiers' political unconscious.[3]

The mechanisation of the men and their bodies is crucial to understanding the application of Jameson's theories of alienation and reification to these memoirs. The effect on bodies is demonstrated in numerous ways. At a basic level, this comprises the physically traumatising effect on the body after a prolonged time spent fighting in the desert environment: '[e]veryone is coughing and has runny noses and weeping, swollen eyes caused by the dust storms' (Wright 238). The marines experience numerous cases of vomiting and diarrhoea, and when they finally see themselves in mirrors, after many days, 'many are amazed by the gaunt reflections staring back at them', having often 'shed five to ten pounds' (Wright 238). At a deeper level, the training which prepared the men for war – both physically and in terms of forging a mental attitude of homosocial camaraderie and submission to authority – represents a clear example of reification, the transformation of people into usable things. Often, there is surprisingly little effort made to conceal either the processes of reification or their purposes. Wright, for example, describes how the men's aggressive impulses are encouraged, against any better natures they may possess: '[t]he hope is that by making the Marines more aggressive on the ground, they can scare up better information from the villagers' (266). Even more crudely, the overall strategy of the officers in ultimate command over the battalion is transparently to send the marines forward into battle as fast as possible, acting as shock troops or even, sometimes, as bait. Given this overt reification of the men, it is hardly surprising that they experience traumatic symptoms, for example through disgust at the civilian casualties, as when one marine witnesses the appalling death of a young girl shot by his team while she was hiding in the back of her father's car, and is reportedly 'devastated', saying that '[t]his is the event that is going to get to me when I go home' (283). If the ROE were supposed to prove the moral rectitude of the American forces' actions and thus protect the soldiers from guilt and perpetrator trauma, they are shown to have signally failed. The reification of these human subjects as tools of war is demonstrably traumatising.

As well as individuals, the marine company itself is described in explicitly mechanised terms. 'Despite all its disparate elements, the column functions like a single machine,' according to Wright, '[t]he cogs that make up this machine are the individual teams in hundreds of vehicles, several thousand Marines . . . The invasion all comes down to a bunch of extremely tense young men in their late teens and twenties, with their fingers on the triggers of rifles and machine guns' (195). Later, Wright revealingly likens the marines' reified task to precisely the kind of deskilled factory job that produces Jamesonian alienation: '[o]nce the initial excitement wears off, invading a country becomes repetitive and stressful, like working on an old industrial assembly line' (296). The language used here is extremely telling, explicitly connecting the typically alienating deskilled civilian employment of late capitalism with the reifying processes of military mechanisation.

Reification here is clearly linked to the insidious character of perpetrator trauma, since the processes whereby the soldiers are mechanised and dehumanised, from their training and on into combat, are again gradual. According to Jameson, it is a self-recognition of the distorting effects of reification that produces alienation in the individual under late capitalism. It is precisely this same dawning awareness on the part of the soldiers that they have been used in this way – in both their training and in battle – which produces in them an alienating and ultimately traumatising effect. In other words, the individual soldier gradually recognises that their bond with their colleagues, and the attendant need constantly to prove their masculinity, is what keeps them usable, that is, reified and mechanised. As Phillips suggests, the men are disabused of one key myth of war, 'that it provides men an opportunity for autonomous action', when in fact, as these memoirs generally demonstrate, 'mechanized battle pins men down more than it lets them act' (178). Realising this, they become disillusioned, and it is this gradual recognition of a political unconscious that, for some of the soldiers, insidiously produces perpetrator trauma.

Espera again supplies evidence of this process of growing awareness and its resultant alienation. Following a failure of an Iraqi truck to stop at a US roadblock, Espera describes how it was fired upon with overwhelming force by the marines. As part of this operation, Espera describes how at the time he felt 'cold-blooded as a motherfucker', whereas afterwards, given time to reflect, he 'seems to wallow in a black, self-flagellating mood. "Dog, whatever last shred of humanity I had before I came here, it's gone"' (Wright 281). Espera's previously suppressed political unconscious exists in the gap between the praise received from those in charge of his unit and the reality of dehumanisation and mechanisation as recognised by Espera himself, as he 'offers his own assessment of the battalion's performance . . . "Do you realize the shit we've done here, the people we've killed? Back home in the civilian world, if we did this, we would go to prison"' (Wright 352). There is a sense in which Wright positions Espera as the consciousness of the platoon, and certainly Espera is the one who most clearly perceives the ideologies used in order to make men fight. Above all, Espera reveals the suppressed political unconscious of the troops, beginning to appreciate more clearly the reifying processes that have insidiously dehumanised and traumatised them.

KAYLA WILLIAMS'S *Love My Rifle More than You*

While the hyperbolic military masculinity discussed above is not a direct personal issue for Williams, a plethora of additional problems arises for her as a woman in such an institutionally misogynistic environment. These include direct threats to her of rape and other variously sexist behaviour, which her own and others' testimony reveals represents typical experiences for women in the military. Alan Petersen notes the extreme 'expectation of heterosexuality' in the military, as a kind of hyper-masculinity that 'can be seen in the tolerance (if not encouragement) of prostitution and in forms of sexual discrimination, harassment and exploitation (for example, sexist jokes and rape)' (53). This is borne out by the experience of Williams and other female combatants considered in this section.

Williams's memoir suggests that perpetrator trauma in combat is experienced differently by women. Although her text attempts a similar movement from perpetrator to victim status, the profoundly sexist structures of the military make this far more convincing, since female warriors are doubly victimised, not only by the same incompetence of their commanding officers and the reifying structures of the military, but also through threats from their male peers. At one point, for example, Williams receives an entirely unexpected and unwelcome proposition from one of her male fellow soldiers to 'break the back axle of that Humvee there on you' (72), underlining how '[f]emale soldiers live in a complex web of power and powerlessness as members of the U.S. military' (Feinman 79). As with other accounts, Williams's thus describes an insidious accretion of slowly traumatising processes. While the insidious nature of Williams's trauma is very similar in manifestation and cause to that experienced by her male counterparts, her empathic ability is noticeably more pronounced than, say, Swofford's, despite his apparent efforts. This is due not least to the fact that Williams speaks Arabic (her primary role in the army was an interpreter) and before joining the army was in a long-term relationship with a Lebanese man. Above all, however, her status as a woman – disempowered, disdained and abused by the military structures of which she is a part – enhances her capacity to empathise with other victims of the US forces.

In terms of Williams's liminal condition, the reader witnesses something close to transference, as if Williams's burden of being part of the perpetrator organisation brings on victim status. 'We come to assume the worst about everyone,' she explains, with reference to the increasingly violent resistance to US forces, and admits that 'there are times I am feeling overwhelmed by the situation' (238). This is followed by a passage which reveals that the worsening situation and related erosion of the ROE as a mechanism of moral restraint significantly exacerbates the ebbing of Williams's capacity for empathy. Instead, she seems afflicted by perpetrator trauma while completely eschewing her former affinity for the Iraqis: '[w]hen we think about the local population now, we're thinking: What are you people doing? We're here to help you! And you're trying to kill us! Are you insane? Do you even *want* peace? Or freedom? Or democracy? . . . What is wrong with these people?' (238). This lack of insight, where Williams had formerly shown a marked aptitude for empathy with the locals, demonstrates the extreme effect of the violence brought to Iraq by the Americans.

As well as the shifting ROE, the insidious trauma suffered by Williams can be attributed in part to her sense of the incompetence of her commanding officers. Again, this is similar to that noted in the other memoirs, but takes on an additional strongly gendered dimension because of Williams's female status. Williams is disgusted when successive female COs cry when put under pressure or are criticised for their decisions, since she is aware that women in the army are under greater scrutiny not to be prey to such gender stereotypes. If Williams, like her male counterparts, is plagued to the extent of traumatisation by the demonstrable incompetence of her COs, this process is exacerbated in her case by feeling 'let down' by their behaviour under pressure, as it reflects badly upon her status as a woman in the services.

Williams suffers a distinct sense of traumatisation following her reifying induction into the army, indeed even more strongly than her male counterparts, both because of her female status in such a strongly patriarchal environment and because of the precise way in which women are used by the military. This is especially clear when Williams is twice co-opted to participate in interrogations of Iraqi men. A number of contributors to Tara McKelvey's collection *One of the Guys*, published in the wake of Abu Ghraib, discuss similar episodes. Jumana Musa observes that the 'decision to use female guards and interrogators for male detainees' exploits gendered expectations and also 'takes advantage of the military women' (86). In other words, the process of coercing female soldiers into the interrogation process has the side-effect of conflating their perpetrator–victim status. Aziz Huq's essay explicitly addresses this liminal status and the idea that in becoming involved in military interrogations, '[w]omen thus have found themselves in morally clouded roles, as both perpetrator and victim in different measures' (126). Reinforcing points made with regard to the dangers of conflating analysis with moral judgement at the start of this chapter, Huq goes on to suggest that in these circumstances, 'it is far from clear that there is only one victim here. To condemn a perpetrator, after all, does not mean ceasing to understand and empathize with her, for there may be multiple villains and many victims even in a simple story' (126). Huq concludes that '[t]he female interrogator or soldier asked to deploy her sexuality . . . is placed in a morally cloven position . . . asked to betray what most people believe to be elementary moral commitments, asked to turn her body into an *instrument* of torture, and asked to deploy her sexuality in ways that degraded her and others' (133, emphasis added). In other words, the use of female soldiers in interrogations is precisely another element in the general reification of the soldier, but in a gendered and sexualised manner.

These observations are particularly pertinent to Williams's involvement in interrogations. Williams is twice used in the interrogation of Iraqi male subjects, and these episodes constitute key sections of her memoir's treatment of the fluid distinctions between perpetrator and victim trauma. Significantly, Williams's first involvement with interrogation is closely followed in the narrative by an episode in which a previously friendly male soldier attempts to rape her, and this in turn is followed by what appears to be temporary mental incapacity on her part. Williams's status at this point slides rapidly from perpetrator-victim to unequivocal victim, and the episodes suggest again that her traumatic experience of the army is directly related to being a woman. Like numerous other women in the forces, Williams is prey to an 'enemy in the ranks'.[4] She is also used for interrogations purely because she is a woman, in order to humiliate the male Iraqi prisoners. These elements in combination make her experience categorically different to that of male soldiers.

Although at first reluctant to participate in the interrogations, Williams does become actively involved: 'I found myself yelling. I found myself calling this jerk every insulting name I knew' (204). The depersonalisation or alienation from self here – 'I found myself' – is particularly telling, and speaks of an awareness, at the moment of writing if not at the time of the actions, that she was overstepping a moral line. Again, this fits another element of perpetrator trauma related to Nash's 'moral injury' which, he explains, can be caused by 'damage to your deeply held beliefs about right and wrong' (qtd in Pilkington). Williams continues,

> I don't even want to repeat what I said; it sickens me now to think about it.
> I grabbed a broom handle and banged it loud on some pipe attached to the wall . . . Yet yelling at this guy did also feel perversely good. Because it was not something I was allowed to do . . . I don't like to admit it, but I enjoyed having power over this guy. (205)

As her involvement becomes sadistically sexualised, before separating herself from this process Williams expresses a kind of guilty and appalled fascination with her actions:

> I was uncomfortable with these feelings of pleasure at his discomfort, but I still had them. It did occur to me that I was seeing a part of myself I wouldn't have seen otherwise.
> Not a good part. (205)

Throughout this episode Williams is, as Musa and Huq above suggest, suspended between perpetrator and victim, both exploited and exploiting. This reification process, whereby she is coerced to exercise violence and thereby employed as an instrument, produces trauma. As with the examples from male authors discussed above, Williams expresses this trauma in part through alienated dissociation, as if she is witnessing herself as a separate subject committing these acts.

Williams's complex traumatised status is redoubled by the following episode when, as mentioned above, she is assaulted by a male fellow soldier who tries to rape her (206–8). After all this, and at the end of this chapter (entitled 'Losing It'), Williams experiences a range of trauma symptoms which recall, inter alia, the incident where she attempts to help victims of the suddenly detonating unexploded ordnance:

> I began to experience intrusive images. They were like snapshots. Sudden and disturbing shots of Baghdad on patrol in the spring with Delta Company. The man in pain, bleeding to death in front of me. Or sometimes they were movie clips. A short film in which I watched myself watch him die. And I'm helpless to save him. Utterly powerless to make a difference here. I watch the flies hover. The blood on his legs. The medic. Me running. Attempting to calm the crowd. Like I said, these could be short films, but mainly they were snapshots. A lot of intrusive snapshots. (212–13)

Again the language used here revealingly suggests alienation and dissociation: 'I watched myself watch him die.' Moreover, the memories are particularly intrusive as they occur 'day or night', and not as dreams but 'during [her] waking life' (213). These are quite conventional symptoms, but they strike Williams with particular force given her previous impermeability, so she thought, to signs of what she takes to be weakness. The description of symptoms continues until the breakdown culminates thus: '[i]t was around this time that I contemplated offing myself. It could all be over in a moment. It would be too easy' (215). The episode, a little later, where one of Williams's compatriots indeed commits suicide (223–4) suggests that this is no idle threat.

Interestingly, given her perpetrator-victim status, Williams remains unsure of the cause of the intrusive symptoms which seem, ultimately, overdetermined. The sexual assault on her, the increased length of her deployment, and her weight loss are all posited as reasons but she is at this point suspiciously silent about her involvement in the interrogation. Structurally, however, given its placement in such close proximity to her breakdown, Williams's involvement is implied as a further cause. This is important, as it suggests that at least an element of her trauma is related to perpetrator guilt. It is again insidious in character, gradually brought on by the worsening situation experienced by the US troops, Williams among them, but also catalysed by her involvement in the interrogations. It is apparently this involvement that brings her to recognise her reified status in the army, especially since she is used primarily because she is a woman rather than for any particular skills she possesses. And it is this realisation, as with some of the memoirs discussed above, which produces an alienating sense of trauma, as the previously suppressed political unconscious is uncovered.

Having separated herself once from the interrogation process, Williams is asked to join again. Reluctantly, she does so, but more as a witness than a participant (246–8), although even this observer role is implicated with her female status, as her presence is again used to humiliate the male Iraqi prisoners. Williams this time witnesses worse abuses – lit cigarettes are flicked at prisoners, who are also struck in the face – and again separates herself from the process before protesting against the practices to her superiors (249). These protests are possibly not entirely ineffectual, since the 'cage' where she witnessed these abuses is investigated (250). On this second occasion, it is perhaps Williams's more steadfast reaction that minimises traces of perpetrator guilt. She is also more able to maintain her empathy with the Iraqis, which, as she acknowledges, she retains in part due to her Lebanese ex-partner, whom she imagines in the place of the prisoners.

More successfully surviving her second involvement with the interrogations allows Williams to reflect in a more detached way on the various damaging effects these processes have on the interrogators. Focusing explicitly on perpetrator trauma, Williams asks, '[w]hat kind of psychological damage does this kind of work do?'

How long does it take to recover from a situation where [the interrogator] gets used to being suspicious of everyone and where he uses threats and intimidation to get what he wants?' (206), and suggests that the exercise of this type of violent interrogation, 'for as long as our interrogators had been required to do them . . . fucks you up in ways we can only guess' (251). The use of 'required' constructs the interrogators not fully as perpetrators because, again, their position in the army coerces them into actions that reify them as instruments.

Williams's recognition of the damaging effects of perpetrator trauma on interrogators is matched by a number of other commentators. In an essay from McKelvey's collection, whose title, 'Pawn, Scapegoat, or Collaborator', neatly encapsulates the liminal perpetrator-victim status which armed forces operatives assume, Barbara Foley argues that America's widespread adoption of brutal interrogation tactics in the Middle East has constructed something like a timebomb in terms of

> the potential impact that the torture, degradation, and humiliation of other human beings will have on young soldiers themselves. What will be the impact on their families, their communities, and our nation when they return having learned to practice extremes of cruelty and violence? Will men who have treated others (including some women prisoners) savagely come home to be kind, gentle lovers, husbands, and fathers; or will they believe that violence is a legitimate way to deal with others? (212)

Foley concludes that, '[a]t the very least, both men and women who participated in these horrors will carry the images in their minds throughout their lives, with unknown consequences for their mental, spiritual, moral, and physical well-being and that of those around them' (212). The 'images in their minds' very much suggests intrusive symptoms of trauma. As we have seen throughout this chapter, perpetrators of traumatic events are prone to experience lasting and damaging after-effects, albeit often taking different forms to more generally recognised manifestations of trauma.

CONCLUSION: CUBICLE WARRIORS

Similar questions about perpetrator trauma have recently been posed with regard to America's use of so-called cubicle warriors. These remote operators, generally working in Nevada for the CIA, control the Predator drone aircraft that carry out missions – often involving assassination – in other parts of the globe. Cubicle warriors initially conduct 'study of life' patterns which involve long periods of surveillance in order to confirm the identity of their targets. They may then be given clearance to launch remote missile attacks on these targets. Following such attacks, the operators are required to revisit the site with remote video devices and assess the impact of the attack, including the counting of bodies. Whereas Foley, above, identifies the potential difficulty of returning soldiers resuming a conventional family life, for the cubicle warriors this problem is more immediate. As a number of studies have reported, these operatives are expected, after they may have been carrying out remote killings or counting body parts, to 'drive home to have dinner with their families' (Mayer). The disjunction between the two worlds inhabited by the cubicle warriors has brought increasing interest to studies of perpetrator trauma since, as Royakkers and van Est suggest, 'the use of remote controlled military robotics causes operators to live in two worlds at the same time: both a "normal" life in the civil world, and a virtual life of combat. As a result, these virtual warriors constantly experience radical shifts in contexts: from battlefield to private family life' (293). Some have argued, moreover, that contrary to what one might expect, remoteness from battle has little effect in terms of diminishing the perpetrator trauma experienced by cubicle warriors: 'some Predator pilots suffer from combat stress that equals, or exceeds, that of pilots in the battlefield. This suggests that virtual killing, for all its sterile trappings, is a discomfiting form of warfare' (Mayer). In other words, while these might be, on one level, 'virtual soldiers' (Royakkers and van Est 293), the technology which puts them in touch with the battlefield also exposes them to similar levels of emotional fatigue, and roughly equivalent consequent stress and trauma to those soldiers actually on the ground. The increased use by the US of cubicle warriors fighting through remote control means that further work is needed in the study of perpetrator trauma, both in terms of the dangers of mixing military and domestic life, and the effect on moral decisions taken by the virtual soldiers. Cubicle warriors may be added to the list of sufferers of perpetrator trauma discussed in this chapter, whose trauma is related in part to guilt and in part to their reified military role. As this chapter has suggested, the reifying processes involved in turning humans into mechanised agents of war can be a slowly alienating and traumatising experience. While the conflation or sliding of status from perpetrator to victim is particularly visible in the texts discussed in this chapter, this echoes a much wider phenomenon in contemporary American society noted at the end of the previous chapter. Indeed, the inversion attempted in a number of these texts – the transformation of the victims of American foreign policy into perpetrators (and vice versa) – is perhaps the epitome of a more general appropriation of victim status in the US post-9/11 through a popularised discourse of trauma. The trauma genre, discussed more extensively in the Introduction and in Chapter 3, is complicit in this process, employing normalised tropes of trauma discourse and thereby perpetuating the sense of victimhood. A consequence of this is that the reluctance by academics to consider perpetrator trauma in any depth (until relatively recently) is not only a dereliction of duty but functionally political (in effect, if not intention), as the above discussion of LaCapra and Rothberg suggested. In erasing or marginalising the colonised victim of American aggression overseas, these texts, and this negligent critical practice, represent a denial of the US's wider status as perpetrator. In retrospect, Rothberg's 'category error', discussed at the start of this chapter, is something far more sinister and purposeful: if trauma is deliberately and exclusively associated with victimhood, then this dangerously excludes the possibility that if one suffers trauma one can be a perpetrator.

NOTES

1. An increasing number of commentators number the 1980–88 Iran–Iraq War as the First Persian Gulf War, but this has not yet fully penetrated western discourse, and that conflict is outside the scope of this study. This chapter therefore adopts western convention and generally labels the 1991 war as the Gulf War and that from 2003 onwards as the Iraq War.

2. The phrase 'perpetrator trauma' is used throughout this chapter to a degree under erasure, or for want of a better term. Regardless of an undesirable degree of moral judgement implicit in the term, it is preferable in its flexibility and applicableness to associated terms (such as Ben Shephard's 'atrocity guilt').

3. In *Jarhead* Swofford is similarly and, in this example where he experiences the crude oil from the burning Kuwaiti rigs raining down, symbolically ambivalent about the US's true motives for being in the Gulf: 'I look at the sky and the petrol rain falling on my uniform. I want the oil in and on me. I open my mouth. I want to taste it, to understand this viscous liquid' (214). Swofford not only allows himself again to be 'invaded' by the country whose borders he is in fact breaching, but here by the product which motivates the war. Becoming one with the oil perhaps suggests recognition of his complicity in this operation.

4. See also, for example, Christy L. Clothier, 'The Controller' and Elizabeth Keough McDonald, 'Every Night Is Footsteps', both in Bowden and Cain (eds) (68–77, 82–3).

CHAPTER 5

It Could Happen Here:
Trauma and Contemporary
American Counterfactuals

In Don DeLillo's *Falling Man* a young boy, Justin, lives temporarily in a 'failed fairy tale' where the World Trade Center towers
remain standing (102), while *Extremely Loud and Incredibly Close*,
as discussed in Chapter 3, concludes with Oskar's retreat into a scenario where his father avoided the attacks. Even *In the Shadow of
No Towers* flirts with this idea, Spiegelman imagining that 9/11 has
actually thrown him into an insane alternative world. Meanwhile,
Ken Kalfus's *A Disorder Peculiar to the Country* concludes with a
fantastic alternative reality wherein, in the spring of 2003, a successful U.S. military campaign in Iraq ends 'with unprecedented
speed and dexterity' (229). Saddam Hussein is captured, tried and
executed by a new Iraqi democratic government, weapons of mass
destruction – the chimera that spuriously motivated the American
war on Iraq in our world – are found, 'some of them already
loaded on medium-range missiles' (230), democracy appears to
be gaining support in Syria and Iran, and finally crowds gather
at Ground Zero to celebrate the capture of Osama bin Laden
(234–7). Kalfus's novel is of some interest in relation to the three
counterfactual history novels discussed in more detail in the following chapter. Predominantly concerned with the lengthy and
acrimonious divorce of its protagonists, Joyce and Marshall, the
novel plays out against a backdrop of post-9/11 America that only
slides towards fantasy shortly before the ending described above.
This ending contrasts the futility of the couple's marriage with an

unlikely harmony in the Middle East. More importantly, the interplay of family romance and geopolitics gestures towards the theme shared by the three novels discussed in this chapter.

In short, it might initially be puzzling that respected novelists Paul Auster, Michael Chabon, and Philip Roth, in the traumasuffused years of the post-9/11 Bush administration, adopted the generally disparaged form of the alternative history or counterfactual novel (albeit perhaps less so for Chabon, who has previously demonstrated an affinity for genre fiction). All three of their novels – respectively *Man in the Dark* (2008), *The Yiddish Policemen's Union* (2007), and *The Plot Against America* (2004) – as with Kalfus's, engage with the form of alternative history primarily as a means to explore the potentially traumatic effect of domestic and international politics upon family life. It is necessary to investigate the reasons behind these writers' choice of genre, especially as counterfactual narratives, being motivated by specific questions, are generally employed as means to particular ends.

The turbulent political landscape of early twenty-first-century America may lead one to conclude that these novels represent a retreat from the traumas of 9/11, the Bush administration, and the wars in Afghanistan and Iraq. Indeed, Richard Gray's *After the Fall* argues that post-9/11 American literature is characterised by such a retreat, an attempt 'simply [to] assimilate the unfamiliar into familiar structures. The crisis is, in every sense of the word, domesticated' (30). This is a facile but nevertheless attractive explanation, given that, as explored in Chapter 1, American writers have typically used techniques such as procrastination, distraction and displaced subjectivity in order to avoid the subject of trauma. The alternative history form in this sense may be envisaged as an extended exercise in shifting subjectivity from first to third person. Auster, for one, has employed this technique in order to write about trauma in *The Invention of Solitude*, and more recently in *Invisible*, and so it is plausible to understand Owen Brick – the invention of *Man in the Dark*'s protagonist, August Brill – as a literal manifestation of this phenomenon, comprising a new subject position for Brill in an alternative and, at least initially, less dangerous universe.

In terms of trauma, the counterfactual history form may also be seen as marking a retreat in its sometimes wistful contemplation of alternative scenarios. This recalls the attempt in *Extremely Loud* of Oskar and his grandmother to force time to flow backwards to a period that predates and circumvents their traumas. Philip, the more or less autobiographical child protagonist of Roth's *Plot Against America*, expresses a similar desire, 'that not uncommon childhood ailment called why-can't-it-be-the-way-it-was' (173). The imagining of alternate histories and counterfactual worlds lies in close proximity to this urge to rewind history. In both cases, the yearning is motivated by an ultimately futile desire to escape the consequences of a traumatic series of events. Alternative scenarios may be used here, however, in order to demonstrate that historic actuality is thoroughly non-deterministic and highly contingent.

Walter Benn Michaels, writing about Roth's novel, also diagnoses a form of escapism as the motivation for the alternative history mode. He suggests that the source of enjoyment for readers in alternative histories in general and *The Plot Against America* in particular is rooted in a retreat from the discomfort of apprehending and addressing real-world economic inequality. Michaels argues that texts disparaging racism enable the reader to feel superior and to be reassured, while simultaneously representing an ideological distraction from inequalities of wealth (297). Dan Shiffman, by contrast, doubts whether Roth's novel represents a retreat from his more familiar topics of 'self-examination, invention, and reinvention' (63). Indeed, he specifically raises the question of escapism in order to dismiss it as a motivation for *The Plot Against America*, which instead 'dramatizes how America can never be fully protected from widespread terror and that there is no escaping into a mythic and ahistorical America' (70). Roth's novel, especially in its ostentatiously perfunctory restoration of the status quo at its conclusion, foregrounds how America was and remains vulnerable to extremist internal threats. This reading is also germane to Auster's novel, which dramatises an unsuccessful attempt at escapism: the failure of Brill's invention of a fantasy alternative world as a means to blot out the horrors of the one he inhabits. It is thus naïve and reductive to read these novels merely as retreats from the horrendous realities of early twenty-first-century life.

In referring to the illusions of a 'mythic and ahistorical America', Shiffman's reading also implicitly raises another key issue that links these novels' exploration of trauma through the medium of counterfactual history, namely Dominick LaCapra's division of trauma into the concepts of absence and loss. Each of these novels emphasises the potentially devastating effect of historical rupture upon the individual and/or the family. In exploring this theme, these writers tread the indeterminate border between absence and loss. LaCapra discusses the two concepts most fully in *Writing History, Writing Trauma* (2001), and given their central importance to the novels explored in this chapter, it is worth considering his arguments in some detail.

LaCapra contends that in a great deal of earlier trauma theory critics tended to conflate absence with loss. 'By contrast to absence', which LaCapra defines as structural and causally intangible, loss is concrete and particular, 'situated on a historical level and is the consequence of particular events' (64). Absence is non-specific in origin and thus associated with a more universal or foundational sense of traumatic hurt resulting from a subject's 'inability to master his or her signification either from him- or herself or others. It is the absence of this mastery . . . that becomes the negative pivot of the subject's neurotic constitution' (Ball xxxii–xxxiii). Loss, on the other hand, is a response or reaction to specific historical events. Distinctions between the two can be extremely difficult, however, and LaCapra adds numerous caveats to his initial definitions. Though there are 'particular losses in all societies and cultures', for example, 'the ways in which they might be confronted differ from the responses more suited to absence' (64). Here, as elsewhere, although definitions are useful, the slightly opaque distinction between loss and absence poses certain difficulties. LaCapra admits that absence and loss should be regarded not as binary opposites, but rather 'problematic distinctions' (47) which 'interact in complex ways in any concrete situation' (48). The characteristics of these situations, LaCapra explains, may themselves help to blur or conflate the two conditions, 'particularly in post-traumatic situations or periods experienced in terms of crisis' (48). Despite this difficulty, LaCapra warns against the conflation of absence and loss, an action which has a number of potentially negative consequences, including inducing a situation for the traumatised subject whereby 'melancholic paralysis or manic agitation may set in' (64). There are occasional examples of this conflation and its attendant 'melancholic paralysis or manic agitation' in the novels in question. Philip, in *The Plot Against America*, as we shall see in more detail below, is regularly unable to distinguish between the specific effects of official anti-Semitic policy and more universally occurring intra-familial disruptions.[1] In other words, for this traumatised protagonist, if not for his author, distinctions between historical loss and generalised structural trauma become blurred.

Before examining LaCapra's concepts in relation to these novels it is necessary to probe more fully the distinctions that he constructs, and assess how successfully this taxonomy of loss and the more nebulous concept of absence survive under close examination. According to LaCapra, Fredric Jameson is one among a number of critics and theorists (also including Walter Benjamin) who turn absence to loss, fantasising in *The Political Unconscious*, a 'lost' total community in place of the non-specific or universal sense of absence (57, n.17). This implicitly raises certain questions about LaCapra's concept of absence: whether it is indeed universal and, moreover, whether it possesses universally consistent elements. Indeed, for absence not to constitute loss, all humans must experience it in more or less the same way and to the same degree. What experiential differences of absence suggest is that absence may be loss endured at a more foundational level. Its causes may be more difficult to determine than in the cases of overt historical losses, since they are generally chronic rather than occasional, and frequently concealed through complex ideological formations. They may nevertheless be detectable in societal structures. Indeed, we might take this a step further, asking whether LaCapra's concept of absence is itself ideological in its masking of causation and thus, at least potentially, of political and economic structures of oppression that produce trauma. If this is the case, then the prime danger regarding conceptualising trauma lies not so much in, as LaCapra maintains, converting loss into absence (or otherwise conflating the two), but in anaesthetising concrete historical loss by transforming it into something entirely illusory, that may be concealed underneath the ideological construction of an allegedly universal human experience labelled 'absence'. Reversing this transformation – and LaCapra indeed discusses in detail the concomitant dangers of transforming absence into loss – we risk constructing some tangible, albeit mythological, foundation for community out of something that does not actually exist. Since absence proves so difficult to define in terms of universal applicability, it is fundamentally weakened as a phenomenological concept. What this critique potentially exposes is that the notion of absence arises from a historical lacuna, or a proposition that trauma may somehow exist outside history. Thus LaCapra's critique of the conflation of absence and loss – in particular, those who convert loss into absence – may not actually concern the substitution of one type of trauma for another, but be more accurately perceived as converting a real type of historical trauma (loss) into an illusory structural one. Indeed, since LaCapra concedes that the conflation of absence and loss is most likely to occur in a post-traumatic condition, this conversion may be comprehended as one method through which victims begin to process their trauma, by de-actualising, universalising, and thus humanising and diminishing their condition's exceptional and overwhelming status. Similarly, what for LaCapra is the opposite case, the conversion of absence into loss, may in fact be the transformation of one type of more recondite and elusive (and maybe even illusory) loss into one which becomes recuperable through the addition of identifiable causes (even if these are actually spurious). The result, as in LaCapra's formulation, may be scapegoating, whereby a section of society is erroneously held responsible for a mythical loss. The cause, however, is subtly different: not absence being converted into loss, but merely a loss with obscure and overdetermined causes that is converted into a concrete and simplified set of phenomena. Notably in this respect, LaCapra's discussion of 'structural trauma' (as opposed to 'historical trauma'), which is closely related to but not precisely the same as the idea of absence, is so vaguely defined that it fails to designate a phenomenon that may be described as traumatic in any recognised sense.

To be fair to LaCapra, he is more cautious in asserting the 'problematic distinction' between absence and loss than critics who have subsequently drawn upon his ideas, and who have tended to understand the terms precisely as binary opposites. Indeed, LaCapra himself expresses certain doubts about the universality of absence, asking, 'Do all cultures and societies have some modality or intimation of absence at the origin . . .? Or is this kind of absence limited to . . . certain cultures or societies in a manner that is nonetheless transhistorical' (48, n.7). Similarly, LaCapra admits that when 'absence itself is narrativized' it is extremely difficult not to begin talking of losses, suggesting that such narratives, 'at least in conventional forms, must be reductive, based on misrecognition, and even close to myth' (49). Ultimately, LaCapra is cautious about classifying phenomena as either absence or loss (for example, the child's recognition of separation from the mother [50, n. 10]) and, perhaps overly so, of providing any convincing examples of absence.

Notwithstanding these reservations, absence and loss nevertheless provide a mutually illuminating framework for exploring the three novels. A key theme uniting these works is the infringement or incursion of large-scale historical events (some of which happened in our world, and some of which are part of the counterfactual dimension) into the personal. Part of the purpose of this chapter is to explore how these writers depict this clash of the global-political (or LaCapra's 'historical traumas') and the personal (which commonly include LaCapra's 'structural traumas') in ways that examine, challenge, or collapse the 'problematic distinction' between absence and loss. Given the way in which this formulation – the potentially violent irruption of the global-political into the personal-familial – echoes the anxieties of post-9/11 America, this investigation pays attention to the political and cultural context from which these texts emerged.

It is important also to take specific account of the employment of the alternative history form in these works and recognise that this achieves considerably more than mere retreat from the vicissitudes of early twenty-first-century life. Instead, the key point here is to consider these alternative histories as a form of neo-naturalist experiment, constructed by these authors as a means to distance their characters from the world we recognise. This enables an analysis of the effects – both global and local – of a specific alternative or imagined event. In other words, just as naturalist writers from the late nineteenth and mid-twentieth century constructed scenarios and characters and (purported to) let them play out as they will, so Auster, Chabon, and especially Roth apply variations to history and existing historical traumas as we recognise them (meaning that our history may be regarded as a kind of control experiment). These counterfactual narratives are thereby used, precisely, as a means of isolating ways in which traumas, both structural and historical, are experienced by individuals and families. The alternative history approach and neo-naturalist form adopted in these novels can be seen to complement one another aesthetically. One typical attribute of the alternative history narrative noted by Karen Hellekson is a reliance on a surplus of descriptive detail – much like Barthes's 'reality effect' – in order to construct convincing alternative scenarios for the reader (35). This excess of realistic detail overcomes readers' resistance to a history different to the one in their world and also questions the very assumptions that readers have adopted in constructing a notion of real history. This is akin to the function of Linda Hutcheon's 'historiographical metafiction', and also closely allied to the neo-naturalist project adopted by these writers, since it helps to paint a wholly realised world in which the characters can be placed for the experiment to play out. We see the best examples of this surplus of detail in *The Yiddish Policemen's Union*. As well as minutely detailed scene-setting descriptions, these include broader verisimilar elements of the alternate world Chabon builds, such as 'the dropping of the atomic bomb on Berlin in 1946' (136), the marriage of President John F. Kennedy to Marilyn Monroe following the death of Jackie Kennedy in Dallas in 1963, and the Cuban War, 'notorious for its futility, brutality, and waste' (341) that stands in for our world's Vietnam. This detail constructs a rich portrait of an illusory world, as Michiko Kakutani notes: 'Chabon has so thoroughly conjured the fictional world of Sitka – its history, culture, geography, its incestuous and byzantine political and sectarian divisions – that the reader comes to take its existence for granted' ('Looking for a Home'). This effect in part accrues through a sense of the uncanny, as events are at once familiar and alien. Although this does not figure in producing trauma in the characters, unlike the ontological unease discussed in relation to *House of Leaves* in Chapter 2, the uncanny nevertheless constructs discomfort in certain characters, to the extent that they feel they are not properly in the world. One character in Chabon's novel thus has '[t]he face of a man who feels he was born into the wrong world. A mistake has been made; he is not where he belongs' (282). As Anna Richardson suggests, '[t]he narrative is permeated by a sense of unease and foreboding and by the very impossibility of its own existence (for, in a world where most of the characters in the narrative would never have been born, the idea of their murder becomes an impossibility)' (166). In investigating the traumas suffered by these characters in their 'wrong' worlds, the following chapter thus focuses on the purposes of the authors' neo-naturalist counterfactual experiments and the formal devices through which they are achieved.

'THE WEIRD WORLD ROLLS ON': PAUL AUSTER'S *Man in the Dark*

As with the other novels considered in this chapter, *Man in the Dark* concerns the traumatic impact of global political events upon a family, here consisting of August Brill, an elderly retired book critic, his daughter Miriam, also a writer, and her daughter Katya, a film student. Katya's former boyfriend, Titus, has recently been brutally beheaded while working for American contractors in Iraq, and August, Miriam and Katya are attempting to deal with the traumatic symptoms of having witnessed graphic footage of his final moments. Miriam is also suffering the effects of an acrimonious divorce, while August is recuperating from a car accident that has left him nearly immobile in bed and from persistent feelings of guilt related to his treatment of his now-dead wife, Sonia. Of the three novels, Auster's is the one most overtly focused on trauma, with the embedded counterfactual history explicitly framed as a means for August to address – or more accurately to avoid – various traumatic memories. The first half of the novel thus comprises August's imagined alternative history scenario concerning a character named Owen Brick, who awakens in an America where a number of states have seceded from the Union after the contested presidential victory of George W. Bush in 2000. Although in this imagined America the events of 9/11, and subsequent excursions into Afghanistan and Iraq, have not occurred, it is embroiled in a second civil war, in which Brick finds himself an unwilling participant. The complex narrative structure adopted by Auster is compounded when the Brill and Brick layers begin to bleed into each other. Brick discovers that his assigned mission is to return to his world (a diegetic level more or less equivalent with our own) and assassinate the 'author' of the civil war, Brill, in order to end the war, which in effect amounts to Brill seeking 'ever more artful and devious ways to kill [him]self' (102). In combining a type of inscribed narration – Brill takes decisions about the Brick narrative as it is communicated to us – with counterfactual history, Auster produces a challenging narrative structure through which the characters' numerous experiences of trauma are explored. And yet there are ways in which this traumatic metafiction is formally both the most and least conventional of the three books discussed in this chapter. In terms of the former Auster may be accused of drawing upon familiar trauma aesthetics in employing repetition and procrastination (in the continual skirting around descriptions of Titus's fate), decentring of subjectivity (in the numerous overlaps between Brill and Brick), and shifts in tense (the final graphic description of Titus's beheading is related in abrupt present tense). On the other hand, the unconventionally hybridised form of alternative history, metafictionally framed within layers of discourse and inscribed by Brill, suggests a more innovative set of practices. The story of Titus's death (and its witnessing by August and Katya) is, as convention tends to dictate, broached relatively cautiously to begin with. There are however, enough knowing asides and brute facts supplied by Brill even at the outset to suggest an attempt to avoid formulaic treatment of trauma.

While the key focus of *Man in the Dark* is the potentially traumatising effect of global events upon the individual and family, Brill's response is to search desperately for distractions from this assault. August is candid about the purpose of his fiction-making from the beginning, admitting that the stories he invents, including the Owen Brick narrative, 'might not add up to much, but as long as I'm inside them, they prevent me from thinking about the things I would prefer to forget' (2). While August's tales indeed act as an avoidance tactic, however, as John Brenkman notes, 'the very movement of his stories inevitably unearths, dredges up, and discloses bits and pieces of his life and memories.' Although Brill's stories aim towards burial of his traumatic memories, the reader witnesses the return of the repressed, as key themes reflecting August's traumas – infidelity and violence – continually reoccur and overlap. Shared characteristics of the tales that Brill relates – to himself, to the reader, and to Katya – reveal much about the nature of the traumas explored in this novel. A number of the stories culminate in devastating violence, often involving untimely death, and more often than not are united by the theme of the traumatic effect of geopolitics on the individual. Brill recalls, for example, his brother-in-law Gil, who died prematurely, having witnessed appalling scenes in a Newark race riot (79–82), and this echoes Gil's father's premature death (83) and anticipates that of Gil's wife (and Brill's sister), Betty (87). Even these are apparently screen memories, warding off recall of Sonia's early death from cancer (101). These morbid tales underline the failure of Brill's strategy to ward off traumatic memories, since the violence of the world nevertheless intrudes into his personal experience.

This intrusion is particularly marked at the point of Brick's violent death within Brill's narrative. Brill here reaches an impasse and acknowledges the failure of his attempt to bury memories of Titus. Owen Brick, by this point, is involved in a story of violence, war, infidelity and betrayal – again reflecting Brill's traumatic memories – while the carnage of the civil war imagined by Brill has begun to rival even the violence of our world. It is therefore not entirely shocking that Brill abruptly abandons his counter-factual narrative. This is again marked by episodes of extreme violence, voiced by a suddenly misanthropic Brill, who appears now resigned to confront the violence of Titus's death. 'My subject tonight is war, and now that war has entered this house, I feel I would be insulting Titus and Katya if I softened the blow,' he declaims, '[t]his is the heart of it, the black center of the dead of night' (118). Brill finally wearies of distraction tactics, recognising this as the return of material inadequately stifled by the stories he was inventing: '[w]ar stories. Let your guard down for a moment, and they come rushing in on you, one by one by one' (119). Following Brick's demise, as if to prove Brill's point, we encounter another series of violent stories: the brutal murder of a female concentration camp captive (121), a peculiar tale of a young girl saved from the concentration camps by a single 'humane' Nazi (123–5), and the violent defenestration of a French secret service agent, 'one of the last casualties of the Cold War' (128). Besides the violence which underscores at least two of these stories, the theme uniting them with the murder of Titus – to recall, the story in his own life that August has been attempting to suppress – is again the traumatising effect of geopolitics on the individual. These are clearly losses rather than absences, in LaCapra's terms, but they are juxtaposed in the latter half of the novel with less extraordinary but perhaps more insidious incidents of trauma, mainly concerning the results of August's infidelities. The family traumas that have more directly affected August – many of which he is at least partially responsible for, such as his treatment of Sonia – are less clearly historical, sometimes evincing elements of LaCapra's structural trauma. More accurately, they are still losses rather than absences (albeit chronic rather than historical or punctual in form), but August attempts to recuperate them as absence, as suggested by his repeated quotation of Rose Hawthorne's 'the weird world rolls on', or in his feebly defeatist response to his granddaughter's question of why life is so horrible: '[b]ecause it is, that's all. It just is' (163).

Brill's perpetrator-sufferer status is significant in numerous ways. It accounts, for example, for his attempts to convert loss to absence, since blame is much harder to apportion in the latter case. Secondly, as with cases cited in the previous chapter, it is a contributory factor in his lack of amnesia. Rather than forgetting and unconscious acting out, as in the case of *Nachträglichkeit*, it is the insistence of conscious recall that troubles him. This perpetrator status is confirmed when Brill narrates his infidelities regarding Sonia, and also with regard to Titus, about whom Brill feels guilty for failing to talk him out of going to Iraq. The constantly repeated themes of violence and infidelity in the stories he tells thus function as key indicators of his perpetrator trauma. Even in the Owen Brick story, which is supposed to act as a shield against memories of infidelity and violence, Owen first has extra-marital sex (115–16) and then violently perishes in a hail of bullets (118), in a graphic display of August overcompensating for his own infidelities. Themes of infidelity and violence begin to dominate the stories which Brill had been relating ostensibly as a distraction from feelings of guilt attached to these subjects. This process is a clear indication that Brill's perpetrator guilt is primarily manifested through a refusal of traumatic material to disperse from conscious memory.

August's perpetrator guilt is also a key to the precise form of the Owen Brick story. The Brick narrative is precisely neo-naturalist in its experimental counterfactual form, and this has significant implications for a character such as August, who is attempting to diminish feelings of guilt. The comparative lack of agency exercised by writers of naturalism – at least according to manifestos dating back as far as Zola's 'The Experimental Novel' – is echoed in the way August constructs the basic scenario of Brick's story but purports not to shape its denouement. August is thus able to eschew much of the responsibility that he has come to fear, through constructing a bare framework and then ostensibly allowing the narrative to play out. In the novel's characteristically solipsistic first paragraph, August describes himself in bed, 'turning the world around' (1), as if he exerts control over his fictional scenario. Yet he subsequently repudiates this power, later describing returning to his story to 'discover' (44) what happens to Brick. When this narrative arrives at an impasse August's fear of agency arises again: 'I'm treading water because I can see the story turning in any one of several directions, and I still haven't decided which path to take' (88). August's reluctance to be accountable for Brick's story is thus embedded in the form of narrative that Auster presents. Notably, Brick's story is related in the present tense, which evokes not only a précis of a fuller narrative, but also inevitably conveys the impression that the plot is being constructed (or, according to August's assertions, 'allowed to play out') as we read it. In effect, of course, this is precisely the case, thus we encounter alternative history, with all its shared naturalist theoretical grounding, as inscribed narration. This hybrid and strikingly aleatory exercise in serious play thus dramatises the contingencies in writing about the relationship between history and trauma.

The form adopted in August's construction of Brick's alternative world illuminates conflicting impulses that result from his traumatic experiences, as both perpetrator and victim. On the one hand, his invention of another world allows him a measure of control, as opposed to the real world which, as the repeated refrain in the novel suggests, 'rolls on' in dangerously unpredictable ways. On the other hand, after creating Brick's world, August is reluctant to assume agency over it, understandably given the disastrous consequences of decisions taken in his real life. August's solution is thus doubly inflected – inventing a world he can control and then refusing that control – the contradictions an indication of his conflicted victim-perpetrator status. This raises the familiar Auster trope of chance, implicitly questioning how many of the outcomes in this world – such as Titus's death – are the result of Brill's actions, and therefore the extent to which he is culpable. The complex relationship between chance and agency is a familiar theme in literary naturalism, where diminished free will renders questions of responsibility debatable. The neo-naturalist form of August's narrative enables him to begin to examine his own culpability and address feelings of guilt arising from his traumatised perpetrator status. This strategy appears not entirely unsuccessful; there are signs that August begins to recognise, address and overcome feelings of shame. He invents a world which ostensibly is better because it lacks the attacks of 11 September 2001 and the subsequent Afghanistan and Iraq wars, but in the substituted civil war it arguably turns even worse for Brill and America. In this sense, we might ask whether August is actually as disingenuous as many other naturalist writers, in fact shaping his narrative in this way precisely to absolve himself from blame, to show that despite his failings and resultant feelings of guilt in the real world, it is better than certain imaginable alternatives. Thus while Auster's novel is not itself a retreat from the real world, it depicts the attempt, and the inherent dangers, of just such a retreat.

'STRANGE TIMES TO BE A JEW': MICHAEL CHABON'S
The Yiddish Policemen's Union

Michael Chabon, too, has been accused of retreat, Alan Berger finding in his work a tendency to employ escapism in relation to the Holocaust (81). The richly textured alternative history in *The*

Yiddish Policemen's Union, however, is not an escape, but functions both to examine the traumatic impact of global events on individuals and families, and as another neo-naturalist experiment, this time concerning the shades of fundamentalism that characterise America's relationship with the Middle East. LaCapra's 'problematic distinction' between absence and loss is again significant in this respect. As we shall see, the extremist Jews in this novel are motivated to carry out terrorist acts through an ideology which has conflated absence and loss. In terms of family trauma, unlike the families in the other two novels in this chapter, the central family in Chabon's novel is already broken at its outset. The protagonist, Meyer Landsman, a dissolute police detective, recently split with his wife, Bina, following their decision to abort a foetus incorrectly diagnosed as suffering from irregularities. Both Landsman and his aborted son, whom they had named Django, come to represent the homeless condition of the Jews in the book, in which the state of Israel is stillborn.

For in the alternative scenario presented in *The Yiddish Policemen's Union*, attempts in 1948 to establish the state of Israel fail. The Jews are granted temporary refuge in the Sitka district of Alaska, and the novel is set sixty years later, as this interim sanctuary is about to end, and the resident Jews face an uncertain future. Chabon blends the counterfactual with an adept pastiche of hard-boiled crime fiction, as Landsman seeks to discover the murderer of a fellow inmate of the seedy Hotel Zamenhof. The complex investigation takes Landsman to the heart of a conspiracy to re-establish a Jewish state in the Middle East. To make matters more uncomfortable, Landsman is forced to follow this investigation under the supervision of his ex-wife, newly appointed as his supervisor. The novel also follows their gradual recovery from trauma and tentative reconciliation.

The Yiddish Policemen's Union is clearly a trauma text, with its broad background of the Holocaust and massive displacement of refugees, and, on a smaller scale, the familial and professional traumas of Landsman. Personal trauma symptoms manifest in a comparatively conventional way. Isidor Landsman, Meyer's father, is a Holocaust survivor who is resultantly withdrawn, 'oblivious to the raucous frontier energy of downtown Sitka' (30). Meyer

Landsman is thus linked to the Holocaust, and 'suffers the weight of the Shoah and the knowledge of near-extinction' (Dubrow 146). Conforming to Marianne Hirsch's observation of traumatised 'postmemory' in children of Holocaust survivors, and following his father's suicide when Meyer was a child, Landsman develops into a despondent and morose boy: 'He wet the bed, got fat, stopped talking. His mother put him in therapy with a remarkably gentle and ineffectual doctor named Melamed' (34). Landsman's inherited postmemory triggers acting out and repetition – for example, when he uses Nembutal for sleep (158) where once his father had used it for suicide (154). The traumatic symptoms arising from Landsman's personal traumas – most notably the violent death of his sister and guilt over Django's abortion – are similarly conventional, comprising flashbacks and repeated tendencies to act out.

More significantly, the traumas originating in Landsman's connections to the Holocaust, via his father, firmly link his history to that of the wider Jewish community in the novel. The decision to abort Django echoes other themes in the book, including the transgenerational trauma Landsman experiences from his father's death, since one factor in the abortion may be Landsman's reluctance to perpetuate his own genes and, given the Jews' precarious existence in Alaska, to pass on traumatic experiences to yet another generation. In this sense, Landsman is linked to those characters in the book identified by Anna Richardson who, because of its being an alternative world, find it difficult or impossible 'to cope with the fact of their own existence' (166). The symbolic link between the abortion of Django and the failed state – the stillborn child – of Israel, is thus merely one of a number of similar links between the fate of Landsman and that of the Sitka Jews. This, in turn, underlines links between individual and collective trauma that characterise all the novels discussed in this chapter and their overarching theme of the traumatic interdependence of world events and the family/individual. Landsman's status as a policeman, rather than a private investigator, is significant in this respect. A number of critics and reviewers mention this attribute of Chabon's central character but fail to explore it further. The point may be that in contrast to Chandler's PI Marlowe and other independent investigators, Landsman, as a cop, is a slightly more establishment figure.

Although he is disrespectful and insubordinate, Landsman's status as a police detective positions him as an official part of the community, thus reinforcing his representative role. Clearly, this is an extended analogy that Chabon aims to pursue. Landsman is also linked to the fate of the Jews when he is delivered of an eviction notice from his hotel, just as the Jews' tenuous existence in Sitka has become more uncertain, and '[n]obody's status is clear' (19). And like Landsman, as discussed above, the uncertainty hanging over the Jews diminishes their agency, a process which is one catalyst for the plot to regain Israel. These are, as the repeated mantra goes, 'strange times to be a Jew' (3), an uncertain period of extended and collective trauma. The Jews' condition in this book indeed echoes that of oppressed communities discussed by a number of contemporary postcolonial trauma theorists. These theorists have noted firstly the insidious rather than sudden character of this type of trauma, which can be produced by 'infrastructural systems such as apartheid . . . long-term endurance of racial segregation or long-term exposure to the threat of abuse' (Baxter 20). Secondly, non-western experiences of trauma have a marked propensity for transcending individual experience and therefore being more convincingly defined as collective (see Craps and Buelens 4). That these modes of trauma clearly characterise the Jews' experience in *The Yiddish Policemen's Union* underlines the extent to which Chabon has constructed a convincing echo of our own world. With the euphemistic 'upcoming Reversion' (7) for the Jews of Alaska comes a collective unease; as Landsman notes early on, '[e]verybody has a funny feeling these days' (2). This is underlined by the range of bizarre visions that members of the community have allegedly witnessed: an aurora borealis with 'the outlines of a human face, with beard and sidelocks', and a talking chicken that announces, 'in Aramaic, the imminent advent of Messiah' (13). Falling back on such superstitions only emphasises the broad and traumatic experience of helplessness: 'This half-island they have come to love as home is being taken from them. They are like goldfish in a bag, about to be dumped back into the big black lake of Diaspora' (202).

As with *Man in the Dark* and again in common with many previous works of naturalism, a central theme in *The Yiddish Policemen's*

Union is agency, in the case of this novel especially bound up with issues of gender. The abortion of Django is particularly significant in this respect. Late in the novel, Bina is taken aback when Landsman suggests that he made her abort the baby, dismissively insisting instead that it was her decision: 'The day you *ever* have that much control over my behavior, it will be because somebody's asking you, should she get the pine box or a plain white shroud?' (409). Bina also unconsciously digs her nails into Landsman's hand at this point. On the one hand, this intimate physical contact helps to assuage some of Landman's feelings of guilt, but it could also be interpreted as a (mild) attack and, in combination with Bina's utterance, questioning Landsman's agency and thus, in conventional terms, his masculinity. This reinforces a general challenge to the gender norms of hard-boiled detective fiction throughout the novel, where women including Bina and Landsman's sister Naomi are notably stronger, more assertive, and more capable than Landsman. By contrast, he is impotent (including sexually) or inadequate to the tasks of his job. Landsman's phobia of 'lightless or confined spaces' (10), for example, raises the question of just how hard-boiled he really is, and this is reinforced by his strong moral sense (not unlike Philip Marlowe's) and his propensity to depression and – albeit sometimes alcohol-fuelled – tears. Every death affects Landsman and, in contrast to the supremely capable Bina, he is vacillating and often wrongheaded. During the course of the novel, Landsman is first stripped of his badge and his gun, following which he continues an unauthorised pursuit of his investigation. This ends disastrously, as he is taken captive, stripped of his clothes and thus any remaining dignity. Landsman manages to escape, naked in a freezing environment, and is only saved through the serendipitous intervention of an old police associate, Willie Dick, whose ludicrously phallic name only serves to underline Landsman's comparative lack of agency (272–5). Although these scenes serve comic effect, they also underline the way in which Landsman's traumas, in particular the abortion of Django and subsequent breakup of his marriage, have undermined his agency, his ability to function, not least since he ends this episode himself naked and helpless as a newborn baby.

If Chabon's novel is, thematically, a relatively conventional

trauma text, its unorthodox form – a hybrid of the naturalist counterfactual and the detective noir – produces more unusual results,
not least in terms of its politics. An example of this unconventional
form serves to illustrate subtler effects than may have been previously appreciated, particularly in terms of the novel's overriding
determinism. Especially striking in this respect is the way in which
Chabon employs flashbacks. The principal narrating voice in the
novel is articulated in a continuous present tense, granting the
action a compelling immediacy, if not the same level of contin-
gency as in Brill's narrative in *Man in the Dark*. When a character
is called upon to spill their story in order to provide information
for Landsman's investigation, however, Chabon tends to end a
chapter as they begin narrating. The subsequent chapter – that
character's backstory – switches to a past-tense heterodiegetic
voice. Employing this, rather than the homodiegetic voice of the
actual character, underlines the inescapable nature of the historical
micro-narratives, almost all of which are traumatic to some degree.
This is similar in effect to Anne Whitehead's interpretation of the
way in which some trauma texts employ intertextuality in order to
represent entrapment in patterns of repetitive behaviour (85). The
authoritative past tense here similarly serves to present characters
as prey to determined and uncontrollable fates.

In terms of the political positions constructed through Chabon's
unusual form, Sarah Philips Casteel notes the sense of disorientation in the Jews' life in Sitka, the 'failed utopia that besets them',
as producing a troubling 'territorializing project' that seeks to
displace, in their turn, first the Tlingit Indians and second the
Palestinians, in their bid to (re)create Israel (797). As a response to
trauma – here the collective trauma of displacement and chronic
uncertainty – this position tellingly calls forth LaCapra's notions of
absence and loss. 'When absence is converted into loss,' LaCapra
maintains, 'one increases the likelihood of misplaced nostalgia or
utopian politics in quest of a new totality or fully unified community' (46). If the Sitka Jews hold that there is a failed utopia
– an ideal which parallels Israel in our world – in the world of
The Yiddish Policemen's Union the Holy Land remains, 'remote or
unattainable . . . a wretched place ruled by men united only in their
resolve to keep out all but a worn fistful of small-change Jews' (17).

This collective sense of failed utopia is a crucial part of the Sitka Jews' conversion of absence into loss, in a way, moreover, that motivates a forceful bid for new territory. This process is perverted into a desire to usurp the Tlingit from their lands, as if Chabon's characters 'have *not* learned the lesson of diaspora' (Casteel 797). And if securing a permanent home in Alaska is impossible, the collective trauma of being 'tossed out of the joint . . . with savage finality in 1948' (17) prompts extreme measures to try to re-establish a Jewish homeland in the Middle East.

Again, the way in which the traumatic experiences of Landsman and the Sitka Jews are repeatedly connected is significant and, to the extent that this risks conflating absence and loss, troubling. Landsman, as we have seen, has suffered numerous clear and identifiable traumatic losses. Facing imminent eviction from the Hotel Zamenhof, Landsman's fate again mirrors that of the wider Jewish community, which is due, in the novel's euphemistic language of American bureaucracy, to 'revert' and be forced to quit Alaska. While Landsman's traumas are concrete in origin, and thus clearly characterised as instances of loss, the trauma of the Jews – as is generally the case with the more contested and diffuse concept of collective trauma – is more elusive in origin. The leaders of the Sitka Jewish community may be seen as having conflated structural and historical trauma – or, more precisely, as converting absence into loss – and it is this conflation that produces the sense of 'failed utopia', the consequential land grabs and, ultimately, acts of terror. While the Jews have collectively suffered huge losses – the Holocaust occurs in the world of this novel too – there is also an ideological shift from absence to loss, a process LaCapra notes as fundamental in the production of founding myths. As the remainder of this section suggests, the Hasidic sect's plot to bomb the mosque in Jerusalem allows Chabon to illustrate the dangers of using such an ideological basis of absence-as-loss as a founding myth.

Whereas in *Man in the Dark* there are various polemical asides, such as Titus describing Iraq as a 'phony, trumped-up war, the worst political mistake in American history' (172), in Chabon's novel, political critique is embedded in the denouement of the alternative history scenario. The absence of Israel in this novel encourages the reader to construct analogies with contemporary American–Middle East politics and the emergence of various forms of fundamentalism. There is a noticeable merging of our world and that of the novel, for example, in Landsman's speculation that the US government's motives in helping the Alaskan Jews 're-establish' Israel are 'all really about oil . . . securing their supply of the stuff once and for all' (322). The most dramatic and significant of these likenesses occurs near the novel's end, in the Sitka Jews' terrorist attack on the Qubbat As-Sakhrah in Jerusalem, which is loosely analogous to the real world's 9/11. The mosque is bombed to destruction, resulting in an image 'that will soon be splashed across the front page of every newspaper in the world. All over town, pious hands will clip it and tape it to their front doors and windows. They will frame it and hang it behind the counters of their shops' (358). The image is thus commemorated and commodified in similar ways to images of the attacks on the World Trade Center, and consumed through the same media, as Landsman witnesses the destruction through a repeated 'image on a television screen' (359). Similar narratives are constructed around the attack to those that resulted from 9/11, including conspiracy theories regarding US involvement (363), or speculation that it is due to fighting between various Muslim factions. Tellingly, these are used as an excuse for aggressive intervention by US administration: '[t]he president was on, saying they might have to go in. Saying it's a holy city to everyone' (370). In terms of the various shades of fundamentalism that have also affected our world, the appropriately named Christian fundamentalist Cashdollar, who is one of the key architects behind the attack, describes Islam as 'a venerable religion', but one which is 'completely mistaken on a fundamental level' (365). The use of the word 'fundamental' is no accident, as Cashdollar's subsequent suggestion that 'the end times are coming' confirms: 'I for one very much look forward to seeing them come. But for that to happen, Jerusalem and the Holy Land have to belong to the Jews again. That's what it says in the Book. Sadly, there is no way to do that without some bloodshed, unfortunately . . . That's just what is written' (366). The reliance on fundamentalist interpretation of the Bible and the clumsy redundancy in the 'Sadly . . . unfortunately' sentence perhaps allude to the absolutist and stilted rhetoric of Bush's 'crusade' speeches about the Middle East, and the 'War on Terror'.

Certainly, the bombing of the Qubbat As-Sakhrah in *The Yiddish Policemen's Union* may be convincingly read as a thinly veiled attack on the contemporary American regime, not least since the whole scheme is ultimately attributed to 'the divinely inspired mission of the president of America' (339). But Chabon's scope is wider, as he uses the counterfactual mode as a means to draw parallels between and demonstrate the evils of all shades of fundamentalism, whether in our world or the alternative world of his novel. As this novel suggests, fundamentalism works partly through the ideological conversion of diffuse structural trauma (or absence) to a politically charged sense of historical loss. This mirroring of Jewish terrorism in the counterfactual world with Islamic terrorism in ours also illustrates the dangers of absence converted to loss as a founding myth, specifically in terms of a belief in entitlement to land.[2]

Another rich consequence of Chabon's employment of the counterfactual form is the way in which arbitrary distinctions between forms of violence are thrown into sharp relief. Varying definitions of 'terrorism' that Chabon's strategy highlights recall Judith Butler's position in *Precarious Life*, wherein she notes that the Geneva Convention (notwithstanding that it was, in any case, flouted by the Bush administration) is actually complicit in legitimising violence, in that it allows for 'a distinction between legal and illegal combatants' (87). This relativism posing as absolutism is located in the idea that, '[l]egitimate violence is waged by recognizable states or "countries," as Rumsfeld puts it, and illegitimate violence is precisely that which is committed by those who are landless, stateless, or whose states are deemed not worth recognizing by those who are already recognized' (87). Authorities deemed illegitimate by powerful states thus wage 'terrorism', even though the violence is indistinguishable in nature to that waged by, for example, the USA and Israel. The world of *The Yiddish Policemen's Union*, through its dispossession of the Jews, demonstrates the problematic nature of such distinctions.

'IT'S SO HEARTBREAKING, VIOLENCE, WHEN IT'S IN A
HOUSE': PHILIP ROTH'S *The Plot Against America*

Philip Roth's *The Plot Against America* posits an America where
anti-Semitic aviator Charles Lindbergh is nominated for the
Republican ticket in the 1940 presidential election, in which he
defeats the incumbent Roosevelt on a platform of non-intervention
in the European war. Lindbergh signs a non-aggression pact with
the Nazis, and embarks on a number of domestic policies with the
apparent aim of discriminating against and undermining America's
Jewish communities. In October 1942, Lindbergh disappears while
on a flight. Roosevelt is re-elected as president, America enters the
war, and history resumes a course similar to (if a little behind) that
of our world. Formally, the book is not only a counterfactual, but
also plays with the novel and autobiographical forms, being related
by an older narrator, named Philip Roth, looking back on his family's experiences in Jewish Newark of the Lindbergh administration while he was a child.[3]

Roth chooses a highly innovative form for this book, which relates
in revealing ways to other works within his oeuvre. Roth has, of
course, toyed with merging the forms of fiction and autobiography
before. For instance, *The Facts* (1988), despite its title, is an artfully
constructed hybrid which walks the tightrope between fiction and
autobiography with the same deftness as *The Plot Against America*.
Indeed, a playful relationship between the two texts is constructed
from the beginning of the later book. Whereas the narrative of *The
Facts* begins (following the Prologue) with a description of a relatively secure childhood menaced only by vague threats 'from the
Germans and the Japanese' abroad and from 'gentile America' at
home (20), the opening of *The Plot Against America* presents these
threats as real: '[f]ear presides over these memories, a perpetual
fear. Of course no childhood is without its terrors, yet I wonder if
I would have been a less frightened boy if Lindbergh hadn't been
president or if I hadn't been the offspring of Jews' (1). This not
only plays intertextually off the earlier work but also immediately
introduces Roth's hybrid form, in that although the work purports
to be an autobiographical memoir, its second sentence refers to the
fictional presidency of Charles Lindbergh. As Matthew Schweber

suggests, contrasted with *The Facts*, *The Plot Against America* 'projects a mirror image of the author and his childhood' (130). Further implications of Roth's combining the hybrid fiction-autobiography mode with the counterfactual are explored later in the chapter. Suffice to say for now that the application of the alternative history to real people close to its author adds considerable depth to this novel's neo-naturalist experiments into the effects of trauma on the individual and the family.

A particular scene concerning the departure of the Roths' neighbours – the widowed Selma Wishnow and her son, Seldon, whom Philip has reluctantly befriended – encapsulates the way in which Philip's status as both victim and perpetrator complicates his trauma to the extent that he grievously conflates absence and loss. Through an intervention with his Aunt Evelyn, who has assumed an administrative role in Lindbergh's government, Philip has engineered the relocation of the Wishnows to Kentucky, as part of Lindbergh's Homestead 42 program aimed at dispersing Jewish communities. As they depart, Philip is surprised at being unable to stop crying, as he recalls an incident that occurred when he was six years old. At this time, predating Lindbergh's presidency, Mrs Wishnow was 'just another watchful member of the local matriarchy whose overriding task was to establish a domestic way of life for the next generation' (256–7). If this suggests stereotypical gender norms, we soon witness how the precipitous events overturn them, but in a violently intrusive, rather than a progressive way.

Philip remembers an incident in the Wishnows' apartment when he inadvertently becomes locked in their bathroom. (In fact, the door was unlocked, which mirrors the narrator's ambivalence about the true extent of danger the American Jews are in from the Lindbergh administration, and that the narrative never absolutely establishes whether Philip's father is overreacting.) Mrs Wishnow talks through the bathroom door to Philip in order to calm him down, just as Philip's mother later talks Seldon through the real trauma of his mother's murder in Kentucky over the telephone in an episode which, like this one, adroitly juxtaposes terror and comedy. As well as embodying the theme of entrapment followed by release that structures the entire narrative, this episode also comprises a series of mishaps that befall Philip, mirroring the numerous disasters that dog the adults throughout. And just as the narrative as a whole is characterised by evasiveness and reluctant confession, so the series of events that beset Philip in the bathroom prompt him to tell a number of lies. Initially, Philip is unable to work out how to unlock the bathroom door, despite instruction. Mrs Wishnow encourages him to remain calm and to take a glass of water, but he cannot do this, as the glass he finds is dirty (he lies about this). Philip is then advised to open a window for air, but is again unable to do so, instead accidentally drenching himself in the shower. He finally fails to open the towel closet to dry himself off (he lies about this too). Philip is finally released when it emerges that the door was not actually locked.

The sheer number of lies Philip finds himself telling in this episode suggests that the recollection may have been subconsciously prompted by the more important lie that Philip told to his Aunt Evelyn in order to have the Wishnows banished from Newark. Thus the bathroom scene is emblematic of Philip's guilt. He continually portrays himself as entrapped, and able to follow no alternative course of action. This suggests an attempt to expiate shame over the Wishnows' fate, something akin to a Freudian screen memory, albeit more consciously constructed. That Philip's entrapment turns out to be illusory suggests that the continual denials of agency in this scene (and, by implication, elsewhere in the narrative), are similarly deceptive. The unspoken implication of this scene is that in fact Philip does exercise agency in his cruel and ultimately deadly treatment of the Wishnows, and it is this perpetrator trauma that does much to shape the book's narrative. This guilt is confirmed only much later in the novel, when Philip steels himself enough to admit how patient, strong, and like his own mother Mrs Wishnow was, '[a]nd now she was inside a casket, and I was the one who had put her there . . . I did it. That was all I could think then and all I can think now. I did this to Seldon and I did this to her' (336). The denial of agency by Brill in *Man in the Dark* and Philip here enables us to draw a useful distinction between the traumatic experiences of perpetrators and victims. Marilyn Bowman and Rachel Yehuda note that a feeling of maintained agency is important as a resistor to trauma, since 'PTSD is often correlated with the belief that control is exercised by external forces' (23). While this is true for unequivocal victims, it would appear that quite the opposite is the case for perpetrators, who do everything possible to deny responsibility for events. This in turn helps to explain the neo-naturalist form of Brill's and Philip's narratives, wherein the protagonists are largely denied free will.[4]

It would, of course, be unfair to consider eight-year-old Philip entirely a perpetrator, or expect him to foresee the disastrous consequences of his actions regarding the Wishnows. Indeed, this incident is another example of characters being overtaken and overwhelmed by broader political events. For much of *The Plot Against America* the intrusion of the outside world is characterised as an assault on the Roths' previously cherished status as assimilated Americans. Thus Lindbergh's nomination is first reported in the novel as a potential attack on Philip's Americanness, 'that huge endowment of personal security that [he] had taken for granted as an American child of American parents in an American school in an American city in an America at peace with the world' (7), and during the early days of Lindbergh's presidency Philip notes 'the incredible speed with which our status as Americans appeared to be altering' (56). On the supposedly reassuring but ultimately soured trip to Washington – the capital city setting clearly intended to underline the challenge to the Roths' and other Jews' sense of belonging in America – Herman Roth is insulted as a 'loudmouth Jew' (65). Looking back at the statue of Lincoln, Philip consequently feels that it becomes 'impossible any longer to feel the raptures of patriotism turning me inside out' (66). The language here is revealing; if patriotism is no longer adequate to the task of making Philip feel turned 'inside out', this is because there is something far more damaging turning his world, rather, upside down. This process is soon systematised through a series of newly created government departments and programs, including the Office of American Absorption, whose covert task is to coerce Jews to disperse into Gentile America, thus both weakening their position as a cohesive community and undermining their sense of belonging in America.

As this suggests, the novel's principal focus of the effect of Lindbergh's anti-Semitic policies becomes the Roth family, and the disruption to their former lives. This interpretation is supported by Roth's comments about writing the novel: 'the subject of the book that interested me was . . . how much pressure can you bring to bear on this family, and what will happen when you bring maximum pressure to bear on them' ('Conversation' with Brown). In other words, Roth sets up the alternative scenario, and uses characters drawn from his immediate real life, in order to carry out an extended neo-naturalist experiment into human behaviour.

That this is indeed an upside-down world in which events for Philip are no longer comprehensible is demonstrated again when Rabbi Bengelsdorf, a quisling pro-Lindbergh figure and fiancé to Philip's Aunt Evelyn, comes to dine at the Roths' house. Philip's reflections make this abundantly clear: 'in my own house – where I was supposed to wear anything *except* my good clothes – I had to put on my one tie and my one jacket to impress the very rabbi who helped to elect the president whose friend was Hitler' (107). World events thus overturn norms even in Philip's 'own house', again constituting an attack on his family's sense of belonging in America: '[s]omething essential had been destroyed and lost, we were being coerced to be other than the Americans we were' (108). This intrusion of overwhelming outside events into the family realm is reinforced when Philip sees his brother Sandy making a face disparaging his father's criticism of Lindbergh to the Rabbi, 'a face that revealed how far he'd spun out of the family orbit merely by making the ordinary American's adjustment to the new administration' (109). The juxtaposition of 'family' and 'American' again illuminates the intrusion of politics into the family, Roth's bringing 'maximum pressure to bear' upon them.

As Philip aptly phrases it, 'history's next outsized intrusion' (184) is the invitation that Rabbi Bengelsdorf and Aunt Evelyn receive to the reception for von Ribbentrop at the White House, which is also extended to Philip's brother, Sandy, but vociferously rejected by their parents. Herman, as noted by Philip, explicitly recognises the intrusion of the political into their family life that this episode represents and, moreover, that it is a deliberate policy of the Lindbergh administration: 'our private turmoil was exactly the sort of dissension that the Lindbergh anti-Semites had hoped to stir up between Jewish parents and their children' (196). The fallout from this invitation includes an incident so shockingly out of character that it aptly demonstrates how far events have intruded into the nuclear family, when Bess, Philip's mother, repeatedly slaps Sandy after he sullenly objects about his father's behaviour. Philip's response to this is revealing in metafictionally addressing the text's counterfactual status: '"She doesn't know what she's doing," I thought, "she's somebody else – *everybody* is"' (194, original emphasis). Worse violence is to come, in the extremely violent fight – again very much out of character – between Herman and his nephew, Alvin, which takes place, significantly, in the Roths' 'ordinary family living room – traditionally the staging area for the collective effort to hold the line *against* the intrusions of a hostile world' (295, original emphasis). Finally, the domestic world of the Roths is turned upside down physically rather than figuratively. This intrusion of violence is completed, literally, when their Italian neighbour forces his way into the Roths' apartment to quell the fight, holding a gun (295–6). It is here that we encounter the reflection used as a heading for this section: '[i]t's so heartbreaking, violence, when it's in a house' (296).

Not surprisingly, given the domestic location of so many of the traumatic events in *The Plot Against America*, the parents' conventional gender roles are particularly challenged. We have already seen, with reference to Mrs Wishnow and Bess Roth, that conventional matriarchal structures are compromised by the Lindbergh administration's various covert assaults on the Jewish community and family. But the effects of these attacks are also seen in terms of the steady diminishment of Herman Roth's ability to exercise conventional masculine authority and freedom. Agency is once more at issue, and the fight with Alvin may be read on one level as Herman's last desperate attempt to assert attributes associated with masculinity, after we have witnessed him insidiously stripped of agency by the effects of the Lindbergh administration. This process may be traced back to the trip to Washington, and his humiliation when the family is ejected from their hotel (70). Another more serious eviction arises when the Homestead 42 programme threatens the Roth family with forced relocation to Kentucky (the placement ultimately filled, after Philip's intervention, by Selma and Seldon Wishnow). Until this point, Herman's resistance to the Lindbergh regime has been staunch and outspoken, but Philip notes how this final attack on their status seems to defeat him. Revealingly, the scene is played as a reversal of the more conventional gender roles Bess and Herman had taken in the hotel lobby in Washington, where she urged conciliation, while he stood his ground. The world is turned upside down once more, as Bess 'refus[es] to resign herself' (207), whereas Herman seems defeated, making Philip realise how his father's 'authority as a protector had been drastically compromised if not destroyed' (209). In contrast to Herman's earlier resistance to a forced relocation, he now concedes that 'confrontation was futile and our fate out of his hands. Shockingly enough, my father had been rendered impotent' (209). The word 'impotent' here is, of course, telling, and draws on similar notions of diminished agency as afflicted Landsman in *The Yiddish Policemen's Union*. Bess and Herman subsequently argue a number of times over whether to stay, to move, or to flee to Canada. While she urges the latter, Herman refuses to move, once more affronted by the assault on their status as Americans. Bess replies that the country is no longer theirs, and the effect of this statement upon Herman is again couched in language evoking emasculation and impotency:

> the nightmare immediacy of what was mercilessly real forced my father, in the prime of his manhood, fit, focused, and undiscourageable as any forty-one-year-old could possibly be, to see himself with mortifying clarity: a devoted father of titanic energy no more capable of protecting his family from harm than was Mr. Wishnow hanging dead in the closet. (226)

Even the child Philip is sufficiently aware to register the change in his father's status, as Herman chooses to remain in Newark, giving up his insurance sales career to work for his brother in the market. Philip is 'dumbfounded . . . by the abrupt decline in [his] father's vocational status' (238), as he notes '[a] family both declassed and rerooted overnight' (239).

The numerous ways in which broader historical events have a damaging effect on the Roths in *The Plot Against America* bear closer examination in terms of Roth's depiction of trauma. There are countless occasions where LaCapra's structural traumas – conventional disagreements, even tragedies, related to the western family economy or to growing up – are suddenly overtaken by unusual and extraordinary historical traumas of loss, which derive externally from the family. Although LaCapra warns against conflating the two, Roth instead juxtaposes historical and structural trauma, partly as a means to demonstrate their imbrication. This careful layering of loss onto absence is in fact one of the key effects of presenting this novel as a hybrid part-autobiographical alternative history. A key episode in this respect occurs when Philip's father, Herman, returns from visiting the wounded Alvin in Canada. Relating the story of the visit to his wife and children, Herman breaks down into tears. 'It was the first time I saw my father cry,' declares the narrator, '[a] childhood milestone, when another's tears are more unbearable than his own' (113). The language here subtly challenges the distinction between structural and historical trauma. The 'childhood milestone' suggests that Herman's tears represent a conventional structural stage associated with maturation, but in the uncanny alternative world of the Lindbergh presidency, it is palpably connected to a specific historical event and therefore to a concept of loss. The world-turned-upside-down trope as a shaping metaphor for *The Plot Against America* is again apposite. The stark alternate history constructed through Roth's experimental hybrid form here begins to blur the lines between absence and loss, or between structural and historical trauma.

David Brauner also writes extensively on *The Plot Against America* in terms of trauma, but his reading differs significantly from that presented here. Firstly, his focus is much more on the effect of events from the perspective of Philip than from the family as a whole, and secondly he pays little attention to Roth's employment of the counterfactual form. That these differences lead him to overlook the novel's sophisticated treatment of structural and historical trauma is evident in his interpretation of the sequence set in Washington, wherein the Roths encounter overt anti-Semitism and consequent exclusion from what they believed was their America. Focusing specifically on Philip, Brauner reads this episode as signalling structural rather than historical loss: 'what disturbs Philip most is not the feeling of being cast out from a Utopian ideal of America that never really existed, but of being thrust suddenly from his own previous state of childish innocence (and ignorance) into the adult world of experience (and corruption)' (204–5). The being cast out, the trauma resulting from a specific historical incident, is downplayed here compared to Philip's (structural) emergence from innocence to experience.

Similarly, Brauner suggests that the effect of the parents' episodes of panic upon Philip is that he 'can never return to any sort of childhood. Now that the vulnerability of both his parents has been exposed, Philip is no longer a child at all' (205). Through sidelining the significance of the counterfactual mode, this is couched in terms that fail to appreciate fully the exceptional character of the events in this novel. One must ask whether the vulnerability Philip witnesses in his parents would have been exposed (at that time and in that way) without the specific historical intervention of Lindbergh and his administration. If the answer is no, as is clearly the case, then it is accurate to characterise the novel's predominant focus as the effects of historical loss rather than, as Brauner seems to suggest, absence and/or structural trauma. This is the case even if we are discussing an insidious rather than sudden incidence of loss. By more or less ignoring the experimental freedom that Roth grants himself through his employment of the quasi-autobiographical counterfactual hybrid, Brauner misses the subtler ways in which the novel shades loss and absence. In fairness, distinction between the two types of trauma is never precise in the novel – and as stressed earlier, even LaCapra admits that absence and loss are always difficult to separate – but the overall emphasis of Brauner's reading, centred as it is on the subjectivity of Philip, is placed mistakenly on structural trauma at the expense of historical loss, and thus somewhat depoliticised.

It is also important to retain the clear distinction between Roth the author and Philip the narrator-protagonist. While Roth, as suggested above, constructs telling juxtapositions of absence and loss, structural and historical trauma, using them as mutually illuminating phenomena, he does not thoughtlessly conflate them. This latter trend may be detected, however, in the consciousness of Philip. LaCapra suggests that the tendency to conflate may

itself be a symptom of traumatic disorientation: '[t]he very conflation attests to the way one remains possessed or haunted by the
past' (46). This seems to be precisely the experience of Philip; he
describes his father's newly-revealed powerlessness in terms that
lament his loss: '[a] new life began for me. I'd watched my father
fall apart, and I would never return to the same childhood' (113).
Philip thus conflates the structural trauma of the 'individual's
necessary separation from the parent' (Kauvar 139) with the historical trauma of the discrimination carried out against his family
and community. LaCapra warns that, '[i]n converting absence into
loss, one assumes that there was . . . some original unity, whole-
ness, security, or identity that others have ruined, polluted, or con-
taminated and thus made "us" lose' (58). A lost ideal such as this,
replaced by the 'terror' of the 'relentless unforeseen' (113–14) is at
the heart of Philip's laments, but not of Roth's. This is achieved
through the novel's employment of the alternative history form,
which separates Roth from the only semi-autobiographical Philip.

Philip's conflation of structural and historical trauma continues
right to the end of the crisis, as the family finally agrees to flee to
Canada: 'quite incredibly, we'd been overpowered by the forces
arrayed against us and were about to flee and become foreigners.
I wept all the way to school. Our incomparable American childhood was ended' (301). Again, the stress is on a lost ideal which
is mythologised through a combination of structural ('childhood')
and historically and geographically specific ('American') trauma.
Even when the Lindbergh administration is brought to an abrupt
end Philip's mythically ambrosial childhood is left permanently
scarred: 'never would I be able to revive that unfazed sense of
security first fostered in a little child by a big, protective republic
and his ferociously responsible parents' (301). The complexity of
Roth's form here bears rich fruit, as the actual historical trauma
(the Shoah) is overlain with an imagined one (Lindbergh's election) and this in turn is conflated by the narrative's central figure,
Philip, with the impact upon the conventional family economy and
all its more normative structural traumas. This complex matrix of
trauma is worked through by merging it with or transforming it
into more mythical losses, in particular Philip's idealised prelapsar-
ian America. A result of this is the 'perpetual fear' which opens the

work, wherein the devastating historical trauma is transformed by Philip from loss into an absence with which he is more able to cope. Roth's employment of a form which slides between autobiography and fiction is clearly key here, not least in relation to the consequently difficult but important distinctions to be made between Philip and Roth. Of course, Philip's nightmarish experience of the Lindbergh administration never actually occurred for Roth. Should we therefore assume that the 'sense of security' quoted above as now missing from Philip's life, due to the betrayal by his country and revealed frailties of his parents, remained and remains present in Roth's? Certainly the earlier comparison of the openings of *The Facts* and *The Plot Against America* suggests this is the case. Questions such as this reveal the richness that is added by this text's drawing on real people (that is, going beyond famous figures such as Lindbergh and Roosevelt by also depicting Roth's own family). Blake Morrison appropriately labels this strategy a 'stroke of genius', since it grants Roth an unprecedented experimental platform of a more serious order or intent than Auster's embedded fiction, as it is based on identifiably real people. The use of real family members in this autobiographical alternative history enables a revitalised form of naturalist experiment which, in turn, allows Roth's deconstruction of the structural and historical categories of trauma. Indeed, *The Plot Against America* is arguably a more thoroughly rigorous naturalist experiment than Zola et al. ever carried out: although the scenario is imagined, many of the participants are not arbitrary fictional constructs, but based on real people, intimately familiar to the author. Roth's comments bear out reading this novel as a counterfactual experiment similar in nature to those of earlier naturalists: '[j]ust change the outcome of the 1940 election and make everything else as close to reality as you possibly can, which is why I chose my family as the family to whom all this happens. And that excited me because it opened up a question which is: How would we have behaved in these circumstances?' ('Conversation' with Brown).

The complexity of this experiment becomes clear at various points, not least from the resultantly unusual narrating perspective that emerges. Early on, for example, Philip-the-narrator describes his younger self as a 'good child, obedient both at home and school

– the willfulness largely inactive and the attack set to go off at a later date' (24). This statement humorously relies on the reader's epitextual knowledge of the real Philip Roth (who is not – quite – the narrator), even as we are presented with an overtly fictional counterfactual history of America.[5] Neither does this playfulness apply solely to Philip; Herman's refusal of the enforced Homestead 42 move says something not only about his character in the (fictional) circumstances of the counterfactual scenario, but also in relation to Roth's feelings about the real man: 'I only then understood that he had quit his job not merely because he was fearful of what awaited us down the line should we agree like the others to be relocated but because, for better or worse, when he was bullied by superior forces that he deemed corrupt it was his nature not to yield' (255). Alternative histories are by definition allied to naturalism's experiments in human behaviour, but Roth's blending of this form with his autobiographical-fiction hybrid makes this a compelling experiment into the effects of extraordinary and traumatic events upon an ordinary family.

CONCLUSION: THE COUNTERFACTUAL AS REDEMPTION NARRATIVE?

While the notion of retreat from the reality of early twenty-first-century America into alternative scenarios is initially attractive as a rationale for these writers adopting the counterfactual form, it is clearly simplistic. The motivation of these authors is directed towards analysing trauma rather than retreating from it. This is true even in *Man in the Dark*, where August, but not Auster, is in retreat, and *The Plot Against America*, where Philip, but not Roth, is trying to mitigate the effects of trauma. As with Roth's novel, distinctions between absence and loss, and structural and historical trauma, are also relevant, if less central, to *Man in the Dark*. There is, for example, the debate over whether 'every family lives through extraordinary events' (converting historical to structural trauma), or whether it is only true for some families (122). While the counterfactual narrative is framed in Auster's novel, the impact of historical trauma upon family life is felt both within it (by Owen and his wife) and externally (by Brill and his family). The alternate history is constructed by Brill primarily to avoid thinking about both structural and historical trauma, but it fails spectacularly, most obviously because it, too, rapidly assumes the same theme – the impact of historical trauma – that Brill is trying to repress.

If absence and loss are kept more distinct in Auster's novel, a consequence of the bracketing function of the framed narratives, the result of this may be the tentative signs of working through at the novel's conclusion. Debra Shostak notes that Auster characteristically 'explores the possibility that loss is a historical, and hence potentially narratable, condition' (66). While this allows a limited working through of trauma, Shostak does sound a useful note of caution: '[c]ontrary to the now commonsense view of storytelling as therapeutic, Auster suggests that the attempt to control experience by telling stories can make one lost rather than found' (82). Although she is here discussing *Oracle Night*, the point stands just as well for *Man in the Dark*. There are signs at the novel's conclusion that Katya is recovering, 'coming along now . . . Bit by bit by bit' (179), but any redemption is nascent and equivocal.

Chabon's novel concludes on a similar note of limited optimism with regard to recovery. Of the three novels discussed, the contrast between the global and the personal is felt most keenly in *The Yiddish Policemen's Union*. While the global situation appears precarious, with years of unrest in the Middle East the most likely outcome of the extremist Jews' bombing of Jerusalem, the rapprochement between Landsman and Bina signals a measure of personal redemption. For Landsman in particular, there are signals of recovery from his various traumas. He now possesses some closure over the mystery of his sister's death, he has – at least for now – stopped drinking, and has reunited with Bina, who has absolved him from blame in the abortion of their unborn child (409). Landsman finishes the novel 'ripe for the grand gesture' (407), which is initially throwing away his cigarettes, but ultimately consists of phoning an investigative journalist in order to bring to public attention the collusion between the Sitka Jews and the American government (410–11). This act may contribute towards addressing the global situation and redressing the extremist Jews' ideological and opportunist conversion of absence into a narrative of loss.

In *The Plot Against America*, the parents – if not the family as a whole – are redeemed through principled stoicism under intense pressure. This novel's ending, however, with its rapid deposing of Lindbergh in favour of Roosevelt, history's rightful president, came under criticism from reviewers as perfunctory and rushed.[6] Certainly, the alleged 'perpetual fear' which opens the novel is displaced and banished remarkably quickly, with the return to a historical narrative we recognise. On one level, this might be understood as a conservative reaffirmation of American values that are seen inevitably to contain the intrusive subversion of the fascist regime. On the other hand, as Elaine Safer contends, the unlikely circumstances of the ending actually indicate that we should not find it reassuring, and instead heed 'Roth's warning that there is always a threat of totalitarianism gaining control in a democracy' (161). To read the novel's conclusion as conservative is also to ignore the perpetuation of the traumatic effects of the Lindbergh administration which are, it is suggested, felt for long afterwards. As Parrish observes, '[a]t the novel's close, the figure of Sheldon [sic] remains in Philip's bedroom (and looms in Philip's memory) as the embodiment of the potential truth of Philip's worst fears' (99). Philip remains haunted by this physical embodiment of his status both as a victim of the dark days of the Lindbergh presidency and as a perpetrator-collaborator in arranging for the Wishnows' deportation to Kentucky. It is, ultimately, naïve to read as canny an author as Roth in such a straightforward way, and the recovery provided at the end of this novel is, as with the other two, provisional and precarious. As Roth points out in his article on the composition of the novel, the ending is resolutely not triumphant or conclusive, with Seldon Wishnow remaining 'the book's most tragic figure, a trusting American kid who suffers something like the European Jewish experience. He is not the child who survives the confusion to tell the tale but the one whose childhood is destroyed by it.'

All three of these counterfactuals offer a tentative measure of redemption through signs of recovery from trauma. And in all three novels some form of family is the motor for recovery and therefore at the centre of the (equivocally) redemptive narrative conclusion. It is necessary to ask, as Richard Gray suggests of many

9/11 novels, whether this makes them in some ways complicit with the conservative ideology of the nuclear family. This is an interesting and persuasive conclusion to reach, especially given the retrenchment of family values in America in the immediate wake of 9/11. In this sense, one might ask whether these novelists are merely part of a zeitgeist that fetishises the family unit as the principal defence against disruptive (global) forces. Benjamin Hedin, for example, notes that the family arena in *The Plot Against America* is 'an Edenic refuge . . . a child's final bulwark against the evils of humanity' (106). While this risks caricaturing Roth's novel, and the others discussed in this chapter, it may be useful to consider a comparison with another noted twenty-first-century American novel, one which posits a dystopian future, rather than an alternative past/present: Cormac McCarthy's *The Road*. In this novel, the family may be interpreted as a more destructive force: the mother commits suicide, leaving the father paranoid and aggressive in the defence of his sole surviving relative, the small boy. And the supposedly redemptive ending of this novel, as the boy is relocated once more within a nuclear family, albeit with no long-term hope of survival, may be read as a critique of the short-sightedness of the family values to which the three novels discussed in this chapter appear to offer tacit support. In narrating such extreme traumatic events from which recovery seems impossible, McCarthy's novel offers up an altogether bleaker version of the neo-naturalist experiment, and one which is perhaps more sceptical about the redemptive potential of the nuclear family.

NOTES

1. In order to avoid confusion, and in common with other critics writing about this work, I refer to its narrator-protagonist as 'Philip' and to its author as 'Roth'.
2. The parallels Chabon draws are sometimes overly simplistic, and this has not gone without comment. Amelia Glaser suggests that 'Chabon's message might be read as a critique of fundamentalism across the board, although his invention of illegal Jewish settlers outside of Sitka who breed an extreme,

latter-day Zionist project is hardly a subtle response to contemporary Israeli policy' (160). Ruth Wisse, who like Glaser objects to the novel's implicit critique of Israel, worries that 'The Arab alternative version of Jewish history, which erases Israel from the map of the world while simultaneously fantasizing a gigantic Zionist-American anti-Arab crusade, has been making inroads in the "progressive" circles to which Chabon belongs' ('Slap Shtick' 76).

3. This novel has been tirelessly examined for contemporary parallels, as if it represents a thinly-veiled allegory of the Bush administration. Roth, in 'The Story Behind *The Plot Against America*', denies that it should be taken 'as a roman à clef to the present moment in America . . . I set out to do exactly what I've done: reconstruct the years 1940–42 as they might have been if Lindbergh, instead of Roosevelt, had been elected president in the 1940 election. I am not pretending to be interested in those two years – I am interested in those two years.' As unequivocal as this seems, nearer the end of the article Roth describes Bush as 'a man unfit to run a hardware store let alone a nation like this one'. Questions regarding contemporary reference are largely irrelevant for this chapter. The novel is clearly more than (and not especially usefully read as) straightforward allegory or satire, elements which are present, but overall provide a reductive way of interpreting the novel. See especially Berman, Coetzee, Kellman and Shiffman for discussion of this issue.

4. In this sense, it might be argued that the novels themselves in this chapter, all of which employ some form of deterministic neo-naturalism, support the perpetrator's attempt to deny their free will. If this is the case, then these works may be as complicit as the trauma genre texts and criticism mentioned in the conclusion to Chapter 3 with attempts to appropriate victim status for America. On closer examination, however, this is not the case. August Brill's neo-naturalist narrative is framed within a text which overall is not thoroughly naturalist. Thus we have a portrait of a not entirely sympathetic character largely failing to appropriate victim status through an overtly constructed neo-naturalist narrative. In *The Yiddish Policemen's Union* naturalism is less pronounced. Moreover Landsman, who indeed

suffers restricted agency, is scarcely a perpetrator, while the extremist Jews are beset by events but nevertheless portrayed as responsible for their actions. While *The Plot Against America* is a neo-naturalist narrative, the only example of a perpetrator character seeking to overturn this through denying free will is Philip who, as stated below, can hardly have been expected to foresee the consequences of his actions. Overall, there is little sense that these writers use this genre as a means to map victim status onto America.

5. Matthew Schweber notes the interesting results of the playfulness regarding Roth's use of his name against his own literary career: 'herein lies much of the novel's piquant meta-irony. After all, this "frightened boy," harassed because he's Jewish, bears the namesake of the literary *enfant terrible* whose early stories certain hysterical rabbis, paranoid critics, and pious activists once fantasized as posing the very danger to Jews the Lindbergh Presidency in *The Plot* actually constitutes' (131). In this sense, Schweber argues, the novel works as 'an instructive fable about the political conditions which *would have had* to prevail in America for Roth's early stories to have been recklessly provocative, let alone dangerous' (132, original emphasis).

6. Michiko Kakutani described this ending as 'an abrupt conclusion that only underscores the slapdash contrivance of Mr Roth's historical projections' ('Pro-Nazi President'), while Ruth Wisse declared that, 'Roth's animating political conceit fizzles in two pages like a spent firecracker' ('In Nazi Newark' 68).

Conclusion

This conclusion briefly revisits some of the arguments made during the course of this book, before looking towards possible developments in trauma studies and the literature of trauma.

THE PRESENT STATE OF TRAUMA STUDIES

Running through this study is a general critique of widely accepted tenets of trauma representation in the humanities, deriving both from the pervasive concept of PTSD and the work of Cathy Caruth. The PTSD model is felt to be overly prescriptive in terms of its diagnostic power and to place too many restrictions on artists' representation of trauma. As this study has demonstrated, countless critics and a number of artists work unquestioningly with models of trauma provided by PTSD in a circle which reinforces both each other's texts and the dominant theoretical model. As argued in the introduction, a number of critics working in cultural trauma studies seem unaware of the controversies surrounding the acceptance of PTSD as a connected set of symptoms, instead assuming that the contested model is scientifically validated. In seeking to supplement the work of critics of the PTSD model such as Allan Young, Susannah Radstone, Ben Shephard, Roger Luckhurst, and Ruth Leys this study aims to add to their vital epistemological challenge, and to encourage critics and theorists of trauma to consider the origins of PTSD before blindly following its precepts.

Key critiques of elements of the dominant model in cultural trauma studies, deriving from Caruth's work, should be reiterated here. As examples throughout this study have suggested, the phenomenon of *Nachträglichkeit*, the belatedness of traumatic memory due to temporary amnesia, is far less ubiquitous than often suggested, despite its importance to Caruthian trauma studies. As for claims that ultimately recovered traumatic memories capture the event exactly, as argued in the work of Bessel van der Kolk, such exactitude is in fact highly contentious. The belatedness and literality claims – cornerstones of Caruthian criticism – have helped to produce a limiting set of aesthetic formulae for the representation of trauma. Instead of either belatedness or the literality of recovered memory, this study indicates that what actually seems much more common is a persistent if partial, but certainly conscious memory, often a kind of synecdoche standing in for the traumatic event. This is what has been referred to in previous chapters – for example in relation to the use of blue in *House of Leaves* – as a kind of coded shorthand denotation of trauma. This synecdochal shorthand is also seen in Yossarian's recalled memory of comforting Snowden, 'there, there', in *Catch-22*, in 'so it goes' in *Slaughterhouse-Five*, in the repeated short phrases Toni Morrison habitually uses, in the countless images of the planes crashing into the Twin Towers in numerous 9/11 representations, and in the sand of the Gulf War accounts. Rather than the absence resulting from repression or dissociation, synecdochal memory implies a conscious persistence. Neither is the shorthand coded memory a literal recall, even though it is generally available to consciousness. Instead it may be just a representative part, sometimes a partial screen, or perhaps the most distressing element of the traumatic memory that is consciously present. The key point, as these literary works suggest, is that the symptomatology varies a great deal more than current dominant models allow.

The event-based model of trauma, equally important to Caruthian and PTSD conceptions, has also been the subject of significant critique, both within this study and without. Postcolonial theorists in particular have revealed the event-based model as laden with western bias. The colonial and postcolonial experience has thus been frequently shown to comprise everyday traumatic experiences of inequality, oppression, and racism. It is welcome that this critique is now central to a more widespread interpretive model for studies of trauma representation. As a result, the punctual model of Caruth (and related ideas such as LaCapra's distinction between historical and structural trauma) must undergo significant adaptations and revisions in order to remain relevant in the analysis of non-western trauma. What this study has demonstrated is that American texts, often written from anything but the margins, can also illustrate the invalidity of the event-based model. As we saw in Chapter 4 (and which is discussed further below), perpetrator trauma is also more typically characterised as insidious rather than event-based.

The restrictive modes of representation approved by dominant trauma theory have also been critiqued in this study, most notably in my identification of a damagingly formulaic body of literary production and attendant criticism, the trauma genre. As suggested in the introduction, the stringent demands from theorists that writers produce texts that are formally avant-garde, and which aim to transmit rather than represent trauma, has led to a narrow, derivative, and only superficially experimental genre of works. This in turn has helped to nurture a body of criticism that at its worst can be termed 'tick-box' (see Chapter 3 for examples pertaining to Jonathan Safran Foer), and which sees dominant theories confirmed by their appearance in works of literature. This vicious circle of conventional artistic works compliant with an approving body of criticism reinforces particular ideas about trauma, and constructs a skewed model of how trauma actually manifests. Key problems with this notion that trauma is unrepresentable except through a prescribed avant-gardism are that this aesthetic is now so reified that it is not at all experimental, and secondly that it bars other forms of representation, such as the neo-realist or neo-naturalist texts discussed in this study.

Indeed, the dangers of trauma genre criticism, as Chapters 3 and 4 concluded, go considerably deeper than restricting artists' choices. Firstly, the Caruthian model, deriving from her noted reading of Tasso, tends to substitute passivity for agency, suggesting that trauma sufferers are by definition victims. This perspective is especially the case, as we saw, when considering collective trauma and its dangerous manipulation into a sense of victimhood and desire for revenge. Mainstream trauma theory professes abhorrence of the perpetrator, but this might also be used covertly to deny perpetrator status. Trauma theory is thus implicated in post-9/11 events, enabling the reconfiguration of the traumatised US body politic as absolute victim, since perpetrators are excluded from suffering trauma. A quotation from an article published in the year I write this concluding chapter bears this out: '[v]ast forces assault Americans at every turn – two seemingly endless wars, an economy that seems inexplicable, natural and human-caused disasters – so much so that the nation is exhibiting the symptoms of clinical depression' (Vanderwerken 48). The spuriousness of this flagrant appropriation of victim status is underlined by the hyperbolic tone and the questionable mapping of individual symptoms onto an entire society. Similar rhetoric of victimhood was detected in the combat narratives discussed in Chapter 4, wherein the attempted inversion of the invading American troops into victims epitomises the US's broader assumption of victim status post-9/11. The frequent employment of many of the conventions of trauma genre writing aims to appropriate the victim status generally conferred in such texts. As stated in Chapter 4, the reluctance of academics to discuss perpetrator trauma – or to consider texts such as these as examples of perpetrator trauma – is thus effectively political, in helping to erase the actual victims of aggressive American foreign policy.

FUTURE DIRECTIONS FOR TRAUMA STUDIES AND TRAUMA LITERATURE

The trauma genre may itself be characterised as exhibiting the ubiquitous trauma symptom of repetition. It is there in the intertextual transmission of tropes from trauma text to trauma text, and writer's aping of earlier works, in critics' unquestioning repetition of theoretical tenets, and in the vicious circle of mutually reinforcing criticism and narratives. In all its repetitive form and inward-looking acting out, the trauma genre itself seems neurotic, self-perpetuating, and self-destructive, locked into a kind of stasis that it purports to analyse. If trauma genre criticism is acting out, then new approaches are required to break this circle (to work it through, as it were).

As I hope this book has demonstrated, the breadth of contemporary American literature on trauma transcends the narrow theoretical models critiqued above. Genuinely innovative writing on trauma, which borrows little if at all from what have become the tired techniques of postmodernism, exists in a number of forms. Chapter 2 discussed the emergence of traumatic metafictions, works which go beyond conventional disruptions to elements of narrative such as narrating voice and linear chronology. In works such as *House of Leaves* we see an engagement with the ontologically unsettling philosophical perspectives of postmodernism, rather than just a routine appropriation of its aesthetic. The inscribed narrator in these works serves to demonstrate the temporal dimension essential to the narration of and recovery from trauma. These works typically draw on trauma discourse in order to parody and question it rather than to reproduce its representational norms. Traumatic metafictions may also be defined by their attempts to unsettle readers through less conventional narrative techniques, to the extent that – as in the examples of *The Zero* and *The Exquisite* discussed in Chapter 2 – readers are unable to fully resolve the text into a single, coherent narrative. Trauma is thus positioned plurally, as an undecidable: narratable and representable, but impossible to assimilate. While this threatens to return trauma to conceptions popularised by dominant trauma theory, the representational means are more genuinely experimental and often parodic than those employed in trauma genre writing. While a description of traumatic metafiction risks establishing these attributes too, as norms, the point is that although these texts so far share certain characteristics – such as the use of inscribed narration – they also vary considerably, and are perhaps better considered as a mood, an attitude or approach (sceptical, sometimes parodic), rather than a set of aesthetic criteria.

Besides traumatic metafiction, we have also discussed the (re-) emergence of forms of realism and naturalism, partly as a reaction to the proliferation of ostentatious experimentation in trauma genre texts. Lorrie Moore's neo-realism, most recently expressed through *A Gate at the Stairs*, ably demonstrates that trauma may be avoided and then indirectly approached in more subtle ways than the now-familiar circular narratives of postmodernist trauma texts. In this novel as in some other more recent post-9/11 texts (such as the later works of Carol Shields, Don DeLillo's *Point Omega*, and certain short stories in Jhumpa Lahiri's *Unaccustomed Earth*), the traumas of contemporary America, in particular its overseas wars and relationship to the developing world, exist as a thematically cohesive undercurrent before emerging more fully into the narrative.

As for neo-naturalism, its appearance goes further than just the counterfactual form discussed in Chapter 5, and is detectable in texts as diverse as Cormac McCarthy's *The Road*, Andre Dubus III's *The Garden of Last Days* and, certainly, Moore's novel. The re-emergence of realism and naturalism has not gone without comment or criticism. David Holloway, for example, lauds Frédéric Beigbeder's *Windows on the World* in familiar fashion, as a trauma text whose experimental techniques address the alleged unrepresentability of trauma, and confirm 'the limits of literary realism' (120). In this novel, Holloway continues, 'the old idea that realism could be a moral force in society, helping glue it together by depicting a world that would appear equally "real" to all readers, however diverse, looked like just another trick of hubristic modernity' (123). Clearly, though, this vastly misrepresents what realism vouches for itself, and what post-9/11 neo-naturalism tends to demonstrate. Moreover, the daringly unconventional form Holloway perceives in *Windows on the World* is actually familiar pseudo-experimentation. Indeed, the turn to naturalism in the work of Philip Roth and the other writers mentioned signifies a rejection of the meretricious avant-gardism in trauma genre texts such as Beigbeder's.

One should not unguardedly celebrate the emergence of neo-naturalism in reaction to the trauma genre without considering possible drawbacks. Firstly, the reappearance of naturalism might be taken as a conservative return to comforting forms of the past and, moreover, it may itself become tired and conventional through overuse. This is not yet a problem since neo-naturalism is, currently at least, a rejection of the anti-realist approach to trauma found in countless trauma genre texts. In this sense, time will tell. Secondly, naturalism encourages a view of humankind at the mercy of larger forces, lacking free will and agency, and therefore responsibility. This deterministic and blameless condition is ripe for the appropriation of victim status as criticised above. This is a valid concern, and thus its employment as a form for the representation of trauma needs to be carefully scrutinised.

This book has been critical of a formulaic mode of criticism that has restricted representational possibilities by approving and therefore encouraging writers to adopt a limited range of aesthetic choices. While too much of this criticism, and the type of fictional narratives it validates, persists, as I write this conclusion there is pleasing evidence of a widening diversity of theoretical and critical approaches to trauma. In other words, as well as emerging literary forms which challenge trauma genre representation, there is a growing body of criticism that dares to dissent from formulaic models of trauma, and the resultantly restrictive aesthetics. This is necessary for a number of reasons, not least that if it does not develop more agile responses to emerging literature, then trauma criticism risks becoming irrelevant. One need only consider radically hybridised works such as *The Plot Against America* or outspokenly pluralistic ones such as *In the Shadow of No Towers* to appreciate that current critical frameworks struggle to comprehend these texts' representation of trauma. As suggested above, a more flexible and responsive criticism will also help to free writers from what they currently perceive as approved ways of representing trauma.

Conferences on cultural representations of trauma provide evidence of a new generation of trauma scholars developing more sophisticated paradigms for the study of its representation and effects. Journal special issues on trauma, such as *Continuum*'s 'Interrogating Trauma' (2010) and *Studies in the Novel*'s 2008 double issue on postcolonial trauma representations provide further proof of a widening scope of critical paradigms. In particular, the interventions of postcolonial critics have made a valuable contribution towards challenging the event-based model of trauma, and gaining recognition of the insidiously traumatic experiences of many living under oppressive, unequal or racist regimes. It is hoped that this book contributes to that widening perspective in a number of ways. Firstly, the focus on perpetrator trauma and my questioning the often unhelpful introduction of ethics into such discussions is intended to prompt further debate. This is a relatively new direction for trauma studies and one which is important in terms of scrutinising the way in which notions of victimhood can be manipulated and distorted. Secondly, this may be linked to my investigation of collective trauma and its potential dangers. As we saw in Chapters 4 and 5, both perpetrator trauma and collective trauma are crucially linked to the notion of agency, in particular the denial of agency, as a means to slough off responsibility. This, too, merits further investigation, especially in terms of America's aggressive reaction to the events of 9/11. Finally, trauma criticism needs to address its potential complicity in the manufacturing of a sense of victimhood, both in terms of its tendency to depoliticise causes of trauma – wresting focus away from social inequalities – and the way in which it diminishes a sense of agency and thus responsibility in the perceived trauma sufferer. This study eagerly anticipates a more pluralistic trauma criticism that is not just (as is already the case) interdisciplinary, but which also recognises a wider range of representations of trauma. Only then will theory and criticism adequately reflect the reality of literary production and widen the potential for future artists.

Bibliography

11'09"01, film, directed by Mira Nair et al. UK/international: CIH Shorts, 2002.

Alexander, Jeffrey C. (2004), 'Towards a Theory of Cultural Trauma', in Jeffrey C. Alexander, Ron Eyerman, Bernhard Giesen, Neil J. Smelser, and Piotr Sztompka, *Cultural Trauma and Collective Identity*, Berkeley: University of California Press, pp. 1–30.

Alexander, Paul (1999), *Salinger: A Biography*, Los Angeles: Renaissance Books.

Anker, Elizabeth S. (2011), 'Allegories of Falling and the 9/11 Novel', *American Literary History* 23.3: 463–82.

Atchison, S. Todd (2010), '"Why I am writing from where you are not": Absence and presence in Jonathan Safran Foer's *Extremely Loud and Incredibly Close*', *Journal of Postcolonial Writing* 46.3: 359–68.

Auster, Paul (2004), *Oracle Night*, London: Faber.

Auster, Paul (2008), *Man in the Dark*, New York: Henry Holt.

Bal, Mieke, Jonathan V. Crewe, and Leo Spitzer, eds (1999), *Acts of Memory: Cultural Recall in the Present*, Dartmouth: University Press of New England.

Ball, Karyn (2007), 'Introduction: Traumatizing Psychoanalysis', in Karyn Ball (ed.), *Traumatizing Theory: The Cultural Politics of Affect In and Beyond Psychoanalysis*, New York: Other Press, pp. xvii–li.

Barthes, Roland (1977), 'The Death of the Author', in *Image, Music, Text*, trans. Stephen Heath, London: Fontana, pp. 142–8.

Baxter, Katherine (2011), 'Memory and Photography: Rethinking Postcolonial Trauma Studies', *Journal of Postcolonial Writing* 47.1: 18–29.

Begley, Adam (2004), 'Image of the Twin Towers Ablaze Haunts Narcissistic Cartoonist', *New York Observer*, 12 September 2004, <http://observer.com/2004/09/image-of-twin-towers-ablaze-haunts-narcissistic-cartoonist/> (last accessed 7 January 2014).

Beigbeder, Frédéric (2005), *Windows on the World*, trans. Frank Wynne, London: Harper.

Berger, Alan L. (2010), 'Michael Chabon's *The Amazing Adventures of Kavalier & Clay*: The Return of the Golem', *Studies in American Jewish Literature* 29: 80–9.

Berman, Paul (2004), 'The Plot Against America', *New York Times*, 3 October 2004, <http://www.nytimes.com/2004/10/03/books/review/03BERMAN.html?pagewanted=all&_r=0> (last accessed 7 January 2014).

Borges, Jorge Luis (1998), *Collected Fictions*, trans. Andrew Hurley, Harmondsworth: Penguin.

Bowden, Lisa, and Shannon Cain, eds (2008), *Powder: Writing by Women in the Ranks, from Vietnam to Iraq*, Tucson: Kore Press.

Bowman, Marilyn L., and Rachel Yehuda, 'Risk Factors and the Adversity-Stress Model', in Gerlad M. Rosen (ed.), *Posttraumatic Stress Disorder: Issues and Controversies*, Chichester: John Wiley and Sons Ltd., pp. 15–38.

Brauner, David (2007), *Philip Roth*, Manchester: Manchester University Press.

Brenkman, John (2008), 'Tender Is the Night in Paul Auster's *Man in the Dark*', *Village Voice*, 27 August 2008, <http://www.villagevoice.com/2008-08-27/books/tender-is-the-night-in-paul-auster-s-man-in-the-dark/full/> (last accessed 7 January 2014).

Brick, Martin (2004), 'Blueprint(s): Rubric for a Deconstructed Age in *House of Leaves*', *Philament* 2, <http://sydney.edu.au/arts/publications/philament/issue2_Critique_Brick.htm> (last accessed 7 January 2014).

Brienza, Susan (1995), 'Writing as Witnessing: The Many Voices of E. L. Doctorow', in Melvin J. Friedman and Ben Siegel (eds), *Traditions, Voices, and Dreams: The American Novel since the 1960s*, Newark, DE: University of Delaware Press, pp. 168–95.

Brooks, Peter (2003), 'If You Have Tears', in Judith Greenberg (ed.), *Trauma at Home: After 9/11*, Lincoln: University of Nebraska Press, pp. 48–51.

Brown, Keith, and Catherine Lutz (2007), 'Grunt Lit: The Participant-Observers of Empire', *American Ethnologist* 34.2: 322–8.

Brown, Kevin (2011), 'The Psychiatrists Were Right: Anomic Alienation in Kurt Vonnegut's *Slaughterhouse-Five*', *South Central Review* 28.2: 101–9.

Brown, Laura S. (1995), 'Not Outside the Range: One Feminist Perspective on Psychic Trauma', in Cathy Caruth (ed.), *Trauma: Explorations in Memory*, Baltimore: Johns Hopkins University Press, pp. 100–12.

Broyles, William Jr. (1984), 'Why Men Love War', *Esquire* 102: 55–65.

Butler, Judith (2004), *Precarious Life: The Powers of Mourning and Violence*, London: Verso.

Cacicedo, Alberto (2005), '"You must remember this": Trauma and Memory in *Catch-22* and *Slaughterhouse-Five*', *Critique* 46.4: 357–68.

Carmichael, Virginia (1993), *Framing History: The Rosenberg Story and the Cold War*, Minneapolis: University of Minnesota Press.

Caruth, Cathy, ed. (1995), *Trauma: Explorations in Memory*, Baltimore: Johns Hopkins University Press.

Caruth, Cathy (1996), *Unclaimed Experience: Trauma, Narrative, and History*, Baltimore: Johns Hopkins University Press.

Casteel, Sarah Philips (2009), 'Jews among the Indians: The Fantasy of Indigenization in Mordecai Richler's and Michael Chabon's Northern Narratives', *Contemporary Literature* 50.4: 775–810.

Chabon, Michael (2007a), *The Yiddish Policemen's Union*, London: Harper Collins.

Chabon, Michael (2007b), 'Jews on Ice', interview conducted by Sarah Goldstein, *Salon*, 4 May 2007, <http://www.salon.

com/2007/05/04/chabon_5/> (last accessed 7 January 2014).

Chen, Tina (1998), '"Unraveling the Deeper Meaning": Exile and the Embodied Poetics of Displacement in Tim O'Brien's *The Things They Carried*', *Contemporary Literature* 39.1: 77–98.

Chute, Hillary (2007), 'Temporality and Seriality in Spiegelman's *In the Shadow of No Towers*', *American Periodicals: A Journal of History, Criticism and Bibliography* 17.2: 228–44.

Codde, Philippe (2007), 'Philomela Revisited: Traumatic Iconicity in Jonathan Safran Foer's *Extremely Loud and Incredibly Close*', *Studies in American Fiction* 35.2: 241–55.

Coetzee, J. M. (2004), 'What Philip Knew', *New York Review of Books*, 18 November 2004, <http://www.nybooks.com/art icles/archives/2004/nov/18/what-philip-knew/> (last accessed 7 January 2014).

Collado-Rodriguez, Francisco (2005–8), 'Trauma, Ethics and Myth-Oriented Literary Tradition in Jonathan Safran Foer's *Extremely Loud & Incredibly Close*', *Journal of English Studies* 5–6: 47–62.

Cox, Katharine (2006), 'What Has Made Me? Locating Mother in the Textual Labyrinth of Mark Z. Danielewski's *House of Leaves*', *Critical Survey* 18.2: 4–15.

Craps, Stef, and Gert Buelens (2008), 'Introduction: Postcolonial Trauma Novels', *Studies in the Novel*, 40.1 & 2: 1–12.

Danielewski, Mark Z. (2000a), *House of Leaves*, London and New York: Doubleday.

Danielewski, Mark Z. (2000b), 'A Conversation with Mark Danielewski', interview conducted by Sophie Cottrell, *Bold Type* 3.12, <http://www.randomhouse.com/boldtype/0400/danielewski/interview.html> (last accessed 7 January 2014).

Danielewski, Mark Z. (2003), 'Haunted House: An Interview with Mark Z. Danielewski', interview conducted by Larry McCaffery and Sinda Gregory, *Critique: Studies in Contemporary Fiction* 44.2: 99–135.

Däwes, Birgit (2007), 'On Contested Ground (Zero): Literature and the Transnational Challenge of Remembering 9/11', *Amerikastudien/American Studies* 52.4: 517–43.

DeLillo, Don (2001a), *The Body Artist*, Basingstoke: Macmillan.

DeLillo, Don (2001b), 'In the Ruins of the Future', *The Guardian*, 22 December 2001, <http://www.theguardian.com/books/2001/dec/22/fiction.dondelillo> (last accessed 7 January 2014).

DeLillo, Don (2007), *Falling Man*, Basingstoke: Macmillan.

Derosa, Aaron (2009), 'Apocryphal Trauma in E. L. Doctorow's *The Book of Daniel*', *Studies in the Novel* 41.4: 468–88.

Doctorow, E. L. [1971] (1982), *The Book of Daniel*, London: Picador.

Eaglestone, Robert (2008), '"You Would Not Add to My Suffering if You Knew What I Have Seen": Holocaust Testimony and Contemporary African Literature', *Studies in the Novel* 40.1 & 2: 72–85.

Edkins, Jenny (2001), 'The Absence of Meaning: Trauma and the Events of 11 September', *Infointerventions*, 5 October 2001, <http://www.infopeace.org/911/article.cfm?id=27> (last accessed 7 January 2014).

Edkins, Jenny (2003), *Trauma and the Memory of Politics*, Cambridge: Cambridge University Press.

Espiritu, Karen (2006), '"Putting Grief into Boxes": Trauma and the Crisis of Democracy in Art Spiegelman's *In the Shadow of No Towers*', *The Review of Education, Pedagogy, and Cultural Studies* 28.2: 179–201.

Faludi, Susan (2007), *The Terror Dream: Fear and Fantasy in Post-9/11 America*, New York: Metropolitan.

Farrell, Kirby (1998), *Post-Traumatic Culture: Injury and Interpretation in the Nineties*, Baltimore and London: Johns Hopkins University Press.

Feinman, Ilene (2007), 'Shock and Awe: Abu Ghraib, Women Soldiers, and Racially Gendered Torture', in Tara McKelvey (ed.), *One of the Guys: Women as Aggressors and Torturers*, Emeryville, CA: Seal Press, pp. 57–80.

Fick, Nathaniel (2005), *One Bullet Away: The Making of a Marine Officer*, Boston: Houghton Mifflin.

Foer, Jonathan Safran (2002), *Everything is Illuminated*, London: Penguin.

Foer, Jonathan Safran (2005), *Extremely Loud and Incredibly Close*, London: Penguin.

Foley, Barbara (2007), 'Pawn, Scapegoat, or Collaborator', in Tara McKelvey (ed.), *One of the Guys: Women as Aggressors and Torturers*, Emeryville, CA: Seal Press, pp. 199–212.

Forter, Greg (2007), 'Freud, Faulkner, Caruth: Trauma and the Politics of Literary Form', *Narrative* 15.3: 259–85.

Freud, Sigmund [1919] (2003), 'The Uncanny', in *The Uncanny*, trans. David McLintock, London: Penguin, pp. 121–62.

Freud, Sigmund [1920] (2003), 'Beyond the Pleasure Principle', in *Beyond the Pleasure Principle and Other Writings*, trans. John Reddick, London: Penguin, pp. 43–102.

Genette, Gérard (1980), *Narrative Discourse: An Essay in Method*, trans. Jane E. Lewin, Oxford: Basil Blackwell.

Gilbert, Sandra M (2002), 'Writing Wrong', in Nancy K. Miller and Jason Tougaw (eds), *Extremities: Trauma, Testimony, and Community*, Urbana and Chicago: University of Illinois Press, pp. 260–70.

Glaser, Amelia (2008), 'From Polylingual to Postvernacular: Imagining Yiddish in the Twenty-First Century', *Jewish Social Studies: History, Culture, Society* 14.3: 150–64.

Graham, Shane (2008), '"This Text Deletes Itself": Traumatic Memory and Space-Time in Zoë Wicomb's *David's Story*', *Studies in the Novel* 40.1 & 2: 127–45.

Gray, Richard (2011), *After the Fall: American Literature Since 9/11*, Chichester: Wiley-Blackwell.

Hacking, Ian (1999), *The Social Construction of What?*, Cambridge, MA: Harvard University Press.

Hamid, Mohsin (2007), *The Reluctant Fundamentalist*, London: Penguin.

Hansen, Mark B. N. (2004), 'The Digital Topography of Mark Z. Danielewski's *House of Leaves*', *Contemporary Literature* 45.4: 597–636.

Harpham, Geoffrey Galt (1985), 'E. L. Doctorow and the Technology of Narrative', *PMLA* 100.1: 81–95.

Hayles, N. Katherine (2002), 'Saving the Subject: Remediation in *House of Leaves*', *American Literature* 74.4: 779–806.

Heberle, Mark A. (2001), *A Trauma Artist: Tim O'Brien and the Fiction of Vietnam*, Iowa City: University of Iowa Press.

Hedin, Benjamin (2005), 'A History That Never Happened: Philip

Roth's *The Plot Against America*', *The Gettysburg Review* 18.1: 93–106.

Hellekson, Karen (2001), *The Alternate History: Refiguring Historical Time*, Kent, OH: The Kent State University Press.

Heller, Joseph (1962), *Catch-22*, London: Corgi.

Herman, Judith (1997), *Trauma and Recovery* (2nd edn), New York: Basic Books.

Hodgkin, Katherine, and Susannah Radstone (2003), 'Remembering Suffering: Trauma and History: Introduction', in Katherine Hodgkin and Susannah Radstone (eds), *Contested Pasts: The Politics of Memory*, London: Routledge, pp. 97–103.

Holloway, David (2008), *9/11 and the War on Terror*, Edinburgh: Edinburgh University Press.

Huehls, Mitchum (2008), 'Foer, Spiegelman, and 9/11's Timely Traumas', in Ann Keniston and Jeanne Follansbee Quinn (eds), *Literature After 9/11*, New York: Routledge, pp. 42–59.

Hunt, Laird (2006), *The Exquisite*, Minneapolis: Coffee House Press.

Huq, Aziz (2007), 'Bitter Fruit: Constitutional Gender Equality Comes to the Military', in Tara McKelvey (ed.), *One of the Guys: Women as Aggressors and Torturers*, Emeryville, CA: Seal Press, pp. 125–34.

Hurley, Terry (2008), 'The Dead Iraqi Album', in Lisa Bowden and Shannon Cain (eds), *Powder: Writing by Women in the Ranks, from Vietnam to Iraq*, Tucson: Kore Press, pp. 56–60.

Hutcheon, Linda (1988), *A Poetics of Postmodernism*, London: Routledge.

Huyssen, Andreas (2000), 'Of Mice and Mimesis: Reading Spiegelman with Adorno', *New German Critique* 81: 65–82.

Jarvis, Brian (2008), 'Skating on a Shit Field: Tim O'Brien and the Topography of Trauma', in Jay Prosser (ed.), *American Fiction of the 1990s*, Abingdon: Routledge, pp. 134–47.

Jentsch, Ernst [1906] (1997), 'On the Psychology of the Uncanny', trans. Roy Sellars, *Angelaki: Journal of the Theoretical Humanities* 2.1: 7–16.

Kahane, Claire (2003), 'Uncanny Sights: The Anticipation of the Abomination', in Judith Greenberg (ed.), *Trauma at Home: After 9/11*, Lincoln: University of Nebraska Press, pp. 107–16.

Kakutani, Michiko (2004), 'A Pro-Nazi President, A Family Feeling The Effects', *The New York Times*, 21 September 2004, <http://www.nytimes.com/2004/09/21/books/21kaku.html> (last accessed 7 January 2014).

Kakutani, Michiko (2007), 'Looking for a Home in the Limbo of Alaska', *The New York Times*, 1 May 2007, <http://www.nytimes.com/2007/05/01/books/01kaku.html> (last accessed 7 January 2014).

Kalfus, Ken (2006), *A Disorder Peculiar to the Country*, London: Simon and Schuster.

Kansteiner, Wulf (2004), 'Genealogy of a Category Mistake: A Critical Intellectual History of the Cultural Trauma Metaphor', *Rethinking History* 8.2: 193–221.

Kaplan, E. Ann (2005), *Trauma Culture: The Politics of Terror and Loss in Media and Literature*, New Brunswick, NJ: Rutgers University Press.

Kaplan, E. Ann, and Ban Wang (2008), 'Introduction: From Traumatic Paralysis to the Force Field of Modernity', in E. Ann Kaplan and Ban Wang (eds), *Trauma and Cinema: Cross-Cultural Explorations*, Hong Kong: Hong Kong University Press, pp. 1–22.

Kauvar, Elaine M. (2011), 'My Life as a Boy: *The Plot Against America*', in Debra Shostak (ed.), *Philip Roth: American Pastoral, The Human Stain, The Plot Against America*, London: Continuum, pp. 130–44.

Kellman, Steven G. (2008), 'It Is Happening Here: *The Plot Against America* and the Political Moment', *Philip Roth Studies* 4.2: 113–23.

Kellner, Douglas (1999), 'From Vietnam to the Gulf: Postmodern Wars?', in Michael Bibby (ed.), *The Vietnam War and Postmodernity*, Amherst: Massachusetts University Press, pp. 199–236.

Keniston, Ann, and Jeanne Follansbee Quinn, eds (2008), *Literature After 9/11*, New York: Routledge.

Kirn, Walter (2005), '*Extremely Loud and Incredibly Close*: Everything Is Included', *The New York Times*, 3 April 2005, <http://www.nytimes.com/2005/04/03/books/review/0403 cover-kirn.html> (last accessed 7 January 2014).

Klinkowitz, Jerome (2004), *The Vonnegut Effect*, Columbia: University of South Carolina Press.

Kuhlman, Martha (2007), 'The Traumatic Temporality of Art Spiegelman's *In the Shadow of No Towers*', *The Journal of Popular Culture* 40.5: 849–66.

LaCapra, Dominick (2001), *Writing History, Writing Trauma*, Baltimore: Johns Hopkins University Press.

Lansky, Melvin R., and Carol R. Bley (1995), *Posttraumatic Nightmares: Psychodynamic Explorations*, Hillsdale, NJ: Analytic.

Lanzmann, Claude (1995), 'The Obscenity of Understanding: An Evening with Claude Lanzmann', in Cathy Caruth (ed.), *Trauma: Explorations in Memory*, Baltimore: Johns Hopkins University Press, pp. 200–20.

Laub, Dori (1995), 'Truth and Testimony: The Process and the Struggle', in Cathy Caruth (ed.), *Trauma: Explorations in Memory*, Baltimore: Johns Hopkins University Press, pp. 61–75.

Laub, Dori (2003), 'September 11, 2001 – An Event without a Voice', in Judith Greenberg (ed.), *Trauma at Home: After 9/11*, Lincoln: University of Nebraska Press, pp. 204–15.

Leopold, Todd (2004), 'Sketches of the Apocalypse,' *CNN.com*, 9 September 2004, <http://edition.cnn.com/2004/SHOWBIZ/books/09/09/art.spiegelman/> (last accessed 7 January 2014).

Leys, Ruth (2000), *Trauma: A Genealogy*, Chicago: The University of Chicago Press.

Little, William G. (2007), 'Nothing to Write Home About: Impossible Reception in Mark Z. Danielewski's *House of Leaves*', in Neil Brooks and Josh Toth (eds), *The Mourning After: Attending the Wake of Postmodernism*, Amsterdam: Rodopi, pp. 169–99.

Longmuir, Anne (2007), 'Performing the Body in Don DeLillo's *The Body Artist*', *Modern Fiction Studies* 53.3: 528–43.

Luckhurst, Roger (2008), *The Trauma Question*, London: Routledge.

Lustig, Timothy J. (2001), '"Moments of Punctuation": Metonymy and Ellipsis in Tim O'Brien', *The Yearbook of English Studies* 31: 74–92.

Matus, Jill (1998), *Toni Morrison*, Manchester: Manchester University Press.

Mayer, Jane (2009), 'The Predator War', *The New Yorker*, 26 October 2009, pp. 36–45, <http://www.newyorker.com/ reporting/2009/10/26/091026fa_fact_mayer> (last accessed 7 January 2014).

McCloud, Scott (1993), *Understanding Comics: The Invisible Art*, New York: Harper Collins.

McHale, Brian (1987), *Postmodernist Fiction*, London: Methuen.

McNally, Richard J. (2004), 'Conceptual Problems with the DSM-IV Criteria for Posttraumatic Stress Disorder', in Gerald M. Rosen (ed.), *Posttraumatic Stress Disorder: Issues and Controversies*, Chichester: John Wiley and Sons Ltd., pp. 1–14.

Michaels, Anne (1994), *Fugitive Pieces*, London: Bloomsbury.

Michaels, Walter Benn (2006), 'Plots Against America: Neoliberalism and Antiracism', *American Literary History* 18.2: 288–302.

Miller, Laura (2005), 'Terror Comes to Tiny Town', *New York Magazine/Metro*, 21 May 2005, <http://nymag.com/nymetro/ arts/books/reviews/11574/> (last accessed 7 January 2014).

Moore, Lorrie (2005), 'Keeping Your Fingers Crossed Makes it Difficult to Hold a Pen, But I must Say, It's Worth It', *The Believer*, <http://www.believermag.com/issues/200510/? read=interview_moore> (last accessed 7 January 2014).

Moore, Lorrie (2009), *A Gate at the Stairs*, London: Faber and Faber.

Morgenstern, Naomi (2003), 'The Primal Scene in the Public Domain: E. L. Doctorow's *The Book of Daniel*', *Studies in the Novel* 35.1: 68–88.

Morrison, Blake (2004), 'The Relentless Unforeseen', *The Guardian*, 2 October 2004, <http://www.theguardian.com/ books/2004/oct/02/fiction.philiproth> (last accessed 7 January 2014).

Morrison, Toni [1987] (1997), *Beloved*, London: Vintage.

Musa, Jumana (2007), 'Gender and Sexual Violence in the Military', in Tara McKelvey (ed.), *One of the Guys: Women as Aggressors and Torturers*, Emeryville, CA: Seal Press, pp. 81–90.

Mullins, Matthew (2009), 'Boroughs and Neighbors: Traumatic Solidarity in Jonathan Safran Foer's *Extremely Loud & Incredibly Close*', *Papers on Language and Literature* 45.3: 298–324.

O'Brien, Tim [1975] (1999), *If I Die in a Combat Zone*, New York: Broadway.

O'Brien, Tim [1978] (1988), *Going After Cacciato*, London: Flamingo.

O'Brien, Tim (1990), *The Things They Carried*, New York: Broadway.

O'Brien, Tim (1995), *In the Lake of the Woods*, London: Flamingo.

O'Brien, Tim (1998), *Tomcat in Love*, New York: Broadway.

Orbán, Katalin (2007), 'Trauma and Visuality: Art Spiegelman's *Maus* and *In the Shadow of No Towers*', *Representations* 97: 57–89.

Parrish, Timothy (2005), 'The Plot Against America', *Philip Roth Studies* 1.1: 93–101.

Pérez-Torres, Rafael (1998), 'Knitting and Knotting the Narrative Thread – *Beloved* as Postmodern Novel', in Linden Peach (ed.), *Toni Morrison: Contemporary Critical Essays*, Basingstoke: MacMillan, pp. 128–39.

Petersen, Alan (1998), *Unmasking the Masculine: 'Men' and 'Identity' in a Sceptical Age*, London: Sage.

Philadelphoff-Puren, Nina (2009), 'Hostile Witness: Torture Testimony in the War on Terror', in Gillian Whitlock and Kate Douglas (eds), *Trauma Texts*, London: Routledge, pp. 166–83.

Phillips, Kathy J. (2006), *Manipulating Masculinity: War and Gender in Modern British and American Literature*, New York: Palgrave.

Piedmont-Marton, Elisabeth (2005), 'Writing Against the Vietnam War in Two Gulf War Memoirs', in Alex Vernon (ed.), *Arms and the Self*, Kent, OH: Kent State University Press, pp. 257–72.

Pilger, John (2013), 'We've Moved on from the Iraq War – But Iraqis Don't Have that Choice', *The Guardian*, 26 May 2013, <http://www.theguardian.com/commentisfree/2013/may/26/iraqis-cant-turn-backs-on-deadly-legacy> (last accessed 7 January 2014).

Pilkington, Ed (2013), 'US Military Struggling to Stop Suicide Epidemic among War Veterans', *The Guardian*, 1 February 1 2013, <http://www.theguardian.com/world/2013/feb/01/us-military-suicide-epidemic-veteran> (last accessed 7 January 2014).

Prose, Francine (2002), 'Back in the Totally Awesome U.S.S.R.', *The New York Times*, 14 April 2002, <http://www.nytimes. com/2002/04/14/books/back-in-the-totally-awesome-ussr. html?pagewanted=all&src=pm> (last accessed 7 January 2014).

Radstone, Susannah (2003), 'The War of the Fathers: Trauma, Fantasy, and September 11', in Judith Greenberg (ed.), *Trauma at Home: After 9/11*, Lincoln: University of Nebraska Press, pp. 117–23.

Radstone, Susannah (2005), 'Reconceiving Binaries: the Limits of Memory', *History Workshop Journal* 59: 134–50.

Radstone, Susannah (2007), 'Trauma Theory: Contexts, Politics, Ethics', *Paragraph* 30.1: 9–29.

Rasmussen, Eric Dean (2010), 'E. L. Doctorow's Vicious Eroticism: Dangerous Affect in *The Book of Daniel*', *Symploke* 18.1–2: 189–217.

Richardson, Anna (2010), 'In Search of the Final Solution: Crime Narrative as a Paradigm for Exploring Responses to the Holocaust', *European Journal of American Studies* 14.2: 159–71.

Roth, Henry (1994), *Mercy of a Rude Stream, volume 1: A Star Shines Over Mt. Morris Park*, New York: St. Martin's Press.

Roth, Henry (1995), *Mercy of a Rude Stream, volume 2: A Diving Rock on the Hudson*, New York: St Martin's Press.

Roth, Philip (2004a), *The Plot Against America*, London: Vintage.

Roth, Philip (2004b), 'The Story Behind *The Plot Against America*', *New York Times Book Review*, 19 September 2004, pp. 10–12, <http://www.nytimes.com/2004/09/19/books/ review/19ROTHL.html?pagewanted=all> (last accessed 7 January 2014).

Roth, Philip (2004c), 'Conversation: *The Plot Against America*', PBS transcript of interview conducted by Jeffrey Brown, *The News Hour with Jim Lehrer*, 27 October 2004 & 10 November 2004, <http://www.pbs.org/newshour/bb/entertainment/ july-dec04/philiproth_10-27.html> (last accessed 7 January 2014).

Rothberg, Michael (2000), *Traumatic Realism: The Demands of Holocaust Representation*, Minneapolis: University of Minnesota Press.

Rothberg, Michael (2003), '"There Is No Poetry in This": Writing,

Trauma, and Home', in Judith Greenberg (ed.), *Trauma at Home: After 9/11*, Lincoln: University of Nebraska Press, pp. 147–57.

Rothberg, Michael (2008), 'Decolonizing Trauma Studies: A Response', *Studies in the Novel*, 40.1 & 2: 224–34.

Rothberg, Michael (2009), *Multidirectional Memory: Remembering the Holocaust in the Age of Decolonization*, Stanford: Stanford University Press.

Rothe, Anne (2011), *Popular Trauma Culture: Selling the Pain of Others in the Mass Media*, New Brunswick, NJ: Rutgers University Press.

Royakkers, Lambèr, and Rinie van Est (2010), 'The Cubicle Warrior: The Marionette of Digitalized Warfare', *Ethics Inf Technol* 12: 289–96.

Royle, Nicholas (2003), *The Uncanny*, Manchester: Manchester University Press.

Ryan, David (2007), *Frustrated Empire: US Foreign Policy, 9/11 to Iraq*, London: Pluto Press.

Saal, Ilka (2011), 'Regarding the Pain of Self and Other: Trauma Transfer and Narrative Framing in Jonathan Safran Foer's *Extremely Loud & Incredibly Close*', *Modern Fiction Studies* 57.3: 453–76.

Safer, Elaine B. (2006), *Mocking the Age: The Later Novels of Philip Roth*, Albany: State University of New York Press.

Salinger, J. D. [1953] (1994), 'For Esmé – with Love and Squalor', in *For Esmé – with Love and Squalor and other stories*, London: Penguin, pp. 65–85.

Schweber, Matthew S. (2005), 'Philip Roth's Populist Nightmare', *Crosscurrents* 54.4: 125–37.

Shay, Jonathan (1994), *Achilles in Vietnam: Combat Trauma and the Undoing of Character*, New York: Scribner.

Shephard, Ben (2002), *A War of Nerves: Soldiers and Psychiatrists 1914–1994*, London: Pimlico.

Shields, Carol (2002), *Unless*, London: Harper Collins.

Shiffman, Dan (2009), '*The Plot Against America* and History Post-9/11', *Philip Roth Studies* 5.1: 61–73.

Shiloh, Ilana (2011), *The Double, the Labyrinth and the Locked Room*, New York: Peter Lang.

Shostak, Debra (2009), 'In the Country of Missing Persons: Paul Auster's Narratives of Trauma', *Studies in the Novel* 41.1: 66–87.

Siegel, Harry (2005), 'Extremely Cloying and Incredibly False', *New York Press*, 20 April 2005, <http://nypress.com/extremely-cloying-incredibly-false/> (last accessed 7 January 2014).

Silbergleid, Robin (2009), 'Making Things Present: Tim O'Brien's Autobiographical Metafiction', *Contemporary Literature* 50.1: 129–55.

Simpson, David (2006), *9/11: The Culture of Commemoration*, Chicago: University of Chicago Press.

Simpson, Mark (2009), 'Attackability', *Canadian Review of American Studies* 39.3: 299–319.

Slotkin, Richard (1973), *Regeneration Through Violence: The Mythology of the American Frontier, 1600–1860*, Middletown, CT: Wesleyan University Press.

Smith, Rachel Greenwald (2011), 'Organic Shrapnel: Affect and Aesthetics in September 11 Fiction', *American Literature* 83.1: 153–74.

Spiegelman, Art (1986), *Maus: A Survivor's Tale, volume I: My Father Bleeds History*, London: Penguin.

Spiegelman, Art (1992), *Maus: A Survivor's Tale, volume II: And Here My Troubles Began*, London: Penguin.

Spiegelman, Art (2004a), *In the Shadow of No Towers*, New York: Pantheon.

Spiegelman, Art (2004b), 'A Comic-Book Response to 9/11 and Its Aftermath', interview conducted by Claudia Dreifus, *The New York Times*, 7 August 2004, <http://www.nytimes.com/2004/08/07/books/a-comic-book-response-to-9-11-and-its-aftermath.html> (last accessed 7 January 2014).

Spiegelman, Art (2008), *Breakdowns*, London: Penguin.

Sturken, Marita (1997), *Tangled Memories: The Vietnam War, the AIDs Epidemic, and the Politics of Remembering*, Berkeley: University of California Press.

Swofford, Anthony (2003), *Jarhead*, London: Scribner.

Tal, Kalí (1996), *Worlds of Hurt: Reading the Literatures of Trauma*, Cambridge: Cambridge University Press.

Timmer, Nicoline (2010), *Do You Feel It Too? The Post-Postmodern*

Syndrome in American Fiction at the Turn of the Millennium, Amsterdam: Rodopi.

Tokarczyk, Michelle M. (1987), 'From the Lion's Den: Survivors in E. L. Doctorow's *The Book of Daniel*', *Critique* 29.1: 3–15.

Traverso, Antonio, and Mick Broderick (2010), 'Interrogating Trauma: Towards a Critical Trauma Studies', *Continuum: Journal of Media & Cultural Studies* 24.1: 3–15.

Turnipseed, Joel (2003), *Baghdad Express*, New York and London: Penguin.

Updike, John (2005), 'Mixed Messages: *Extremely Loud and Incredibly Close*', *The New Yorker*, 14 March 2005, <http://www.newyorker.com/archive/2005/03/14/050314crbo_book s1> (last accessed 7 January 2014).

Uytterschout, Sien (2008), 'Visualised Incomprehensibility of Trauma in Jonathan Safran Foer's *Extremely Loud and Incredibly Close*', *Zeitschrift für Anglistik und Amerikanistik* 56.1: 61–74.

Uytterschout, Sien (2010), 'An Extremely Loud Tin Drum: A Comparative Study of Jonathan Safran Foer's *Extremely Loud and Incredibly Close* and Günter Grass's *The Tin Drum*', *Comparative Literature Studies* 47.2: 185–99.

van der Kolk, Bessel A., and Onno van der Hart, 'The Intrusive Past: The Flexibility of Memory and the Engraving of Trauma', in Cathy Caruth (ed.), *Trauma: Explorations in Memory*, Baltimore: Johns Hopkins University Press, pp. 158–82.

Vanderwerken, David L. (2013), 'Kurt Vonnegut's *Slaughterhouse-Five* at Forty: Billy Pilgrim – Even More a Man of Our Times', *Critique* 54.1: 46–55.

Vees-Gulani, Susanne (2003), 'Diagnosing Billy Pilgrim: A Psychiatric Approach to Kurt Vonnegut's *Slaughterhouse-Five*', *Critique* 44.2: 175–84.

Versluys, Kristiaan (2009), *Out of the Blue: September 11 and the Novel*, New York: Columbia University Press.

Vickroy, Laurie (2002), *Trauma and Survival in Contemporary Fiction*, Charlottesville: University of Virginia Press.

Vonnegut, Kurt [1969] (2000), *Slaughterhouse-Five*, London: Vintage.

Vonnegut, Kurt (1980), 'There Must Be More to Love than Death:

'A Conversation with Kurt Vonnegut', interview conducted by Robert K. Musil, *The Nation*, 2–9 August 1980: 128–32.

Wallace, David Foster (1993), 'An Interview with David Foster Wallace', interview conducted by Larry McCaffery, *The Review of Contemporary Fiction* 13.2: 127–50.

Walter, Jess (2006), *The Zero*, New York: Harper Collins.

Weigel, Sigrid (2003), 'The Symptomatology of a Universalised Concept of Trauma: On the Failing of Freud's Reading of Tasso in the Trauma of History', trans. Georgina Paul, *New German Critique* 90: 85–94.

Whitehead, Anne (2004), *Trauma Fiction*, Edinburgh: Edinburgh University Press.

Wilkomirski, Binjamin (1996), *Fragments*, trans. Carol Brown Janeway, London: Picador.

Williams, Kayla, with Michael E. Staub (2006), *Love My Rifle More than You: Young and Female in the US Army*, London: Phoenix.

Wisse, Ruth (2004), 'In Nazi Newark', *Commentary*, December 2004: 65–70.

Wisse, Ruth (2007), 'Slap Shtick', *Commentary*, July–August 2007: 73–7.

Wolff, Carlo (2004), '*In the Shadow of No Towers* by Art Spiegelman', *Pittsburgh Post-Gazette*, 19 September 2004, <http://www.post-gazette.com/ae/book-reviews/2004/09/19/In-the-Shadow-of-No-Towers-by-Art-Spiegelman.print> (last accessed 7 January 2014).

World Trade Center, film, directed by Oliver Stone. USA: Paramount, 2006.

Wright, Evan (2005), *Generation Kill*, London: Corgi.

Wyatt, David (2009), 'September 11 and Postmodern Memory', *Arizona Quarterly* 65.4: 139–61.

Wyatt, Jean (1993), 'Giving Body to the Word: The Maternal Symbolic in Toni Morrison's *Beloved*', *PMLA* 108.3: 474–88.

Young, Allan (1995), *The Harmony of Illusions: Inventing Post-Traumatic Stress Disorder*, Princeton: Princeton University Press.

Žižek, Slavoj (2002), *Welcome to the Desert of the Real*, London: Verso.

Index